# VIRTUE ETHICS
# AND MORAL EDUCATION

The post-war revival of interest in virtue ethics has yielded enormous advances in our understanding of moral psychology and development. However, despite the widespread interest of educational philosophers in virtue theorists from Aristotle to Alasdair MacIntyre, it would appear that the theory and practice of moral education have yet to draw upon virtue ethics to any appreciable degree.

This collection of original essays on virtue ethics and moral education seeks to fill this gap in the recent literature of moral education, combining broader analyses with detailed coverage of:

- the varieties of virtue
- weakness and integrity
- relativism and rival traditions
- means and methods of educating the virtues.

This rare collaboration of professional ethical theorists and educational philosophers constitutes a ground-breaking work and an exciting new focus in a growing area of research.

**David Carr** is Reader in the Faculty of Education at the University of Edinburgh. He is editor of *Education, Knowledge and Truth* (Routledge 1998) and is writing a book on *Ethical Issues in Teaching* (forthcoming with Routledge).

**Jan Steutel** is Reader in Philosophy of Education at the Free University, Amsterdam, The Netherlands.

# ROUTLEDGE INTERNATIONAL STUDIES IN THE PHILOSOPHY OF EDUCATION

# VIRTUE ETHICS AND MORAL EDUCATION

*Edited by*
*David Carr and Jan Steutel*

London and New York

First published 1999
by Routledge
11 New Fetter Lane, London EC4P 4EE

Simultaneously published in the USA and Canada
by Routledge
29 West 35th Street, New York, NY 10001

*Routledge is an imprint of the Taylor & Francis Group*

Typeset in Garamond by Curran Publishing Services
Printed and bound in Great Britain by
Biddles Ltd, Guildford and King's Lynn

*British Library Cataloguing in Publication Data*
A catalogue record for this book is available
from the British Library

*Library of Congress Cataloguing in Publication Data*
Virtue Ethics and Moral Education
Edited by David Carr and Jan Steutel

288 p. 15.6×23.4 cm.
Includes bibliographical references and index

1. Moral Education  2. Virtue
3. Ethics – I. Carr, David, 1944–
II. Steutel, J. W. (Jan Willem), 1948–
LC268.V57 1999
370.11'4--dc21        98-47913 CIP

ISBN 0–415–17073–7

# CONTENTS

CONTENTS

# CONTENTS

# FIGURES

# CONTRIBUTORS

**Eamonn Callan** is Professor of Educational Policy Studies at the University of Alberta. He is the author of *Creating Citizens* (Oxford University Press 1997), *Autonomy and Schooling* (McGill-Queen's University Press 1988), and many articles in the philosophy of education.

**David Carr** is Reader in the Faculty of Education of the University of Edinburgh. He is editor of *Knowledge, Truth and Education* (Routledge 1998) and author of *Educating the Virtues* (Routledge 1991) as well as of numerous philosophical and educational articles. He is currently writing a book on *Ethical Issues in Teaching* (also for Routledge).

**Paul Crittenden** is Professor of Philosophy in the School of Philosophy, University of Sydney. He is the author of *Learning To Be Moral* (Humanities Press International 1990) and teaches and writes mainly in ethics and sociopolitical theory, especially in relation to Greek philosophy and recent European philosophy.

**Randall Curren** is Associate Professor in both the Department of Philosophy and the Warner Graduate School of Education and Human Development at the University of Rochester. He is the author of a forthcoming book, *Aristotle on the Necessity of Public Education* (Rowman & Littlefield), and other works in ethics, ancient philosophy, legal and political philosophy, and philosophy of education.

**Nicholas Dent** is Professor of Philosophy at the University of Birmingham where he has worked since 1979. He is presently Head of the School of Humanities in the university. His publications include *The Moral Psychology of the Virtues* (Cambridge University Press 1984) and *Rousseau* (Blackwell 1988).

**Joseph Dunne** teaches philosophy and philosophy of education at St. Patrick's College, Dublin. He is author of *Back to the Rough Ground: Practical Judgment and the Lure of Technique* (University of Notre Dame Press 1993), now available in paperback with a new foreword by Alasdair MacIntyre. Currently completing a collection of essays in 'public philosophy', he also has research interests in history and philosophy of childhood.

**John Haldane** is Professor of Philosophy and Director of the Centre for Philosophy and Public Affairs in the University of St Andrews. He has published widely in various branches of philosophy and is co-author with J. J. C. Smart of *Atheism and Theism* (Blackwell 1996) and *Faithful Reason* (Routledge 1999).

**Bonnie Kent** is Associate Professor of Religion at Columbia University and author of *Virtues of the Will* (Catholic University Press 1995). Her publications include 'Habits and virtues', in *Ethics on the Ethics of St. Thomas Aquinas* (Georgetown University Press, forthcoming), 'Moral provincialism', in *Religious Studies* (1994), and other articles on virtue ethics and its history.

**Joel Kupperman** is Professor of Philosophy at the University of Connecticut, with special interests in ethics. His books include *Character* (Oxford University Press 1991), *Value ... And What Follows* (Oxford University Press, forthcoming) and *Learning From Asian Philosophy* (which is being completed and will be published by Oxford University Press).

**Nancy Sherman** is a Professor of Philosophy at Georgetown University and Visiting Distinguished Chair of Ethics at the United States Naval Academy. She previously taught at Yale University for seven years, and has held visiting posts at the University of Maryland and Johns Hopkins University. She is the author of *Making a Necessity of Virtue* (Cambridge University Press 1997) and *The Fabric of Character* (Oxford University Press 1989). In addition, she has written numerous articles in the areas of ethics and moral psychology.

**Michael Slote** is Professor of Philosophy and department chair at the University of Maryland, College Park. He is the author of *From Morality To Virtue* (Oxford University Press 1992) and, most recently, the co-author of *Three Methods of Ethics* (Blackwell 1997). He is currently working on issues concerning the importance of love in virtue ethics.

**Ben Spiecker** is Professor of Philosophy of Education at the Department of Psychology and Education at the Vrije Universiteit, Amsterdam. His many publications and research interests lie in the areas of moral, civic and sexual education. He is a member of the board of the *Journal of Philosophy of Education* and *Studies in Philosophy and Education*.

**Jan W. Steutel** is Reader in Philosophy of Education at the Vrije Universiteit of Amsterdam. His many publications and work in progress focus on civic and moral education, in particular on virtue theory and the cultivation of the virtues. He is a member of the board of the *Journal of Moral Education*.

**Kenneth A. Strike** is Professor of Philosophy of Education at Cornell University. He has been a distinguished visiting professor at the University of Alberta and is a member of the National Academy of Education. His principal interests are professional ethics and political philosophy as they apply to matters of educational practice and policy. He is the author of over a hundred articles and several books, including *The Ethics of Teaching* (with J. Soltis, Teachers College Press 1985) and *Liberal Justice and the Marxist Critique of Schooling* (Routledge 1989).

**James D. Wallace** is Professor of Philosophy at the University of Illinois at Urbana-Champaign. A graduate of Amherst College, he received his Ph.D. from Cornell University. He is the author of *Virtues and Vices* (Cornell University Press 1978), *Moral Relevance and Moral Conflict* (Cornell University Press 1988), and *Ethical Norms, Particular Cases* (Cornell University Press 1996).

# PREFACE AND
# ACKNOWLEDGEMENTS

A long road has been travelled towards the realization of this project. Indeed, the possibility of assembling a collection of essays along these lines was first discussed by the editors on a rainy night in Amsterdam as long ago as January 1994. The editors already shared a long-standing interest in virtue ethics, especially in possible applications of virtue theory to problems about moral education. In this connection, the need for an exploratory volume of moral educational essays specifically focused on virtue theory seemed pressing; for despite growing recognition in mainstream philosophy of virtue ethics as a serious rival to utilitarianism and Kantian deontology – not to mention widespread contemporary educational philosophical interest in the work of such philosophers as Aristotle and Alasdair MacIntyre – relatively few educational philosophers to date have focused directly upon the practical implications of virtue ethics for moral education. Compared with the wealth of literature produced over the years on research into moral cognition, for example, work on the moral educational applications of virtue ethics has been scarcely more than a drop in the ocean, despite the fact that the post-war revival of interest in the virtues was more or less coincident with the outset of Kohlberg's influential research programme.

All the same, when the idea was first broached, enthusiasm for the project was mixed with doubt, and Steutel's optimism had to contend with Carr's scepticism. In a general climate of declining publishing interest in educational philosophy and theory in general, this topic could hardly appear other than *recherché*. Indeed, although the eventual publishers of this collection had retained enough faith and commitment to the general importance of educational philosophy to launch a new research series on the philosophy of education, the would-be editors were aware that other important work on, or related to, moral education had already been commissioned for this series. This threatened to weaken rather than increase the chances of acceptance of an additional work on a fairly specific approach to moral education. Thus, it is to the enormous credit of Routledge that they did not need strenuously persuading of the potential interest and significance of a work of this kind, and the editors remain extremely grateful for the eventual warm reception of their proposal.

It was a further difficult question who should be approached by the editors to contribute to the volume. As already noted, relatively few professional educational philosophers have to date strayed into the territory of virtue ethics and virtue theory, despite significant growth of mainstream philosophical interest in the topic and the almost hourly appearance of high calibre analytical work (articles, anthologies and single-authored books) in the field. It was clear that, in addition to enlisting the assistance of educational philosophers who had produced quality work focused upon the significance of the virtues for moral education, it would be crucial to have substantial input from mainstream philosophers working at the leading edge of virtue theory. This might have been a problem to the extent that it has not been common, since the earliest days of the post-war analytical revolution in philosophy of education, for the mainstream philosophical community to show any large interest in the messy (and, often enough, not very rigorously addressed) particularities of educational policy and practice. Contemporary collaborations between mainstream philosophers and educational philosophers are all too few and far between. In the event, however, the editors were overwhelmed by the enthusiasm for, and commitment to, this project of so many key players in the field of contemporary virtue ethics.

From this point of view, the editors believe that the present volume represents a pioneering instance of collaboration between two related but often mutually uncommunicative professional communities, which they hope may be judged successful enough to constitute a significant precedent. Effectively, of the fifteen invited contributors to this volume, six (Callan, Carr, Dunne, Spiecker, Steutel, Strike) are educational philosophers in one way or another implicated in the practicalities of professional training, eight (Crittenden, Dent, Haldane, Kent, Kupperman, Sherman, Slote, Wallace) are academic philosophers significantly if not primarily interested in aspects of virtue ethics, and one (Curren), as a professor of philosophy and education, has connections with both these areas of professional concern.

There cannot be any doubt, however, concerning the distinguished reputations in their respective fields of all who finally accepted an invitation to contribute to this volume. Moreover, although the editors were aware from the outset that they were approaching some extremely busy people, all never the less contributed as enthusiastically, conscientiously and graciously as any editors could wish to the production of what we believe to be a show-case of some of the finest original contemporary work on ethics and moral education. The editors are therefore enormously indebted to each and every contributor to this volume for their parts in what we hope may come to be seen as a significant landmark in the philosophy of moral education. Last but not least, we wish to reaffirm our debt to the publishers for their faith in this project, especially to all at Routledge who assisted, so kindly and with such patience and care, in the final production of this volume.

The quotation on page 92 is copyright © 1979 *The Monist*, La Salle, Illinois 61301. Reprinted by permission.

David Carr and Jan Steutel
August 1998

# Part 1

# INTRODUCTION

# 1

# VIRTUE ETHICS AND THE VIRTUE APPROACH TO MORAL EDUCATION

*Jan Steutel and David Carr*

## Introduction

Different approaches to moral education – distinguished, as one would expect, by reference to diverse conceptions of moral educational aims and methods – are to be encountered in the research literature of moral education. In the sphere of psychological theory and research, for example, somewhat different moral educational emphases – on parental influence, behaviour shaping, dilemma discussion – appear to be characteristic of (respectively) psychoanalytic, social learning and cognitive developmental theory.

In general, however, it is arguable that differences between conceptions of moral education are nothing if not philosophical. Thus, notwithstanding modern psychological attempts to derive moral educational conclusions from quasi-empirical research alone, it is difficult to see how such conclusions might be justified without appeal, however covert, to specific epistemological, ethical and even political considerations. Indeed, such familiar modern moral educational approaches as values clarification and cognitive-stage theory – though clearly inspired by psychological research of one sort or another – do not in the least avoid controversial conceptual, normative and/or evaluative assumptions and commitments. The allegedly 'impartial' goal of values clarification, for example, appears to enshrine a deeply relativistic moral epistemology, and cognitive stage theory seems ultimately rooted in liberal ethical theory. Again, more recent moral educational conceptions – associated with ideas of just community, character development and caring – also appear to be fairly philosophically partisan.

In addition to the accounts just mentioned, however, there is evidence of renewed and mounting interest in another, actually more ancient, approach to moral education: which, because it focuses on the development of virtues, may be called the *virtue approach* to moral education. As in the case of other moral educational perspectives, the virtue approach is rooted in a philosophical

3

account of moral life and conduct from which educational aims stand to be derived. All the same, it is not entirely clear that current interest in the virtue approach to moral education has been attended by widespread appreciation of the philosophical status and logical character of the associated philosophical perspective of *virtue ethics*. One consequence of this has been a tendency to confuse the virtue approach to moral education with such quite different accounts as character education, the ethics of care and even utilitarianism. So, in the interests of disclosing the distinctive features of the virtue approach, we need to be rather clearer about the philosophical claims of virtue ethics.

Thus, by way of introduction, we shall try – via exploration of a range of alternative definitions – to chart the conceptual geography of virtue ethics and the virtue approach to moral education. Our main aim will be to try to distinguish different ways in which moral education may be held to be implicated in the development of virtues, diverse conceptions of virtue ethics, and ultimately, what a distinctive virtue ethical conception of moral education might be coherently said to amount to. Although no complete summary of the various contributions to this volume will be given in this introduction, reference here and there to the views of contributors is made for purposes of illustration.

## The virtue approach: broad and narrow senses

At first blush, it might be suggested as the principal criterion of a virtue approach that it takes moral education to be concerned simply with the promotion of virtues. On this criterion, a virtue approach is to be identified mainly by reference to its aims, all of which are to be regarded as virtue-developmental, or at any rate, as primarily focused on the promotion of virtues. What should we say of this criterion?

Despite modern controversies concerning the status of particular qualities as virtues, a reasonably uncontroversial general notion is nicely captured by George Sher's (1992: 94) characterization of virtue as a 'character trait that is for some important reason desirable or worth having'. According to this description, although such qualities as linguistic facility, mathematical acumen, vitality, intelligence, wit, charm, *joie de vivre* and so on are rightly considered of great human value, they cannot be counted as virtues, because they are not traits of character. On the other hand, although such qualities as mendacity, cowardice, insincerity, partiality, impoliteness, maliciousness and narrow-mindedness do belong to the class of character traits, we cannot regard them as virtues because we do not see them as worthwhile or desirable.

Given this general concept, although our first tentative criterion of a virtue approach to moral education does not exclude the possibility of different or even rival virtue approaches, it clearly excludes any approach which does not take moral educational aims to be mainly concerned with the promotion of desirable or admirable character traits. However, insofar as several

4

approaches to moral education mentioned earlier in this introduction would seem to satisfy this initial criterion, one might well wonder whether it is quite demanding enough. Advocates of character education, for example, also define moral education in terms of cultivating virtues and their constituents. The criterion arguably applies even to Lawrence Kohlberg's well known cognitive development theory (Kohlberg 1981), for while at least early Kohlberg was explicitly opposed to any 'bag of virtues' conception of moral education – of the kind beloved of character educationalists – he nevertheless regarded the promotion of one virtue, the abstract and universal virtue of *justice*, as the ultimate aim of moral education.[1] Thus, in pursuit of a more discriminating account of a virtue approach to moral education – one which promises to do rather more conceptual work – we need to tighten the initial criterion.

One promising route to this might be to identify some particular moral theory as the ethical justification or ground of a virtue approach. In short, we might regard as a virtue approach to moral education only one which is based on *virtue ethics*, as opposed to (say) utilitarianism or Kantianism. But what exactly might it mean to found a conception of moral education on an ethics of virtue? Since the very idea of a virtue ethics is itself contested, we may now be vulnerable to the charge of attempting to explain what is already obscure in terms of what is yet more obscure: unless, that is, we can further clarify what might be meant by an ethics of virtue.

We might make a start on this by defining virtue ethics – formally enough – as a systematic and coherent account of virtues. On this view, it would be the aim of such an account to identify certain traits as desirable, to analyse and classify such traits and to explain their moral significance: more precisely, to justify regarding such traits as virtues. Accordingly, to regard virtue ethics as theoretically basic to a conception of moral education, would presumably be to conceive moral education as a matter of the development of such traits, along with promotion of some understanding of their moral value or significance. Hence, whereas the initial criterion takes a virtue approach to moral education to consist in cultivating virtues and their constituents, our elaborated criterion makes a coherent and systematic account of those virtues a condition of the virtue approach.

All the same, this definition of virtue ethics is still a fairly broad one, an account with, as it were, very large scope and relatively little conceptual content. As yet the definition is quite wide enough to comprehend even utilitarian or Kantian views as instances of virtue ethics. Thus, in *Moral Thinking* (1981) R. M. Hare – whose ideas draw heavily on both the Kantian and utilitarian traditions – offers a systematic and substantial account of moral virtues. Drawing a valuable distinction between intrinsic and instrumental moral virtues, Hare takes courage, self-control, temperance and perseverance to be examples of the latter and justice, benevolence, honesty and truthfulness to be instances of the former. Thus, as the bases of our *prima facie* moral principles, intrinsic virtues are to be regarded as not just instrumental to, but constitutive of, the moral life. Moreover, Hare provides a detailed account of their moral significance: both kinds of virtue are to be justified by critical thinking on the score of their 'acceptance-utility'.

Again, in his *Political Liberalism* (1993), John Rawls gives a systematic and coherent account of a clearly articulated set of virtues in the context of a basically neo-Kantian conception of moral life, considering such traits of character as tolerance, fairness, civility, respect and reasonableness as crucial to peaceful coexistence in conditions of cultural diversity. However, a more fine grained taxonomy of moral virtue is also a feature of his account. Thus, Rawls distinguishes civic or political virtues – those presupposed to the effective functioning of liberal-democratic polity – from the virtues of more particular religious, moral or philosophical allegiance. Whereas the latter may have an important part to play in personal and cultural formation, the former are indispensible to the social co-operation required by his principles of justice. These principles are themselves justified from the perspective of the original position or on the basis of wide reflective equilibrium.

In sum, our formal definition of a virtue ethics still appears to cover too much ethical ground. Indeed, it is not just that it lets in neo-Kantians. We could even argue that Kant himself is a virtue ethicist in the sense defined to date, since in the second part of his *Metaphysik der Sitten* (1966[1797]) he offers an account of virtue as a kind of resistance to the internal forces opposing moral attitude or will. In brief, the virtuous person is depicted as the one with sufficient strength of mind to obey the moral law in the teeth of counter-inclinations.

But if we define virtue ethics in such a broad sense, our definition of the virtue approach to moral education must also be a broad one, given that the former is, according to our second criterion, theoretically basic to the latter. Thus, for example, any conception of moral education which endorsed Hare's account of the nature and ethical value of intrinsic and instrumental virtues would be a case of a virtue approach. If Kohlberg's conception of moral education, at least in its final post-conventional stage, is based on a Kantian account of the virtue of justice (as Paul Crittenden plausibly argues in his contribution to this volume) his conception of moral education would also have to be construed as a virtue approach. Such considerations, however, point to the need for a less formal and more substantial interpretation of our elaborated criterion and to a narrower definition of virtue ethics. This would exclude Kantian and utilitarian moral views (and, for that matter, other deontological and consequentialist theories) as well as any and all conceptions of moral education (including Kohlberg's) which are clearly grounded in Kantian and utilitarian ethics. (See Figure 1.1.)

Our initial criterion of a virtue approach referred only to certain general features of the aims of moral education, while the elaborated criterion related more directly to matters of justification. We have also seen that the elaborated criterion of virtue ethics admits of broad and narrow construals. On the broad

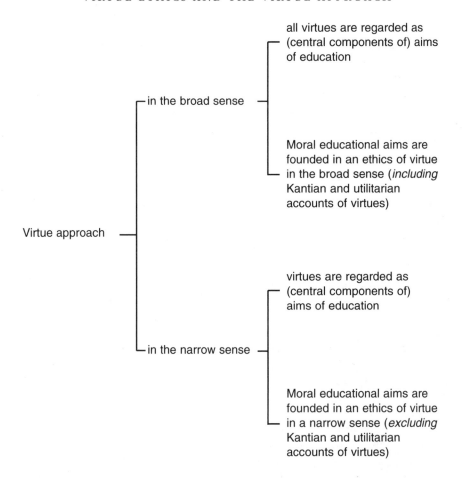

*Figure 1.1* The virtue approach in the broad and the narrow sense

interpretation, a virtue ethics certainly requires us to provide an ethical justification of virtues – some account of their moral significance – but on a narrow interpretation, the ethics of virtue points to a justification of a particular kind: one which grounds moral life and the aims of education in other than utilitarian or Kantian considerations.[2]

## The aretaic basis of virtue ethics

From now on we shall focus – unless otherwise indicated – on the virtue approach defined according to a narrow sense of virtue ethics. Despite philosophical disagreements of detail concerning the precise nature of an ethics of virtue – there would appear to be broad agreement on one important point: that insofar as it is proper to regard ethical theories as either *deontic* or *aretaic*, a virtue ethics belongs in the second of these categories. This classification, in turn, is ordinarily taken to depend on the possibility of a reasonably clear distinction between deontic and aretaic judgements.[3]

The term 'deontic' is derived from the Greek *deon*, often translated as 'duty'. Such judgements as 'one should always speak the truth', 'one ought to keep one's promises' and 'stealing is morally wrong' are typical deontic constructions. 'Aretaic' is derived from the Greek term for excellence, *arete*. Such judgements as 'she has great strength of character', 'her devotion is admirable' and 'spite is most unbecoming' are examples of aretaic locutions. These two types of judgement differ most conspicuously with respect to their principal topics of discourse: whereas deontic judgements are primarily, if not exclusively, concerned with the evaluation of actions or kinds of actions, aretaic judgements are *also* concerned with the evaluation of persons, their characters, intentions and motives. This distinction is not entirely hard and fast since actions may be the subject of *either* deontic or aretaic judgements. But although actions are also subject to aretaic evaluation, such appraisal seems to differ from deontic evaluation insofar as an appeal to rules or principle is a salient feature of the latter. Hence whereas characterising an action as morally wrong suggests that performing it is contrary to some general rule or principle, the focus in aretaic judgements about actions, is more on the psychological or personal sources of agency. To call an action bad or vicious, for example, is to draw attention to the bad inclinations or vicious motives from which it springs.

Again, aretaic predicates ('good' and 'bad', 'admirable' and 'deplorable', 'courageous' and 'cowardly' etc.) differ from deontic predicates ('right' and 'wrong', 'obligatory', 'permissible' or 'prohibited' etc.) by virtue of expressing what can be referred to as *scalar* properties. To be good or admirable, for example, is to possess a comparative quality, since we can speak of better and best, more or less admirable. However, since we lack the comparatives right, righter and rightest – presumably because no very clear sense attaches to appraisal of actions as more or less right – rightness is not a scalar quality (Urmson 1968: 92–6). To this extent deontic evaluations may appear, by contrast with aretaic appraisals, to resemble *legal* judgements, and, indeed, this difference is well explored in Nicholas Dent's insightful contribution to this volume. Whereas moral qualities may be expressed either deontically (by identifying actions as right or obligatory, wrong or forbidden) or aretaically (by identifying actions as friendly or considerate, hostile or unkind), Dent nevertheless shows how the former kinds of characterization incline to a quasi-legal construal of moral imperatives as externally imposed demands or unwelcome constraints.

At any rate, this distinction between deontic and aretaic judgements gives us some purchase on the difference between a deontic and an aretaic ethics. It is characteristic of an aretaic ethics that: first, aretaic judgements and predicates are treated as basic or primary, at least in relation to deontic ones; second, deontic judgements and predicates are regarded as, if not inappropriate or redundant, at least derivative of, secondary or reducible to aretaic ones. The same holds *mutatis mutandis* for deontic ethics.

It should also be clear, however, that these definitions license a distinction between two versions of an aretaic ethics, and by implication, two versions of virtue ethics. On the first version – which might be called the *replacement view* – the claim is that deontic judgements and notions are inappropriate or redundant and should be jettisoned in favour of aretaic ones. Elizabeth Anscombe in her widely celebrated and much discussed paper 'Modern moral philosophy' (1958) seems strongly drawn to some such radical thesis in observing that contemporary philosophers would do well to suspend enquiry into notions of moral rightness and obligation – given their source in a divine law conception of ethics which no longer enjoys widespread modern currency – in default of further clarification of the psychologically grounded vocabulary of received aretaic usage. It seems implied by Anscombe's discussion, not just that we need to make sense of notions of 'intention', 'character' and 'virtue' before we can do the same for ideas of moral obligation – but that not much real sense can be made of notions of moral obligation in conditions of contemporary secularism.

As well as the replacement thesis, however, there is a less radical *reductionist* version of aretaic ethics which, far from proposing to dispense entirely with deontic notions, claims only that aretaic evaluations have ethical primacy over the deontic. It would appear that the majority of contemporary virtue ethicists incline to the reductionist position. According to Rosalind Hursthouse (1996: 27–8) for example, an ethics of virtue does not at all preclude our giving sense to such moral rules as 'lying is morally wrong' or 'one ought to keep one's promises': the point of a virtue ethics is rather that such general deontic judgements find their justification in terms which are basically aretaic. Thus, telling lies is wrong because it is dishonest, and dishonesty is a vice; breaking a promise is something we ought not to do, because it is unjust or a case of betrayal; and so on. Deontic judgements, in short, are treated as derivative from – rather than replaceable by – aretaic evaluations.

Alongside the replacement versus reductionist distinction, there would appear to be a further important difference between types of aretaic ethics. According to William Frankena (1973a: 63; 1973b: 24–5), an ethics of virtue is an aretaic ethics of a *certain kind,* namely an aretaic *agent* ethics. It is typical of such ethics that aretaic judgements about agents and their traits are taken as basic, whereas evaluations of action or kinds of action – irrespective of whether these are aretaic or deontic – are taken to be derivative. On the face of it, this distinction neatly captures the widespread view that an ethics of virtue centres on the goodness or badness of agents and their character, rather than on the rightness or wrongness of actions or kinds of actions. It also seems fully in tune with the ethical theory of Aristotle, who is generally regarded as the prime exemplar of an ethics of virtue: after all, was it not Aristotle who claimed that actions are noble in so far as they are actions that a virtuous or noble agent would perform?

In the event, most modern philosophical commentators on virtue ethics – we may here cite Richard B. Brandt (1981), Robert B. Louden (1984; 1986), Gregory Trianosky (1990) and Gary Watson (1990) as examples – seem to agree with Frankena in regarding it as an aretaic agent ethics. Again, Hursthouse (1991; 1996) not only accepts this definition, but is herself a powerful advocate of virtue ethics so defined, arguing that an ethics of virtue differs from its Kantian and utilitarian rivals primarily in terms of its distinct emphasis on the primacy of good character over right conduct. For Hursthouse too, deontic appraisals of action are derivative of aretaic judgements about agents and their traits, and it is the hallmark of an ethics of virtue that an action is regarded as right if and only if it is what a virtuous agent would characteristically do in the circumstances.

Despite this, the general tendency to define an ethics of virtue as an aretaic agent ethics has not lacked philosophical opposition. J. L. A. Garcia (1990), for example, doubts the possibility of deriving act evaluations from some prior evaluation of character, inclining to the contrary view that the concept of virtuous character is derivative of our notions of virtuous conduct. However, insofar as he also holds aretaic act-evaluation to be more basic than deontic act-evaluation, he subscribes to an aretaic *act* version of virtue ethics.

Michael Slote (1992: 88–93) also appears to have doubts about the general tendency to regard virtue ethics as an aretaic agent ethics, although unlike Garcia he does not exclude the possibility of developing an aretaic agent ethics. Indeed in one of his pioneering publications (1995) he sketches the outlines of an 'agent-based virtue ethics'. It would appear that his main reservation about any exclusive definition of virtue ethics in aretaic agent terms is a general dearth of clear-cut historical examples of any such 'agent-basing'. In his view, even Plato's and Aristotle's ethics are difficult to construe in such terms. Consequently, Slote inclines to an alternative, less exclusive, definition of virtue ethics as agent-*focused* rather than agent-*based*. On this view, virtue ethics seems to include in its basic evaluative repertoire, not only aretaic evaluations of agents and their traits, but also aretaic appraisals of actions. Thus, the ethics which he develops in his *From Morality To Virtue* (1992), though agent-focused, is not (purely) an aretaic agent ethics, insofar as the polar aretaic predicates of 'admirable/deplorable' function as primary terms of act-evaluation.[4] (See Figure 1.2.)

As already observed, insofar as Aristotle's ethical views are commonly taken to epitomise virtue ethics, any definition of a virtue ethics might be expected to embrace his account of virtue. Slote (1992: 89–90; 1995: 239–40; 1997: 178), however, makes out a substantial case for supposing that Aristotle's ethics does not meet the requirements of an aretaic agent ethics; for, according to him, Aristotle characterizes the virtuous agent 'as someone who *sees* or *perceives* what is good or fine or right to do in any given situation' (1995: 240). On the face of it, such language suggests that the virtuous agent does what is

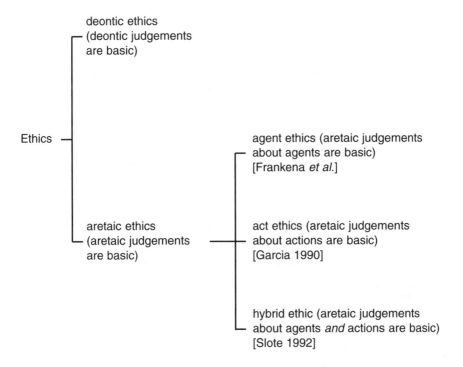

*Figure 1.2* An ethics of virtue as an aretaic ethics

noble or virtuous *because* it is the noble or virtuous thing to do, and this, he says, clearly indicates that act-assessment is not entirely derivative of evaluations of persons or traits.

Is Aristotle's ethics, then, agent-based or only agent-focused, and is it therefore inappropriate to define an ethics of virtue as an aretaic agent ethics in accordance with the standard view?[5] Fortunately, this question may for present purposes be left open, since it is enough for an ethics of virtue to be aretaic irrespective of its precise act-based, agent-based or agent-focused status. It is likely that any satisfactory answer to this awaits further clarification of the philosophical psychology of character, and perhaps especially of the relationship of practical reasoning to virtuous action. Indeed, many of the explorations of the precise mechanics of virtue included in this volume may well constitute progress in this direction. For a start, as Randall Curren shows in his contribution to this volume, Aristotle holds that the intellectual virtue of practical wisdom (*phronesis*) both completes and presupposes moral virtue. His view of the unity of virtue implies not only that one cannot be morally virtuous without also being practically wise, but also that there can be no practical wisdom without moral virtue. On the face of it, this time-honoured way of expressing matters does seem to pull us in the direction of some kind of agent-based ethics; for if being fully virtuous is a prerequisite of being able to discern the ethical features of actions, how then could we know what is right or proper other than by determining what the fully virtuous agent would do in the circumstances? But then, on the other hand, how are we to determine whether or not an agent is fully virtuous without some independent means of ascertaining the ethical value of her actions?

As recent work by Nancy Sherman (1997) and others shows, however, it may be that what here needs questioning is the very nature of practical moral reason, in particular, the modern idea that such reason is purely a matter of intellectual discernment of rules and principles of conduct. On the Aristotelian view such reason seems better patterned on the model of cultivation of a range of sensibilities to the particularities of moral engagement, involving crucial interplay between the cognitive and the affective. From this point of view although we may agree with aretaic act ethicists that we could have little idea what a good character is without some grasp of what constitutes virtuous conduct, we also need to recognise with friends of agent-basing that no such full grasp is possible via purely intellectual discernment of agent-neutral features of action. Any complete grasp of the nature of virtuous action must involve some understanding of it as expressive of personal sensibilities, and this cannot be had other than via the proper cultivation of sensitivity to the particularities of experience. Thus, the issue between agent-basing and act-basing – to which Slote's idea of agent-focusing seems usefully addressed – more than likely turns on further clarification of these important issues.

## The virtue approach: eudaimonia and perfectionism

To date, we have identified two marks of a virtue approach to moral education which seem to go some way towards distinguishing it from other approaches. Our initial criterion was that a virtue approach would have to feature virtues or their constituents as aims of moral education. Several chapters of the present work are devoted to exploring such aims by making basic distinctions between types of virtues. James Wallace offers a perceptive discussion of the vexed relationship between virtues of benevolence and justice, Michael Slote examines the important distinction between self- and other-regarding virtues, and we have already referred to Curren's treatment of the Aristotelian connection between moral and intellectual virtue. Our elaborated criterion, however, more precisely characterized a virtue approach as a conception of moral education grounded in a virtue ethics, and we saw how this may be understood in different ways according to different definitions of virtue ethics. Beside the issues raised by the diversity of these definitions – which we have for the moment left unresolved – there are some remaining questions about the relationship of virtue ethics to other moral theories which should not go unnoticed here.

We earlier argued that to define an ethics of virtue aretaically – in, as it were, the narrow sense – is to offer it as an alternative to Kantian and utilitarian moral views. But it might be asked to what extent an aretaic ethics is a *real* alternative to these two major traditions of modern moral philosophy, especially since, as we have already admitted, there may be Kantian or other non-virtue-theoretical conceptions of virtue. Thus, in order to be clearer about what differences, if any, there are between the virtue-theoretical approach and others, we need to attend more closely to the *justifications* offered for regarding certain traits as virtues. The question is now therefore: are the virtue-ethical reasons which justify virtues really all that different from standard Kantian and utilitarian justifications of virtues?

First, the difference between virtue ethics as such and any form of Kantian ethics seems clear enough; for whereas aretaic appraisals are taken to be basic on a virtue ethics, they are regarded as at least secondary to, or derivative of, deontic judgements in Kantian ethics. Thus, in construing the moral or virtuous life – including assessments of character – basically in terms of a principled appreciation of interpersonal duties and obligations, Kantian ethics is more or less deontic by definition. Eamonn Callan's contribution to this volume may perhaps serve as an example of some such deontic conception of virtue. Insofar as Callan seems to regard the promotion of such liberal virtues as moderation, tolerance and open-mindedness as central aims of moral education – and a high profile is given to aretaic considerations in his theory – his account of moral formation appears to have a distinctly Aristotelian flavour. Nevertheless, to the extent that deontic considerations seem to be fundamental to his account, Callan's virtue approach seems unrepentantly deontological, and the role he gives to such virtues as moderation and tolerance seems ultimately grounded in a liberal ethics of obligation.

Moreover, most versions of utilitarian ethics – though commonly contrasted with deontological theories as forms of teleological ethics – are of a basically deontic character.[6] Thus, although – as with Kantians – utilitarians may regard certain traits as virtues, this is only insofar as their practice contributes to conduct which is independently establishable as conforming to rules or principles of right action. To be sure, utilitarians differ from Kantians in holding that the value of moral rules and principles ultimately depends on their consequences for human happiness, so such principles are not in the least Kantianly self-validating, but are justified in terms of some extra-moral good. However, because deontic considerations are understood on such views to be basic relative to aretaic appraisals, many versions of utilitarian ethics would appear to sit comfortably enough on the deontic side of any aretaic-deontic divide.

At the same time, there is a version of utilitarian ethics – usually referred to as *character*- or *trait*-utilitarianism – which does seem to qualify well enough as a form of aretaic ethics. Character-utilitarianism is undeniably utilitarian – since the extra-moral good of human happiness (or preference-satisfaction) is the principal ground of moral evaluation – but it is not deontic insofar as it takes aretaic appraisals to be more fundamental than deontic evaluations of actions. In contrast with act- or rule-utilitarianism, character-utilitarianism does not appear to require a mediating account of the relation between moral character and human happiness. On this view, in short, certain character traits – broadly the traditional virtues – derive moral significance directly from their tendency to maximize utility.

Insofar as our aretaic characterization of an ethics of virtue fails to distinguish virtue ethics from character-utilitarianism, then, it may still be considered incomplete. If we want to present virtue ethics as a genuine alternative to utilitarianism we need to show that it is aretaic in a different sense from trait-utilitarianism. On closer scrutiny, moreover, the incompleteness of our definition of virtue ethics to date also shows up in our contrast of an ethics of virtue with Kantianism and the deontic versions of utilitarianism. For all these ethical views offer a certain type of justification of virtues – and, consequently, of the aims of moral education – which, we argued, is uncharacteristic of an ethics of virtue aretaically conceived. But as yet we have not given any detailed account of the way in which virtue ethics might itself justify the virtues, and this is precisely what needs to be done if we are to distinguish an ethics of virtue from trait-utilitarianism.

So far as one can see, however, a virtue ethics might be distinguished from trait-utilitarianism in either of two ways. First, an ethics of virtue is sometimes defined as a view according to which the virtues have intrinsic value or worth. On such a view – which can be called perfectionism (Sher 1992: 93) – virtue ethics clearly differs from trait-utilitarianism in terms of its distinctly non-teleological character. Whereas it is characteristic of any form of utilitarianism to regard the virtues as good only insofar as they are productive of the further good of human happiness, perfectionism values the virtues as goods in themselves. Unlike other accounts of the virtues, perfectionism enshrines a non-inferential conception of the moral value of the virtues: that is, virtues do not derive their moral value from any other source such as obligation or the maximization of utility. However, defenders of perfectionism would insist that the alleged impossibility of justifying virtues on any terms other than their own, does not mean that they cannot be justified at all. Perfectionists may therefore incline to this or that form of *non*-inferential ethical justification, claiming, for example, that virtues are naturally fitted to the expression of well-formed human sentiment (as in moral sense theories) or that they are somehow self-evidently good or right to anyone of appropriately developed moral sensibility (as in moral intuitionism) (Sinnott-Armstrong 1996).

A second conception of virtue ethics would construe virtues as traits of character in some sense constitutive of human flourishing (Carr 1991: 100–1; Hursthouse 1991: 219–20). Insofar as Aristotle is commonly associated with such a view, it seems appropriate to refer to it as an Aristotelian virtue ethics. Like trait-utilitarianism, but unlike perfectionism, Aristotelian virtue ethics is teleological: since the value of character traits is held to depend on their relation to human well-being, some non-moral notion of good appears to be taken as primary. But Aristotelian ethics differs from trait-utilitarianism in certain crucial respects. First, whereas the utilitarian justification of virtues in terms of well-being indifferently emphasises the good of *all* who are affected by the possession and exercise of virtues (agents and patients alike), the focus of Aristotelian virtue ethics is primarily – though not exclusively – upon the good of the possessor of virtues (the agent). For the most part, then, an Aristotelian ethics regards as virtues traits of character which are in a significant sense conducive to the agent's own flourishing (*eudaimonia*), bearing in mind that, since personal flourishing on the Aristotelian view has an important social dimension, friendship, sociability and justice are to that extent crucial virtues. A second and more important point is that virtues are conceived on the Aristotelian view as *constitutive* elements of a flourishing life. Since trait-utilitarianism is not just a teleological but a consequentialist ethics, the virtues are invested with moral significance only to the extent that they are causally or instrumentally productive of human happiness. But although Aristotelian virtue ethics is teleological, it is not consequentialist and to that extent construes practice of the virtues as internal to leading a worthwhile life. Unlike the trait-utilitarian who might take or leave virtues according to their expected utility in securing some independently ascertained goal of human happiness, the Aristotelian has no conception of human fulfilment which would exclude practise of the virtues (Steutel 1998).

Such a view is not without its own difficulties, one of which is that any such 'internal' conception of the relationship of virtue to flourishing opens up the possibility of the relativization of virtue. To the extent that different cultural constituencies appear to embody different conceptions of the good life, it would appear that there may rival and incompatible accounts of the virtues. This has, of course, been one of the burning issues of contemporary moral and social theory ever since the publication in 1981 of Alasdair MacIntyre's seminal work *After Virtue*. MacIntyre has himself explored the worrying moral educational consequences of his neo-Aristotelian view of the relationship of virtue to *eudaimonia* in conditions of contemporary cultural pluralism, arguing that since any meaningful initiation into moral virtues cannot but enshrine some substantial conception of the good life, it is impossible to conceive any neutral or impartial moral education reflecting 'a shared public morality of commonplace usage' (MacIntyre 1991). In view of such notions, MacIntyre's work has been widely seen as giving hostages to the fortunes of radical moral relativism, and various contributions to the fourth and fifth parts of this work are concerned to address such issues. However, other recent virtue ethicists, while accepting MacIntyre's basic premise that any view of the virtues cannot but be socioculturally conditioned, have nevertheless argued the possibility of a non-relative conception of virtue which might well constitute a common cross-cultural currency of moral evaluation (e.g. Nussbaum 1988).

Regardless of these further issues and problems we venture to hope that this introduction has succeeded in laying bare some of the main ways of conceiving a virtue approach to moral education, which we may now roughly summarise. In the first place we argued that a virtue approach to moral education would at the very least be one which entertained the promotion of virtues and their constituents as the goal of moral education. But, secondly, since this would not significantly serve to distinguish a virtue approach from other (for example, Kantian or utilitarian) approaches to moral education, we argued that a distinctive virtue approach would be one grounded in a virtue ethics, which, in turn, we characterized as aretaic rather than deontic. Although we left unresolved the question of which of a variety of kinds of aretaic ethics – agent-based, act-based and agent-focused – the genuine virtue ethics might be, we argued that a virtue ethics is *necessarily* aretaic and character-centred. But though it seems necessary to a virtue ethics to be aretaic, we also saw that it may not be *sufficient*, for while trait-utilitarianism does not seem to be virtue-theoretical in the sense of giving a non-instrumental account of the value of virtue, it does seem to be aretaic. In distinguishing trait-utilitarianism from virtue ethics proper, then, we were left with the two strictly virtue-theoretical alternatives of perfectionism and Aristotelian eudaimonism, of which the Aristotelian option is arguably the most plausible.

By no means all contributors to this volume, as already noted, seem inclined to defend this more particular way of conceiving virtue education. Some, indeed, do not appear inclined to defend, as basic to virtue education, any form of virtue ethics in our narrower sense. All the same, we hope that this introduction has at least contributed to a somewhat clearer view of how the virtue-theoretical land lies.

## Notes

1 Elsewhere (see Steutel 1997) it is argued that the virtue of justice, as explained by Kohlberg, encompasses quite a bag of virtues, in particular virtues of will-power (required for bridging the gap between judgement and action) and intellectual virtues (required for appropriate moral reasoning).

2 Frankena (1970: 5–6; 1973a: 65–7) and Baier (1988: 126–7) draw a related distinction between two senses of an ethics of virtue, namely a 'moderate' virtue ethics which is supplementary to Kantianism and utilitarianism, and a rival 'radical' virtue ethics. (See also Slote 1997: 176.) The present distinction between a virtue ethics in the broad and the narrow sense is somewhat different. Whereas moderate and rival virtue ethics are presented as mutually exclusive, a virtue ethics in the broad sense would include all virtue ethics, moderate *and* rival.

3 Although the present account of the distinction between deontic and aretaic judgements draws heavily on Frankena (1970: 9; 1973a: 9, 62, 70; 1973b: 23–4), it is not entirely unproblematic. Still, some version of the distinction would appear to be assumed by all philosophers who argue in favour of a virtue ethics in a narrow sense.

4 However, in a more recent essay (1997), Slote no longer appears quite so wedded to an agent-focused virtue ethics. Although he continues to hold that Aristotle's

ethics is agent-focused more than agent-based, he is less sure 'which form of virtue ethics is likely to fare best and make the greatest contribution in the current climate of ethical theory' (1997: 179).

5  According to Slote, an agent-based ethics treats character evaluation as fundamental and as therefore in no need of further ethical grounding. However, we have defined an agent-based ethics (or an aretaic agent ethics) in a less restricted way: namely, as an ethics which treats act evaluation as secondary to trait-evaluation, irrespective of whether the latter mode of evaluation is considered to be fundamental. Consequently, any ethics which treats act-evaluation as derivative from trait-evaluation – grounding the latter in further considerations of human flourishing – will be agent-based in our own but not in Slote's sense. In this connection, to distinguish such an view from an agent-based (in his sense) ethics, Slote refers to it as an agent-prior form of virtue ethics (1997: 207).

6  This distinction between a deontic and an aretaic ethics should not be confused with the quite different contrast between the deontological and the teleological, since of course, whereas all utilitarian views are teleological, many of them are also deontic. Moreover, though a virtue ethics (in a narrow sense) is by definition aretaic, some versions are not teleological, as explained below.

# References

Anscombe, G. E. M. (1958) 'Modern moral philosophy', *Philosophy* 33: 1–19.

Aristotle, (1925) *Nicomachean Ethics* (Ethica Nicomachea), trans. W. D. Ross. Oxford: Oxford University Press.

Baier, K. (1988) 'Radical virtue ethics', in P. A. French, T. E. Uehling and H. K. Wettstein (eds) *Midwest Studies in Philosophy. Vol. XIII. Ethical Theory: Character and virtue*, Notre Dame: University of Notre Dame Press.

Brandt, R. B. (1981) 'W. K. Frankena and ethics of virtue', *The Monist* 64, 3: 271–92.

Carr, D. (1991) *Educating the Virtues: An essay on the philosophical psychology of moral development and education*, London: Routledge.

Frankena, W. K. (1970) 'Prichard and the ethics of virtue. Notes on a footnote', *The Monist* 54: 1–17.

—— (1973a) *Ethics*, Englewood Cliffs, N. J: Prentice-Hall.

—— (1973b) 'The ethics of love conceived as an ethics of virtue', *The Journal of Religious Ethics* 1, 1: 21–36.

Garcia, J. L. A. (1990) 'The primacy of the virtuous', *Philosophia: Philosophical Quarterly of Israel* 20: 69–91.

Hare, R. M. (1981) *Moral thinking: Its levels, method, and point*, Oxford: Clarendon Press.

Hursthouse, R. (1991) 'Virtue theory and abortion', in R. Crisp and M. Slote (eds) *Virtue Ethics*, Oxford: Oxford University Press, 1997.

—— (1996) 'Normative virtue ethics', in R. Crisp (ed.) *How Should One Live? essays on the virtues*, Oxford: Clarendon Press.

Kant, I. (1797)[1966] *Metaphysik der Sitten*, Hamburg: Felix Meiner Verlag.

Kohlberg, L. (1981) 'Education for justice: A modern statement of the Socratic view', in L. Kohlberg, *Essays on Moral Development, vol. I, The Philosophy of Moral*

*Development: Moral stages and the idea of justice*, San Francisco: Harper and Row.

Louden, R. B. (1984) 'On some vices of virtue ethics', *American Philosophical Quarterly* 21, 3: 227–36.

—— (1986) 'Kant's virtue ethics', *Philosophy* 61: 473–89.

MacIntyre, A. C. (1981) *After Virtue*, Notre Dame: University of Notre Dame Press.

MacIntyre, A. C. (1991) *How To Appear Virtuous Without Actually Being So*, University of Lancaster: Centre for the Study of Cultural Values.

Nussbaum, M. (1988) 'Non-relative virtues: an Aristotelian approach', in P. A. French, T. E. Uehling and H. K. Wettstein (eds) *Midwest Studies in Philosophy. Vol. XIII. Ethical Theory: Character and virtue*, Notre Dame: Notre Dame Press.

Rawls, J. (1993) *Political Liberalism*, New York: Columbia University Press.

Sher, G. (1992) 'Knowing about virtue', in J. W. Chapman and W. A. Galston (eds) *Nomos XXXIV: Virtue*, New York and London: New York University Press.

Sherman, N. (1997) *Making a Necessity of Virtue: Aristotle and Kant on virtue*, Cambridge: Cambridge University Press.

Sinnott-Armstrong, W. (1996) 'Moral skepticism and justification', in W. Sinnott-Armstrong and M. Timmons (eds) *Moral Knowledge? New readings in moral epistemology*, New York: Oxford University Press.

Slote, M. (1992) *From Morality To Virtue*, New York and Oxford: Oxford University Press.

—— (1995) 'Agent-based virtue ethics', in R. Crisp and M. Slote (eds) *Virtue Ethics*, Oxford: Oxford University Press, 1997.

—— (1997) 'Virtue ethics', in M. W. Baron, P. Pettit and M. Slote, *Three Methods of Ethics*, Malden, Mass.: Blackwell.

Steutel, J. W. (1997) 'The virtue approach to moral education: some conceptual clarifications', *Journal of Philosophy of Education* 31, 3: 395–407.

—— (1998) 'Virtues and human flourishing: A teleological justication', in D. Carr (ed.) *Knowledge, Truth and Education: Beyond the postmodern impasse*, London: Routledge.

Trianosky, G. (1990) 'What is a virtue ethics all about?' *American Philosophical Quarterly* 27, 4: 335–44.

Urmson, J. O. (1968) *The Emotive Theory of Ethics*, London: Hutchinson University Library.

Watson, G. (1990) 'On the primacy of character', in O. Flanagan and A. O. Rorty (eds) *Identity, Character, and Morality: Essays in moral psychology*, Cambridge, Mass.: MIT Press.

# Part 2

# GENERAL ISSUES

# 2

# VIRTUE, *EUDAIMONIA* AND TELEOLOGICAL ETHICS

*Nicholas Dent*

## I

Two of the – perhaps the two – great questions of moral philosophy are these. First, is there a real, objective, distinction between what is morally right and good and what is morally wrong and bad? Second, why should we do what is morally right and avoid what is morally wrong? Or, to put it in a more idiomatic way: why should I be moral?

To the first of these questions accrete all the issues around the metaphysics and ontology of moral properties, their relation to 'natural' properties and so on. In addition, questions about whether, or how, we can know what is right or wrong, good or bad, arise in this area, and for this reason it is convenient to refer to this whole cluster of issues as matters of the epistemology of morals, or moral epistemology.

To the second of these questions accrete issues about the reasons for action which would lead someone to behave morally, or about the sentiments and interests which actuate human beings and might lead them to engage with moral purposes and commitments. I shall refer to this cluster of concerns as the problem of moral motivation.

Although most of the questions central to each of these two broad areas are very substantially different and can be considered independently of one another, a theorist's response to one of these groups of questions has often been shaped (wittingly or unwittingly) by their response to the other. This is perhaps most obvious in the case of those for whom the most urgent issue has seemed to be explaining and justifying the (supposed) role of moral requirements as having an overriding claim to govern choices and actions. If it is taken, plausibly enough, that human choices and actions are the upshot of desires, attitudes, will and feeling (our conative and affective powers), it is often concluded that moral requirements can only have the role indicated if they are supposed to be of the same general character as desires, attitudes etcetera. also. The primary notion will be that of accepting a moral requirement or making a moral commitment, and that is conceived in terms of an overriding commitment of the will, or of having a predominant attitude. (Prescriptivist and emotivist moral theories conform to this pattern.) Construing moral commitments in this way secures their motivational role; it could hardly be otherwise, since the construction was made precisely with this end in view. But now the epistemology of moral commitments becomes problematic. Being commitments of the will, enduring attitudes or whatever, they do not appear to involve at all knowledge claims, representations of things being thus and so. Familiarly, prescriptive and emotive theories are referred to as 'non-cognitive' in character, implying that there is nothing to be known (or believed) about what is right or wrong.

This shaping can, of course, work in the other direction. A utilitarian moral theorist, for example, will have a more or less secure epistemological route for identifying actions as right or wrong. But reasons for doing what is morally right, or sentiments leading us to do what is morally right, will be harder to come by, especially if the wish is to show that we have overriding reasons to do what is right. It is very far from being obvious why everyone might have overridingly good reason for placing pursuit of the greatest happiness of the greatest number as their highest priority. So, customarily, this role for moral claims is ceded; moral requirements become requirements which different people may have reasons of differing weight for acknowledging.[1]

I make these perfectly familiar points because they provide a useful context in which to consider what is central to this essay. There are modes of moral thinking and action which have at their core the deployment of deontic notions, notions of what is morally obligatory, morally prohibited and morally permissible. There are also modes of moral thinking and action which centrally involve the notion of a virtue and the notions of particular virtues, admirable and estimable traits of character. If we reflect upon how moral thinking and action articulated in these two differing modes leads us to engage with the question 'why should I be moral?', then, I shall suggest, we may be able to see some deep differences between them. We may be led to think that there are quite strong reasons why moral thought and action articulated through aretaic notions (notions of virtue) promises a more fruitful insight into the significance of the issues of moral motivation, and a more fruitful response to those issues. The question of moral motivation provides us with a way of assessing the differing meaning and force that is given to moral 'norms' (as I shall neutrally and colourlessly call them) through these different conceptualizations of morally normative claims.

The point of application is this. If we focus on the question 'why should I be moral?' – or, lest this appear already to import a deontological articulation, the more indeterminately formulated question 'why be moral?' – then the way in which we might begin to answer this question will depend crucially upon how we see moral norms engaging us: that is, how we see moral norms impacting upon us. It will be central to my argument that moral norms conceptualised in deontic terms engage with moral agents and their activity in a markedly different way from such norms conceptualised through aretaic notions. If we explore these different forms of engagement we shall, I think, see with considerable vividness the scope and limits of each of these different conceptual frameworks for moral thinking and action.

In the next section, I shall try to show more clearly what I have in mind, by looking at the role of moral norms in the life of moral agents when they are articulated deploying deontic notions. After that, I shall attempt a roughly parallel task with reference to aretaic notions; and in a brief final section I touch on a couple of further aspects of the case.

## II

As mentioned above, the core deontic notions by which we formulate and express moral norms are the notions of the morally obligatory, the morally prohibited (forbidden) and the morally permissible. I must stress that I am not here concerned with the cogency of articulating moral norms in these terms, nor with our capability to prove, to know, whether something is morally obligatory, permissible or whatever. I am setting to one side questions of the metaphysics and epistemology of morals. My concern is with how, accepting the cogency of claims articulated in this way, the choosing and acting moral subject stands in relation to them; or with how they address or engage the moral agent.

My guiding thought here is this. Moral norms thus conceptualised and articulated are being represented as requirements that bear down upon the agent, as directives to act or constraints upon action. They are formulated as if they are externally imposed demands which have a coercive role to play in governing conduct. (The case of the morally permissible may seem not to fit this characteristation, but this is a secondary case. The permissible is that which is neither obligatory nor forbidden, and I am centrally concerned with the primary ideas of the obligatory and the forbidden). Moral norms so conceptualised are conceived as a kind of law; indeed, the notion of a 'moral law' is a very familiar one.[2] Admittedly there is no obvious lawgiver, nor apparatus for the enforcement of law, nor are there due procedures for bringing people to judgement before the custodians of the law. But, as I shall go on to argue, the structure of thought, appraisal and action in play here is still in many important respects that appropriate to the structure of law and the role of law.

What is it to confront something in the character of its being an externally imposed requirement? How does something with the significance of a (quasi-) coercive demand engage the will, decision and action of an agent? In the case of a plain, non-controversial instance of a coercive demand ('Your money or your life!') the answer is scarcely elusive though not without its complexities. Where that requirement is a moral one, the demand is the demand of righteousness, and the coercion is powerful but impalpable, the answer is much more difficult. I shall attempt no exhaustive analysis, of which anyway I am incapable. I shall, rather, single out three or four aspects that are particularly material to the comparison with aretaic conceptualisations of moral norms. There will be an element of exaggeration in some of my comments in order to sharpen the points I am after, but I hope the points do not arise only out of the exaggeration.

An agent encountering a norm in the form of an imposed requirement will encounter it as specifying something to be done which does not necessarily, if at all, connect with anything that the agent desires, cherishes or values. To take a familiar type of case, deeds of friendship need not be represented as things one is under an obligation to perform if one is already willing and desirous of doing them. Even if it is the case (and, as I have said, I am not concerned to debate that question here) that friendship has its obligations, the deeds, words and gestures of affection and concern characteristic of friendship are not undertaken and shown in their character as obligations. For the deeds of friendship to be engage someone as morally obligatory, they must be deeds which the agent does not already have sufficient reason to do, or interest in doing, but which he or she requires to be directed to do through the engagement of a (supposed) additional conative power, a 'sense of obligation'. This 'sense of obligation' is supposed, at the very least, to ensure morally appropriate action in the absence of other interests, and, at the most, to override all contrary interests. (Entire moral psychologies have been formulated around the attempt to make sense of this; Kant's is only one of many.)

If there is anything in this, it imports already a very remarkable representation of an agent's relation to moral norms. Moral norms thus conceptualised appear to be disengaged from those interests and concerns which an agent would avow as naturally and spontaneously his or her own, and in principle, and often also in practice, appear to be opposed to those interests and concerns. An agent's relation to obligation appears to be that of obedience or submission to what is demanded. But how extraordinary it is to think that the central postures of moral acceptance are those of submissive obedience. Or, to put it another way, what an extraordinary thing morality must be, if the core responses it invokes are submission and obedience to a moral 'command'. (I am not, plainly, to be taken as arguing that we should never submit and obey; the humbling of pride is often very good. My point is rather that it is worth considering whether this is the emblematic moral posture.)

There is something not entirely straightforward going on here; and that idea can be added to if one reflects that it is customarily held that among the most significant moral demands we face are those that concern the well-being of others, that involve 'respect for persons' (whatever exactly that entails). But if it is thought appropriate to articulate the moral place of others' needs and good in our lives through the ideas of what is obligatory and what is prohibited in our dealings with them, then the implication is that their need and good does not engage us, or does not engage us adequately and sufficiently, on any other footing. To acknowledge their need and good as an obligation is supposed to make it more significant than it otherwise would be. But this, so far from materially engaging us more closely with others' weal and woe, merely causes us to submit to an obligation to respect the weal and woe of others. The obligation actually seems to interpose itself between us and the purported object of moral concern: the living presence of another person. In so far as the idea of the obligatory is involved, it suggests that the moral claim others present is something importunate, something of which we need to be brought to obedient submissive acknowledgement. Other people appear figured as unwanted repositories of imperious demand, and we have to acknowledge these claims of obligation.[3]

I want now to look at another aspect of the case. Infractions of law make the offender liable to punishment. If moral norms are conceived of as having the character of a moral law, they likewise make us liable to blame, to accusations of fault, and to punishment in the shape of pangs of conscience, or censorious condemnation by others. This punitive element surrounding moral failure has profound implications, I believe. I want to attend to just one aspect of it. It presents the moral agent as performing before a panel of judges and assessors who are entitled to pass a verdict upon what he or she has done, and to inflict some penalty in the event of substandard performance. It would seem that in our moral undertakings we are not so much colleagues who are mutually supportive in our common endeavour to achieve some cherished end, but people whose efforts are to be measured and assessed by those whose place is to stand in judgement. Of course, any sensitive and thoughtful judge will hesitate to condemn too quickly and too dismissively, will be conscious of his or her own limitations and weaknesses, and will be as ready to forgive as to condemn. But none of this questions the proposition that the moral agent stands to his fellows as one to be appraised, evaluated and assessed by them, as a person before judges. Indeed it presupposes this. These propositions are all relaxations within this same framework.

Where did this idea come from? How can it possibly be reasonable? Someone who stood in judgement of their friend would be assuming a footing in the relationship which is quite inapposite. But it appears that when moral conduct is in question this is a position which (more or less) anyone may assume in relation to anyone else.

If we place this representation of our standing with others alongside the previously discussed representation of others as sources of importunate demands, it is scarcely surprising that moral conduct involving others can come to seem something we would rather opt out of completely if possible. This is, of course, to create the very image of the heedless amoralist, to curb the waywardness of whom deontic morality puts itself forward. But this image is the product of deontic morality's construction of the case; it is not something that pre-existed deontic morality, or is inevitably so.[4]

In the passage quoted in note 2, Hume pays particular attention to the issue of voluntariness which, he argues, is given undue prominence because of the connection of morals with punishment and reward. I shall not pursue this matter further in detail here; I make just a few comments on it in Section III.

Finally, I want briefly to return to my first point concerning moral norms conceptualised deploying deontic notions. I suggested that the idea of moral obligation most clearly has its application in directing conduct where the agent does not already have sufficient reason to do, or interest in doing, what is specified as obligatory. As I put it, the moral obligation is apprehended as quasi-coercive. But it is a very general truth that human beings are apt to respond to coercion with anger and resentment. The source of the coercion is viewed as something thwarting or controlling, and this bodes ill for any willing moral compliance. The point should perhaps be put more subtly. Because acknowledgement of moral obligations involves setting aside desired objectives, it is apt to be viewed with anger. It is then experienced as being coercive and thwarting, as comprising an unwarranted imposition. It can scarcely be a promising basis for moral development and commitment if the character of moral norms is configured in such a way that this becomes one of the most basic features of their engagement with a subject's readiness to embrace a purpose and to act.

It may be argued that there is no alternative, that the character of human desire and its distance from what is morally appropriate is such that, as I put it before, obedience and submission before the moral law must be the emblematic moral posture. But I am not convinced matters must be viewed in this light; and in the next section I hope to suggest that if we examine how moral norms conceptualised through the deployment of aretaic notions engage with human agents, we shall see that another way of looking at these issues is possible.

## III

Central cases of virtues, as I understand them, would include kindness, generosity, patience, endurance, courage, thoughtfulness and many more. The possession of a virtue comprehends many elements in close integration. In the virtue of kindness, for instance, there is a full-hearted appreciation of the importance of caring for others, of their needs and well-being. The 'full-heartedness' comprises the free and willing giving of attention to other people, a readiness to interpret situations in a way favourable to others' interests, a reluctance to give up on others' problems, and so on. A kindly person does not, see in another's need an importunate demand which drags them away from their own ends. Rather, the opportunity to help is likely to be wanted and accepted with pleasure, valued and found worthwhile. Aristotle writes in his Nichomachean Ethics (NE):

> We must take as a sign of states of character the pleasure or pain that ensues on acts; for the man who abstains from bodily pleasures and delights in this very fact is temperate, while the man who is annoyed

26

at it is self-indulgent, and he who stands his ground against things that are terrible and delights in this or at least is not pained is brave, while the man who is pained is a coward.

(NE 1104b4–8).

I take Aristotle's point to be that someone who, for instance, resented 'having to' do things for someone else's good would, in that very response, reveal that the true centre of their concern lay elsewhere. In contrast, a kindly and good-natured person would do them gladly because they found them good and rewarding. There is both pleasure in the doing, and being pleased at having done.

Virtuous dispositions do not, of course, spring up fully developed in people. (See Aristotle again, NE 1103a14–25 and following.) We may acknowledge, with Aristotle, that there can be 'natural virtue' (NE 1144b1 ff.). For instance, someone who is blessed with an equable and affectionate nature, who makes friends easily and rejoices in their company, will do a thousand and one acts of kindness, consideration and care. But yet this is not 'virtue in the strict sense' which, Aristotle says, involves 'reason'. This involves understanding the overall importance of others' good in a well conducted life, not only in order to inform and consolidate the original bent of temperament, but also in order ensure that the good of others does not come to occupy so very large a place in someone's life that other equally telling goods and objects for proper concern are marginalised or neglected. In many cases we may not be so fortunate in our original natures; we may be fearful, enclosed, distempered people. In this case our distance from someone who is virtuous in the strict sense is even more plain.

How, then, will the requirement to become virtuous and to do the deeds of virtue engage us, make a claim on us? Why is it not simply a case of saying that we have a moral obligation to try to acquire virtuous dispositions and to perform the acts proper to such dispositions? Can there really be any difference between this case and that previously considered, the moral situation of the agent as articulated through deontic concepts?

Of course one can think and say that one has an obligation to be a more kindly, generous or gentle person. However, I would suggest that to the extent to which one has such dispositions and undertakes the acts appropriate to them under the aspect of acknowledgement of an obligation, one has not really succeeded in achieving one's objective. For as I have already indicated, to a kindly person the attitude and acts of kindness are enjoyed. They are found worthwhile and rewarding. Kindly people feel they have meaning and give point to their lives. The whole mode of embracing and incorporating the well-being of others into one's concerns, structure of ends, sense of value and of what it is worth spending time and one's substance on, is strikingly different from that involved when action is taken under the aspect of obligation. In kindness, fostering others' good is not sought and valued only as something proper and good to care about, and corresponding points apply to generosity, gentleness and so on. This is perhaps to make it all sound too laboured and portentous. Thoughts about meaning and worth may lie very much in the background. The ordinary life of virtue consists in easy spontaneity, unforced naturalness, light gladness of offering help, being comfortable with requests and so on.

How can this come about? How can one acknowledge that there is, not only initially but normally throughout one's life, a marked distance between the force and direction of one's desires, feelings, delights and miseries and what virtue requires of one, and yet that the norms of virtue, or norms articulated deploying notions of virtue, do not engage the moral agent as quasi-coercive imposed demands?

In order to explain this I would like to put forward the notion that the acquisition of virtues involves the refinement of attachments. What I have in mind is this. In the great majority of instances, virtues are rooted in emotions (what Aristotle calls passions; see especially NE 1105b19–28). Our emotions disclose our concern with, our tie to, something we feel to be good, important or significant to us. Fear discloses our concern to avoid pain and injury as evils; pity, our concern to ease another's suffering as evil; affection, our care for another's life and well-being as good; and so on. (I am not suggesting that these estimates of importance and significance will be clear, conscious and explicit. Indeed it is often the case that an unexpected flush of shame, or spark of disappointment, is the first revelation that something mattered to us, that we really were caught up with something which had acquired significance for us.)

We ordinarily expect people to be susceptible to a very wide and diverse range of emotions, including not only the fear, pity and affection I have already mentioned, but also hostility, elation, despair, anguish, excitement and so on. In each case, I believe, this is a way of registering the significance and importance of some person, event, occurrence, absence or whatever. Of course, emotions come and go, and with their ebb and flow there waxes and wanes responsiveness to the presence of some good or evil or registration of its significance. But, as I noted before, even early in life there are different patterns in people's reactivity. One child may be affectionate, open, trusting and loving – in general, vividly responsive to the joy of other people – while another may be imperious, short-tempered, volatile, passionate and deeply preoccupied with the force of his presence and the power of his will.

This is all quite familiar. My purpose is to suggest that virtues develop out of such material, with its first small, shifting, fragmentary growths of a sense of value and disvalue, of what urgently matters and what is indifferent, and that moral norms articulated deploying aretaic concepts have in it their point of application.

This development of virtue will involve the consolidation, extension, harmonisation, sifting and integration of all these various registerings of value and importance, which is achieved principally through the regulation and re-direction of our emotions and the attachments they incorporate. A growing conscious awareness of what it signifies to have these patterns of emotional reactivity, in terms of what one finds important, will be a substantial part of this development. This growing consciousness does not merely incorporate reflection on how things stand with one, as if one was an object of curiosity. Rather, it involves seeking out possibilities of greater significance, more enduring meaning and worth; seeking to lay hold on life in abundance. In this way one draws in, or is struck by, ideas, models, examples and precepts which show something of what others have found significance in, or have found sterile and futile. This process shapes and directs the shifting of one's concerns, and guides the refinement of one's attachments. Thoughts, or comments, about what it would be unkind or greedy or considerate or friendly to do – that is, thoughts or comments which formulate moral norms deploying aretaic concepts – feed directly into this ongoing process of change and redirection of concern. They address an instance or pattern of attachment and response, and shape it towards an adjustment, a refinement.

Bare and abstract though this sketch has been, I hope it captures recognizable experiences and responses. I want now to draw out certain aspects of it, which will show up marked contrasts with the way an agent is represented as standing in relation to moral norms which have a deontic formulation.

First, this picture of the roots and character of moral commitment, figured in terms of the growth of virtue, emphasises that this commitment grows out of existing engagements and attachments, out of the subject's own lived sense of what has meaning and worth. The movement towards the embrace of moral norms is inherent in the subject's own developing awareness of what has importance to him or her, why it does, and how attaching importance to this or that may sustain or fail him or her. Although these terms 'meaning', and 'significance' are not his, I would suggest that this is what we can take from Aristotle's claim that a *eudaimon* life, a life in which we are well and do well, is the active life of virtue (see NE 1098a, 15–16, and Book I *passim*)[5] We shall – or so Aristotle contends – procure for ourselves a life we shall enjoy, a life we shall be glad we have lived, in and through apprehending and responding to goods in the way in which we shall if we possess and enact virtuous dispositions. Transposing the idiom, we could say that a moral norm which is articulated deploying artaic concepts indicates, if it is a justified norm, where importance really lies, what holds true and enduring significance. As such, it speaks directly to an agent's fumbling and inchoate sense of this.

The commitment to moral betterment is thus not to be seen as an alien demand, imposed from without, constraining an agent to be and do that in which they have otherwise no investment. Rather, it is an implicit part of the subject's own concern to sort out his or her allegiance, to test the enduringness of the objects of his or her attachment. Of course, all the standard impediments to moral commitment will remain: laziness, selfishness, greed, malice, unthinking habit and so on. But the evil in these will be seen just as well (if it is seen at all: there can never be a guarantee of moral decency in any account of these matters), in terms of the agent's own discovery of the waste, futility, limitation and truncation of life these vices embody, as in terms of any supposed failure to meet an obligatory requirement.

Let me put the matter in a (ridiculously) simple formulaic way. Deontically understood, moral norms work from the outside in; aretaically understood, they work from the inside out. The former curb and repress; the latter shape and redirect. The former impose on an unwilling subject; the latter guide a myopic and stumbling agent.

With this form of account, we may now consider the footing of the moral claim on us that the need and well-being of others represents. Figured in deontic terms, I said in Section II, other people's need established a moral obligation. Represented in this way, it was as if this was an importunate demand which stood as a constraint upon us. But there is no good reason to figure it like this. In the vast majority of cases, everyone will have some fondness, affection and care for at least some other people, and care to strangers and unknowns can come out of this sense of the significance and value of others, and of the enduring reward and meaning that open relations of trust and mutual recognition bring.[6] That other humans have worth is already appreciated and responded to; what is being sought is an extension and enlargement of that responsiveness to reach any person. Someone whose life is centred in contempt for, or fear of, others has not found an alternative way of making sense of their lives; rather they have attachments which promise only impoverishment and despair. It is true, of course, that an engaged response to the need of another may be absent in many cases. But one can have confidence in the cogency of a norm that directs one to care for their well-being, because it is altogether continuous in character with those ties whose meaning and value is appreciated. The requirement to have 'respect for persons' can be seen as building on the care and respect we have for some persons, and not as requiring a completely different mode of moral expression.

I shall touch briefly on two further points of contrast with morality as it is deontically conceived. So far as I can see, there is nothing, in moral norms which are articulated deploying aretaic concepts directly corresponding to the idea of our standing before others as agents to be judged. Of course, moral judgement may still be made. One could be chided for unkindness, censured for cowardice, upbraided for meanness. But the meaning of these failures is in terms of not giving the right place and weight to important goods in one's choice and action. It is not seen in terms of standing before others to be judged as having failed to comply with an obligatory requirement. The whole form of law, with judgement being passed on infractions, is absent. This does not mean that moral failure will be treated more gently or indulgently, although the punitive colouration so characteristic of deontically figured morality may well be absent. Rather, the subject, in his or her moral failure, is not being called to account in the same way before a bar of judges. Instead, he or she is urged to make reparation for the fault and to endeavour more strongly to cleave to the good in view.

Finally, the whole issue of the voluntariness of moral choice and action will be much less significant, since imposition of punishment is not a key element in moral judgement in an aretaic framework. We do naturally admire, praise and esteem people who are kind, considerate, and courageous, and we dislike and condemn those who are mean, thoughtless and cowardly. But we need have no thought that their being so is 'all their own work', which it quite certainly is not. Our sense of repugnance can remain as clear and strong towards someone who is vicious and vindictive as it may be towards someone whom we simply dislike, whose bearing or manner we find repellent. There is, I should say, no sharp discontinuity in character between dislike – which everyone accepts can attach to traits and behaviour which are not directly subject to the will – and moral disapprobation. The thought that there has to be one derives from the idea that such disapprobation represents a quasi-judicial verdict, and that it is critical to discover the responsibility of the plaintiff for the wrong in order to determine the justness of that verdict. Without the context of judgement, the issue need not be so crucial.[7] I am not saying that: to understand all is to forgive all. I am saying that we should not suppose that moral judgement is a matter of calling people to account, and that we sit in judgement on the adequacy of their account. If we are wronged, then we may well demand explanation, apology, reparation. We may sometimes take up the wrongs others suffer, and speak on their behalf. But we are not, as such, inspectors and judges of others' moral performance.

## IV

I have placed at the centre of my discussion the issue of how moral norms engage with the personality, desires, goals, choices and behaviour of an agent, when these norms are articulated deploying deontic notions and when they are articulated deploying aretaic notions.[8] I have argued that the question 'why be moral?' will assume a very different significance depending on whether 'being moral' is conceived principally in terms of obedience to a moral demand or in terms of the refinement of our attachments, and I suggested that we see the promise of a more fruitful response to that question if we approach it on the latter footing.

In conclusion, I shall first take up one issue regarding the contrasts I have been drawing; and second, quote an anecdote of Geoffrey Warnock's which bears on some of my principal themes.

The issue is this. There may be an objection to this account of the nature and role of moral norms articulated deploying aretaic concepts, that the moral 'demand' thus conceived lacks rigour and definiteness, and the claim it makes upon us lacks the imperative peremptoriness which moral requirements properly possess. I have two brief comments to make in reply. First, there are certainly times and places where we want to make very rigorous demands on people's conduct, rigorous in terms both of what is demanded and of the manner of the demand. But it is not self-evident that moral norms exist to serve in this role; and, if they are made to serve in it, this may well involve some distortion or falsification of their significance.[9] Second, there is nothing in the nature of aretaically formulated demands that precludes rigour. Things can be as morally necessary or morally impossible for a person who is kind, generous or patient as they are for someone who believes themselves to be under an obligation to do something or to forbear from doing it. It remains the case that the source of the necessity or impossibility, and the way in which it engages with the desires and deliberations of the subject, is (if I am right) very different.

In a collection of essays on the work of J. L. Austin, G. J. Warnock (1973: 40) tells the following story about discussions in which Austin and others regularly took part, which for a time concerned 'absolutely ground-floor . . . actual moral problems'. Warnock writes that:

> practically no philosophical conclusions were ever explicitly drawn . . . The only explicit impingement on philosophy was that Austin seemed to regard with a certain irony R. M. Hare's attachment to 'principles', and seemed not to think much of what were offered as examples of such things. (I recall the words 'a tatty little principle'.)

The footnote to this passage reads:

> How would one respond, say as an examiner, to the offer of a bribe? Hare (if memory serves) said he would say 'I don't take bribes, on principle'. Austin said: 'Would you, Hare? I think I'd say "No thanks".'

This story can no doubt provoke many different responses. I cite it because, I believe, it effectively illuminates one of my principal themes.

## Notes

1 This point is made very forcefully in, for example, Foot 1978: 157–73.
2 The most interesting modern discussion of this is that of G. E. M. Anscombe in 'Modern Moral Philosophy' (1958). I hope I have managed to learn from this essay. Other relevant material is to be found in Hume. Consider this:

> And here there occurs the *fourth* reflection which I purposed to make, in suggesting the reason why modern philosophers have often followed a course in their moral enquiries so different from that of the ancients. In later times, philosophy of all kinds, especially ethics, have been more closely united with theology than ever they were observed to be among the heathens; and as this latter science . . . bends every branch of knowl-

edge to its own purpose . . . reasoning, and even language, have been warped from their natural course, and distinctions have been endeavoured to be established where the difference of the objects was, in a manner, imperceptible. Philosophers, or rather divines under that disguise, treating all morals as on a like footing with civil laws, guarded by the sanctions of reward and punishment, were necessarily led to render this circumstance, of *voluntary* or *involuntary*, the foundation of their whole theory. Every one may employ *terms* in what sense he pleases: but this, in the mean time, must be allowed, that *sentiments* are every day experienced of blame and praise, which have objects beyond the dominion of the will or choice.

(Hume 1963 [1751]: 322)

Kant is, of course, customarily cited as the moral philosopher who gave the greatest prominence to the idea of a moral law. See, for instance, Kant (1961[1785]: 80–1). For pertinent comment on Kant, see Williams 1973: 226–9 and Schopenhauer (1965: 1841). In a different idiom, my thinking has also been much influenced by Wollheim 1984: Ch. VII.

3 Rousseau tells a story which perfectly illustrates this point in *Reveries of the Solitary Walker* (1979 [1782]): especially 93–9.
4 I discuss this issue as it arises in Rousseau's thinking, in Dent 1995: 239–50.
5 See, in this connection, Wiggins 1987: 132 ff. and *passim*.
6 See, for instance, Williams' (Humean) thoughts on this in Williams 1973: 260 ff.
7 Compare the passage from Hume, given in Note 2, above.
8 On the general notions of the aretaic and the deontic, one of the best discussions remains, I think, that of John Laird (1935).
9 I take this to be part of Hume's point; see the passage given in Note 2. And it is prominent in Foot 1978: 157–73 also (see Note 1 above).

# References

Anscombe, G. E. M. (1958) 'Modern moral philosophy', *Philosophy* 33: 1–19.

Aristotle (1925) *Nicomachean Ethics* (*Ethica Nicomachea*), trans. W. D. Ross, Oxford: Oxford University Press.

Dent, N. J. H. (1995) 'Rousseau as critic of morality', in L. Clark and G. Lafranche (eds) *Rousseau and Criticism*, Ottawa: North American Association for the Study of Jean Jacques Rousseau.

Foot, P. R. (1978) *Virtues and Vices and Other Essays in Moral Philosophy*, Berkeley/Los Angeles: University of California Press.

Hume, D. [1751] (1963) 'Of some verbal disputes', Appendix IV to *An Enquiry Concerning the Principles of Morals*, ed. L. A. Selby-Bigge, Oxford: Clarendon Press.

Kant, I. [1785] (1961) *Groundwork of the Metaphysics of Morals*, trans. H. J. Paton, under the title *The Moral Law*, London: Hutchinson.

Laird, J. (1935) *An Enquiry into Moral Notions*, London: Allen & Unwin.

Rousseau, J.-J. [1782] (1979) *Reveries of the Solitary Walker*, trans. Peter France, Harmondsworth: Penguin Books.

Schopenhauer, A. [1841] (1965) *On the Basis of Morality*, Indiana: Library of Liberal Arts.

Warnock, G. J. (1973) 'Saturday Mornings', in G. J. Warnock (ed.) *Essays on J. L. Austin*, Oxford: Clarendon Press.

Wiggins, D. (1987) *Needs, Values, Truth*, Oxford: Basil Blackwell.

Williams, B. A. O. (1973) *Problems of the Self*, Cambridge: Cambridge University Press.

Wollheim, R. (1984) *The Thread of Life*, Cambridge: Cambridge University Press.

# 3

# CHARACTER DEVELOPMENT AND ARISTOTELIAN VIRTUE

*Nancy Sherman*

## I

Aristotle, more than most ethical theorists, makes it clear that ethical theory is ultimately a practical subject. As he puts it, 'Will not the knowledge of it, then, have a great influence on life? Shall we not, like archers who have a mark to aim at, be more likely to hit upon what we should?' (*Nichomachean Ethics* [NE] 1094a22–4).[1] In the case of his own lectures, Aristotle set a prerequisite for admission to his course: namely, a strong foundation in good moral habits. Of course, not all teachers have this luxury. But as important as early education is, the point of Aristotle's inquiry is to show that it is not enough. Practical wisdom is a lifelong pursuit; the challenges persist, and so too the opportunities for deepening one's moral commitment. When it comes to good character, it simply is false that everything one needs to know can be learned in kindergarten.

Yet however practical Aristotle envisions his own lectures, his teachings, by and large, have yet to figure comfortably in our own practical ethics course. Dilemmas about what is the right thing to do often move between utilitarian and Kantian paradigms, between notions of promoting good consequences and restrictions on the kinds of means one can undertake to bring about those ends. The idea of making a decision on the basis of virtues one would endorse often seems vague, vaguer than the counterpoint of consequence versus principle. Moreover, many attempts to embrace virtue talk seem to return to derivatives of Kantian and utilitarian positions: on the one hand, virtues or motives that commit one to universalizable principles or duties to respect persons, and on the other, virtues and motives that commit one to bringing about certain social goals.

Despite the present state of affairs, I want to argue that Aristotelian virtue theory can and should find a home in practical ethics courses. There are features of the theory, including the conceptions of practical wisdom and the emotions, that lend themselves to fruitful notions in the teaching of ethics.

I want to discuss both themes, with particular emphasis on an Aristotelian account of the emotions. To be virtuous we must hit the mean with regard to both action and emotion. This implies that we have a moral responsibility to develop our emotions, and not merely suffer them as unregulated affects or impulses. Thus, virtue education is, in no small part, education of the emotions. To teach virtue requires that we take seriously the idea that we can become (to a greater degree than we often imagine) 'agents' of our emotional lives.

## II

I begin, then, with practical wisdom (or *phronēsis*).

Aristotle tells us that virtuous action is the action that the person of practical wisdom (the *phronimos*) would choose (*NE* 1169b35–1171a2). That person is one and the same as the person of good character, who in turn is the person who has a full complement of virtues or excellent states of character (*NE* 1144b30–32). To be wise is to know how to exercise those virtues as circumstances require. In the case of courage, it is a matter of knowing what the demands of courage are in particular circumstances, when to be fearful, when to be confident, what counts as having the right mix of each, what ends are worth sacrificing one's life for; in the case of generosity, it is a matter of knowing when and how and toward whom generosity is well actualized, how much to give without leaving oneself destitute, how often is often enough, and so on. In general, wisdom is a matter of seeing the morally relevant occasions for action, and then knowing, sometimes only after explicit deliberation, what to do.[2]

But what specific elements of Aristotle's conception of practical wisdom are useful for teaching ethics? The first is the familiar idea of an exemplar or role model implicit in Aristotle's appeal to the person of practical wisdom. Virtue, on the Aristotelian view, is embodied, made concrete in the flesh. To make virtuous living a goal is to think about virtue actualized, in a person or persons whom one can identify with and appreciate as sharing some of one's life circumstances. The moral importance of friendship, in Aristotle's view, and in particular, the importance of the friendship of good character, reinforces this point.

Some have argued that the role model notion yields little substance for actual practical choices. (Here I am thinking of Rosalind Hursthouse [1991; see also 1997] who asks of the hard choice whether or not to have an abortion, what guidance can an adolescent girl gain from thinking what Socrates would do in such a case?) But her example makes my point. To an adolescent girl, Socrates is no concrete role model. He is an abstraction, little more fleshy than virtue with a capital 'V'. True, the danger in having to be able to identify with another is that one might be thrown back into the narrow world of one's own blindness. 'Mom, what would you know about these matters?' one can hear one's child saying. The plea for relevance can be a plea for close-mindedness, a shabby defence to stick within the limits of one's own horizon. If we assume useful role models can be established for others, then some of what is at issue is indeed packaging: how to become relevant and accessible. But this has been, and always will be, the task of a good teacher, be it in morals or mathematics.

The notion of identifying with others should not be underestimated. The rudiments of our personality are shaped, in no small way, through identificatory mechanisms, by taking in the ways of responding, coping, and interacting that fill our small world (see Stern 1985). While we are more discriminating with age, relationships still shape common pursuits and interests. Specific parts of us come alive and flourish with certain individuals but not others. We take on determinate shape through the history of our relationships.

I have been alluding to the background, psychological role that privileged and constant persons in our lives serve in the moulding of character. Additionally, the force of a role model is that we learn through the concrete, through the narratives, stories, and drama of someone who has been there, faced the music and made choices. Take the case of naval education, in which I have been involved for the past few years. It seems to make a huge difference in the teaching of naval ethics that midshipmen have within their team of teachers experienced officers who have stories to tell from the fleet of real cases where virtue was tested, moral criteria were brought to bear, and choices were made, often in the face of competing moral demands.

I witnessed a recent classroom presentation in which a naval commander, a former fighter pilot, told his students that after a mission flying over the Basrah Road in Iraq, he returned to the aircraft carrier to learn that seven men in his squadron from one eight-person plane had just been killed. A funeral took place, but the next day the bombing missions began again, with each pilot now knowing unmistakably, as they catapulted from the carrier and tailhooked back on the flight deck in the dead of night, just how treacherous the missions were. 'If you are downed over Iraq', they were told, 'you are on your own. We can't get you. You are in enemy territory'.

Here is the courage, as well as the fear, of the warrior laid out before one's eyes. This is especially so because the story was told in role play, with the commander entering class in his 'zoom bag' (aviator jump suit). He gave a 40-minute brief on the mission that 'we' were about to engage in, to destroy the chemical weapon assembly plant 30 miles west of Basrah. The lights were dimmed, the overhead was put on, a time 'hack' was given with watches set to standardized time, the weather conditions over the Basrah Road were reported, and we were told the chaplain would be coming in a few minutes. By the end of 40 minutes we knew the leader, alternative leader and striker leader of the mission, the size of our armaments, the terrain below, what the enemy MIG 29's would look like, how similar they looked to our own F-14's, what the expected threats were, what the code word for 'mission aborted' would be, what would constitute a 'no go' call, and so on.

After this brief, the simulation was lifted and discussion was initiated about themes taken up earlier in the week: about the nature of Aristotelian courage and how it is partially constituted by skill and knowledge (of the sort, in this case, imparted in officer training school), the emotions of the warrior, how we grieve in war, how we compartmentalize our emotions in order to carry out a mission, how we regain our humanity or don't, as in the case of those who go berserk or who never fully recover from post-traumatic stress disorder (Shay 1994).

Not all of us can rely on the drama of war to illustrate courage at work. Not all of us have examples of living on the edge of danger, for the sake of noble ends. But that is not the point. Rather, it is that as teachers, particularly in higher education, we tend to focus on the abstract and forget the riveting power of an enactment to immerse a class in a gripping and nuanced discussion of a moral topic, such as the nature of courage. One can make a parallel point in the use of case studies. It makes sense to teach military ethics with cases drawn from the military and not primarily from, say, medical or business arenas, not because there are not shared themes that run through each, but because the application – the specific details and players – matters if the identificatory process is to take hold.

A second heuristic element of Aristotle's account of practical wisdom is his notion that good moral decisions rest on a grasp of the particulars of the case. Aristotelian particularism emphasizes that a moral judge has an obligation to know the facts of the case, to see and understand what is morally relevant and to make decisions that are responsive to the exigencies of the case. 'The decision rests in perception', as Aristotle famously says (*NE* 1109b23). The thought is captured, too, in Aristotle's definition of virtue. 'It is a state concerned with choice, lying in a mean relative to us, this being determined by reason and in the way in which the person of practical wisdom would determine it' (*NE* 1106b36–1107a3).

I want to focus on the phrase 'relative to us'. To some, this augurs notions of moral relativism and/or subjectivism: that on the one hand, moral choices are relative to the customs of a group and that there is no independent ground for critique, and on the other, that moral judgements are a matter merely of the opinions or tastes of an individual. But Aristotle is making neither point. Rather, the idea is simply that good moral choices are responsive to the circumstances in which an individual finds him- or herself. An agent has a moral obligation to know the facts of the case. This does not preclude the use of general rules, but they are, at best, only rough guides, summaries of past actions, a part of our web of background knowledge useful in understanding a case. The feasibility of their application is itself a study of relevance on the basis of the merits of the particular case. Of course, sometimes over-involvement in details amounts to little more than rationalization and an obsessional way of avoiding the need to make a decision. But this is at the extreme, and does not itself impugn the importance of discerning the case.

A related point is that Aristotelian practical wisdom is linked with a conception of virtue as porous ends, to be specified over time in a cumulative, case by case way. The point here is that moral decision-making requires both a top-down specification of general ends and a bottom-up narrative of circumstances. Thus, to capture context often requires a careful narrative of the overall landscape of a case in a way that highlights salient features. Again, the moral agent must know the details of this case, but the notion of salience is itself often a matter of elaborating and specifying general ends to which we are antecedently committed. We work from both ends at once (Sherman 1997: 271–2).

Aristotelian practical wisdom gives us some insight into how to use moral rules. In my view Aristotle, contrary to many interpretations of Aristotelian ethics, does not outright reject the role of rules in moral education. True, he does not think mature virtue is a matter of applying rules. Rather, under the interpretation I have just given, it is a matter of specifying ends in highly variable circumstances through attention to the details of the case. Still, in the early stages of learning virtue, one typically begins with summary rules, or what he calls, 'for the most part' rules (*NE* 1094b21), that is generalizations about what typically count as the specifications of particular virtues. So, 'generally, facing the enemy is courageous' or 'generally, giving to those more needy than oneself is an act of generosity'. In this way, the virtues correspond in some rough way to rules of thumb. But the qualification 'generally' or 'for the most part' makes it clear that Aristotle means to deny that any action which is a matter of facing the enemy is necessarily courageous or again, that because facing the enemy is morally relevant in one case, it will necessarily have the same relevance wherever it occurs. There are characteristic or paradigmatic contexts for the expression of virtue, and characteristic ways of acting, though these may be defensible. The role of practical wisdom is not to serve prudence (that is, to find the exceptions or loopholes that allow for expedience), but to find the moral accommodations that depend upon more sensitive and nuanced judgements of the case. It may turn out that there are theories and conceptions other than Aristotle's which can help us substantively with these accommodations, such as the natural law notion of double effect in deciding whether one can violate the prohibition on killing in order to save. But Aristotle's contribution is no less important for making clear the more basic point that as heuristic as rules are, they have definite limits in the wise judgement of particulars.

## III

Practical wisdom is a component of the Aristotelian portrait of virtue, but so too is emotional maturity. The virtuous person, on the Aristotelian view, has emotions that hit the mean. That is, he or she has emotions that are appropriate and well-regulated by the judgements of good reason. What account of emotions and emotional development does this presuppose? And what are the various functions emotions serve in the life of virtue?

I begin with the last question. How do emotions figure in morality? There are several functions we can limn, broadly in agreement with the spirit of Aristotle's theory, though again, he is not fully explicit here. The first thing to note is that emotions play a crucial epistemic role in the moral life in their function of recording information. We can think of them as modes of attention enabling us to notice what is morally salient, important, or urgent in ourselves and our surroundings.[3] They help us track the morally relevant 'news'. They are a medium by which we discern the particulars. In the case of grief, what is salient is that humans suffer and face loss; in the case of pity, that they sometimes fail through blameless ignorance, duress, sickness or accident; in the case of empathy, that they need the express support and union of others who can understand and identify with them; in the case of love, that we find certain individuals attractive and worthy of our time and devotion. Moreover, emotions draw us in in a way that grabs hold of our attention and puts to the top of our priority orderings, thoughts or actions regarding these matters. We focus with intensity and impact, making inferences that might otherwise not have arisen or been thought of in as compelling a way (De Sousa 1987).

In addition to their role as modes of attention, emotions play a role in communicating information to others. They are modes of responding. Putting the two together, emotions become modes both for receiving information and signalling it. Through emotions we both track and convey what we care about.

To focus on the second role, manifest affect and attitude are often taken to convey morally relevant information, including important aspects of our moral character: for example, that we value certain persons, are hurt by the prejudice of others, or are moved visibly by certain calls for help. Who we are and what we hold as important are reflected in our emotional communication. This emotional display may be verbal as well as non-verbal, or what some have called gestural articulation, which is important both in early childhood and in our adult relations (Greenspan 1989). It is true, that sometimes these less controlled facial gestures and vocalizations betray what we wish not to show: that we are hurt, annoyed, or have become impatient; that we feel slighted even though we know the injury was not intentional. The gap between how we would like to respond spontaneously and how we in fact do may not be to our liking. Who the real self is becomes something of a conflict, and sometimes, a matter for defence. Others too may feel uneasy about the perceived lack of congruence, not sure what to trust, and vulnerable to the looks and glances that prey on their own emotions. Issues such as these once again raise challenges to the programme of including emotions in an account of moral character. I shall have more to say about this later when I consider just how we are, or can be, 'in charge' of different aspects of our emotional lives.

For the time being it seems uncontroversial that the presence or absence of certain emotions can be morally significant. To take one example, a helping action that is emotionally flat may not be received in the same way as an action conveyed through more positive, affective expression. As recipients, we may judge that it lacks what is important for our well being: namely, that others be engaged with us here and now, and that they view that kind of attention and engagement as itself important. Of course emotional tone is not always to the point. If someone is bleeding profusely, any action aimed at stopping the bleeding would be helpful, whatever its emotional tone. The communication of emotion is neither here nor there. But there are clearly other cases where it matters, and matters a lot. It typically matters in how we comfort a child, how we volunteer services to a student, how we show our willingness to help a colleague who needs our resources. The point of helping in many of these cases is to reassure another that we care: to show patience, availability, considerateness, empathy. Here, the quality of the emotional interaction is inseparable from the act of helping. In the case of a parent or teacher, it is part of how we define the notion of assistance. Mutual aid is in these cases partly emotional tenor, and this may be conveyed by the kind of affective, gestural articulation that we spoke of earlier. We may feel another's attentional devotion because of a smile, or a laugh, or a twinkling eye, or a long and intense gaze. Conversely, we may sense another's disapproval through gaze breaking or a stolid glance, flitting motions, head shaking, or flat intonation. All are signs of how we are being taken by others.[4] Moreover, they form a part of our conduct that is systematically excluded by action and conversation considered more narrowly. They seem to be something we care about when we appraise character and reflect on how persons express their moral commitments and concerns.

There is a danger in my discussion so far of thinking of emotions as primarily instrumental, as epistemological tools whose value is pricipally in terms of accessing and conveying antecedent valuings (Stocker 1996). They come to be mining tools that track and reveal what we already care about. But this distorts things, and it also misses much of the character of emotion. The operations of emotions themselves often create some of what is valued, as well as being valued intrinsically even in their exercise as instruments. To take the first point, emotions do not always reveal what we already care about, but they can themselves invest with value otherwise neutral states of affair. The point is clearest when we think about the kind of 'halo effect' loved or admired ones have over our lives.[5] What we associate with our loved ones often becomes charged with our original attachment to them, so that new things come to take on value for us through the original emotional attachment. A kind of transference is at work that is a familiar part of certain identificatory emotions, such as emulation, respect, and love.[6] The limited point now is that attachment emotions, characteristic of love or friendship, create new objects of care or fear for us. This role of emotions will have crucial importance in moral development, and in learning in general. We learn best from those with whom we can identify and from those whom we value positively. This underlies Aristotle's view that friendship (*philia*) is the central arena in which character development takes place.

Granted, the expression of emotion reveals old values as well as creates new ones. But even aside from these contributions, experiencing emotion itself bears value. A world without humour, laughter, playfulness, flirtatiousness, as well as aggression and fear, would be impoverished; it would be unrecognizable as human. Simply to be an emotional creature and to live with others on an emotional plane (in a life that engages our emotions and in which emotions are part of the social fibre) is an intrinsic part of living humanly. We prize that way of experiencing self and others, apart from whatever else it leads to. Certainly, on the Aristotelian view, a *eudaimôn* life is a life lived emotionally, and part of what is valuable is realizing oneself through emotions. We express our excellent functioning through both action and emotion, and these expressions are valued in their own right (NE 1109a23).

There is a final role for emotions, one probably most emphasized in connection with morality. This is the role of emotions as motives. Emotions can move us to action. They are motivational. We act out of compassion, out of friendliness, out of sympathy. In this role, the emotions are reasons for acting. Kant, as well as the Stoics, cast suspicion on the moral significance of this role, arguing for the unreliability of this sort of motivation for moral action (Kant 1964 [1785]: 66). I shall not say much more here about the motivational aspect of emotion, except to note that an exclusive emphasis on it throughout the history of moral philosophy has obscured the other important roles which emotions serve in our lives. A benefit of pointing out these other roles is that even a philosopher such as Kant, who accords duty the privileged role of moral motive, can still leave room for emotions to play these other roles in a complete account of moral practice.

I have now outlined a number of pervasive functions of the emotions in moral life. I can sum up by saying that emotions are sensitivities that, first, help us to attend to and record what we care about (in both a positive and negative sense). They are modes of recording values. Second, they assist us in signalling those valuings both to ourselves and others. They are modes of conveying values. Third, in some cases they help to establish what we value or detest, rather than merely track or reveal antecedent valuings. They are modes of establishing values. Fourth, emotions can be valued for their own sake, simply as important ways of living a full, human life. They are intrinsically valued. Finally, emotions motivate action. They provide impetus for action. They are motives for action.

## IV

I now want to consider Aristotle's analysis of the emotions, and in the section that follows, I conclude with remarks about the nature of emotional agency.

Aristotle's analysis is best appreciated by considering three alternatives to it. On a commonsense view, emotion is thought to be an irreducible quality of feeling or sensation. It may be caused by a physical state, but the emotion itself is the sensation we feel when we are in that state. It is a felt affect, a distinctive feeling, but not something that is about something else. The view quickly falters, however, when we realize that emotions on this view become no more than private states, something felt like an itch or a tickle, inaccessible to identification in terms of propositional content (that is, a mental representation of what they are about).

A second view, associated with William James and Carl Lange (1884), is that emotions are proprioceptions of visceral or behavioural movements. They are an awareness of bodily changes in the peripheral nervous system. We are afraid because we tremble, angry because of the knots in our stomachs, not the other way round. The view, though rather counter-intuitive, none the less captures the idea that emotions, more than other mental states, seem to have conspicuous physiological and kinaesthetic components. These often dominate children's and adults' reports of their emotional experiences. However, even well-honed physiological feelings do not easily identify specific emotions. Proprioceptions of our skin tingling or our chest constricting or our readiness to flee or fight under-determine just what emotion we are feeling. Many distinct emotions share these features, and without contextual clues, and thoughts that dwell on those clues, we are in the dark about what we are experiencing (Schachter and Singer 1962). The chief burden of the work of the psychologist Walter Cannon (1927) was to show that emotional affects are virtually identical across manifestly different states.

A third view steps outside the privacy of the mind, locating emotions in behaviour (Skinner 1953; also Arnold 1960; Frijda 1986). On this general view emotions are modes of readiness to act, or in Freud's early idiom, discharges of tension. Support for this view comes from the fact that we often experience emotions as excitations in need of release,[7] and we often describe emotions in terms of dispositions to concrete behaviour. 'I felt like hitting him', 'I could have exploded', 'I wanted to spit', 'I wanted to be alone with him, wrapped in his embrace'. Yet the action tendency view seems at best a partial account of emotion. The basic problem here is not that some emotions, such as apathy, inhibition, and depression seem to lack clear activation modes, while others are more a matter of the rich movement of thought so well depicted, for example, in Henry James's novels. It is rather that emotions are about something (internal or external) that we represent in thought. As such they have propositional content. Their identity depends on that content.

This takes us to Aristotle's view, implicit in the *Nicomachean Ethics*, but explicitly developed in the second book of the Rhetoric. At the heart of his account is the view that emotions are about something that we represent in thought. Emotions are intentional states. As such they have cognitive content. They are identified by that content, by what we dwell on, whether it be fleetingly or with concentrated attention. Equally, these states can be beliefs or just musings and construals that are only slenderly based on 'objective' evidence.

Such an account need not exclude other features of emotion, such as aware-ness of physiological and behavioural response or felt sensations. The claim is that these, when present, are dependent on cognitive (that is, descriptive and evaluative) content, and are directed toward that content. Thus, on Aristotle's view, emotions are produced by evaluations, but also and more strongly, emotions are partly constituted by them. It is not just that certain antecedent evaluations typically cause certain emotions. Rather, the connection is a conceptual one. Anger would not be anger without thoughts that one was unfairly injured or the like. Fear would not be fear if there were not some mental content of a threat or danger. Indeed, Aristotle is insistent that closely related emotions, such as contempt, spite, and insolence, are differentiated not by their 'feels', but by their distinct intentional focuses: by what they are about (*Rhetoric* 1378b14).

At this point we can begin to see the broad compatibility between an Aristotelian account of the emotions and an account of the moral significance of emotions, along the lines limned in the previous section. Emotions are not blind sensations, but judgings of what we take to be good and bad in the world. They track the salience in virtue of making evaluations about the world. These evaluations may present reasons for action. Moreover, through emotions we convey to others not just that we are in pleasure or pain, but that we care about something in particular, or are the sort of person who takes certain things to be important. We convey and record determinate informa-tion through our emotions.

Of course, those who hold a sensation theory of the emotions might also see a close connection between certain kinds of evaluations and the emotion as a quality of feeling. They could argue that certain beliefs typically cause those feelings (Oakley 1992: 22). But in so far as the connection is not conceptual but merely contingent, it could be, on such a view, that while fear is typically caused by something appearing threatening, on other occasions that same feeling could be experienced without that characteristic thought or indeed, any cognition paired up with the affect at all. For it is the feeling alone which constitutes the emotion, and anything that it is associated with is purely contingent. Thoughts, such as that cantaloupes are orange, could be connected with fear, so long as the feeling is characteristic. The Aristotelian view of emotions as intentional not only is inherently more plausible, but gives a more natural account of how emotions track salience.

# V

As I have said, Aristotle holds that we are morally assessed not only for our actions, but for our emotions. Both can be praiseworthy and blameworthy, both fine and shameful. But in what sense, according to Aristotle, can we be held responsible for our emotions? In what sense are they 'up to us', or related to choice (*prohairesis*)?

Aristotle assumes that emotions are within our dominion, though he does not explicitly instruct us about how we take charge. His general remarks on habituation are well known. We become just by doing just actions, become generous through generous deeds. As I have argued elsewhere, the plea is not for mindless repetition of behaviour, but for critical practice that develops the cognitive skills constitutive of virtuous choice-making and action (Sherman 1989: ch. 5). Aristotle also holds that critical habituation is part of the development of the emotions, but again does not give us many details. None the less we can fill in the lacunae in keeping with the spirit of his view that through practice, we can come to 'stand well' with regard to the emotions.

Common parlance includes a host of locutions which presume that emotions are 'up to us' in various ways. Thus we exhort ourselves and others in such phrases as 'pull yourself together', 'snap out of it', 'put on a good face', 'lighten up', 'be cheerful', 'think positive', 'keep a stiff upper lip'. In many of these cases, we are being implored to take on the semblance of an emotion so that it can 'take hold' and rub off on our inner state. Practise as if you believe and you will believe. As Ronald de Sousa puts it, 'earnest pretense is the royal road to sincere faith' (de Sousa 1987). Sometimes we 'pretend' through behavioural changes: changes in facial expressions, body gestures and vocalizations that evoke in us a changed mood. If we are fuming, relaxing our facial muscles, ungnarling our fingers, breathing deeply and slowly may put us in the frame of mind to see things in a calmer light. Something like this may undergird Aristotle's notion of becoming by doing. Putting on the look of an emotion may introduce into our thoughts the evaluations that typically constitute such emotions.

Some of the above suggestions involve nuancing an emotional state from outside in: trying on more luxuriant smiles as a way of trying to become more loving. But equally, a newly felt emotion may demand a new look, a concrete and stable realization for oneself and others to behold. Here the nudging works from inside out, though still it is the facial or gestural expression that coaches the emotion. Thus, we can fuel the flames of an emotion by allowing it bodily expression. To weep may intensify our grief, or simply bring us to acknowledge its presence.

Of course we would expect that on an Aristotelian view emotional changes require not merely facial or behavioural alteration, but an evaluative change (that is, a change of the evaluative or cognitive content of emotion). Moreover, the view is that behavioural or expressive changes really prepare us for changes at this level. If this is so, then there are more direct ways to alter emotions through changes of perception or belief. For example imagine Josh, a ten-year-old, who often fumes with anger about how his classmates treat him. A psychologically minded parent or teacher may try to have the child reflect on specific instances, on just what caused the anger and whether it is justified. In some cases it may turn out that there are real external taunts and insults that spark the child's anger. In other cases, the anger may be less the result of his 'enemy's' attitude than his own attitude projected outward on to classmates. The adult who tries to get the child to see this is attempting to make the child self-observant and critical of his own contribution in tracking what is morally salient. He or she helps the child by shifting the gestalt, by recomposing the scene in a way that is more accurate. This is not simply a lesson in psychology, but a lesson in morality, to the extent that a chronically bullying and angry attitude stands in the way of morally finer ways of interacting.

A more general point is that many morally problematic attitudes have at their core emotions that require reform. Racism feeds on irrational hatred, and abuses of power often flow from arrogance and self-righteousness that denote a failure of empathy. Change that penetrates not merely conduct but attitude must work on those emotions and their constitutive evaluations. The aim is to bring these constitutive evaluations in line with reflective and justified beliefs. Of course, a dyed-in-the-wool racist may simply refuse to subject his views to rational assessment. More resourceful methods may be required to break down the habituated attitude. The point still remains that an evaluative change is what is required, and that it is an evaluation that infuses the emotion.

In all these cases, the aim is to expose the implicit judgements that emotions involve. This becomes crucial in the moral education of children as well as adults. If we believe that emotions need not be unregulated impulses for acting out, then we need to empower individuals with capacities to reflect on their emotions so that they can begin to assess the reasonableness of the judgements implicit in their emotions. In essence, the emotions and their impact must enter an individual's discursive world and be examined in terms of their implicit claims and appropriateness.

None of this is earth-shattering. Our virtuous and our vicious conduct relies upon a whole gamut of emotions that inform what we see and how we act. If we are traditional Kantians and believe that emotions are divorced from the full commerce of reason, we retreat at this point. Genuine virtue cannot be grounded in emotion, for emotion can never adequately partake of our rational and discursive sides. The Aristotelian challenges this point. Emotions are ways of judging the world. Some of the ways we regulate them are by arguing against their judgements.

## Notes

1  Citations from Aristotelian texts are from Barnes (1984).
2  At a deeper level, the wisdom may involve understanding that the intrinsic conflict that a virtue like courage regularly brings with it – of experiencing fear in a case of real danger, pitted against the desire to stand one's ground for the sake of some higher good – is a conflict necessary for courage, a noble conflict, and one quite different from, say the struggle that some have to be temperate. In the latter case, what stands against one's desires to be temperate are desires that devalue

temperance, desires that aim for immoderate satisfaction. Whereas it is noble to triumph over fear of real dangers, it is far less noble to have to triumph over desires for excess. Those are temptations, not external threats, and the battle should already be won.

3 On the general issue of moral salience, see Blum 1980; Murdoch 1970; Nussbaum 1986; Dancy 1993; McDowell 1979; Herman 1993: ch. 4; Sherman 1989. Something like this role of the emotions is noticed by Descartes too, but primarily in terms of an account of the objects that cause different emotions, without attention to the intentionality of the emotions. So he notes, objects which move the senses cause 'diverse passions in us . . . because of the diverse ways in which they may harm or help us, or in general be of some importance to us' (Descartes 1955 (1649): Article LII).

4 This is plainest in infants who depend upon gaze and smile for reassurance of love. By tracking smiles they learn to reciprocate in kind, making play a matter of dialogue through pre-verbal gestural articulation. Moreover, Greenspan (1989) has observed that parental expression of emotion at the earliest stages of a child's life (four to eight months) may figure crucially in how a child comes to differentiate his or her own affective proclivities and ultimately, learn self-control. In caregiving environments, where there is active and expressive feedback, children learn to identify their needs and dependencies. By reading parents' faces, they come to know when and where danger lurks and when and where emotions need trimming. In contrast, in those environments where there is little reciprocal feedback, where parents are 'poker-faced', children tend to show more deficits in affective differentiation and control. Without the proper cues from others, they tend to lack the kind of early warning system that helps them to recognize and control their own responses. For further discussion of emotional expression, see Darwin 1872;Ekman 1973; 1982.

5 A similar point may be made about negative valuing, and may be at the heart of insidious forms of discrimination. See Piper 1990.

6 Aristotle himself (*Poetics* IV) emphasizes the importance of identification (or mimēsis) as a learning method, and combines this in the books on friendship with the importance of an empathetic, responsive relationship as a context for learning.

7 In this regard, there is similarity between behaviourism's push outward and the classical Freudian notion of the release of drive, though Freud was by no means offering a behavioural account that reduced the mental to outward movement.

# References

Arnold, M. (1960) *Emotion and Personality*, New York: Columbia University Press.

Barnes, J. (ed.) (1984) *The Complete Works of Aristotle: The Revised Oxford Translation*, Vols.1 and 2, Princeton: Princeton University Press.

Blum, L. (1980) *Friendship, Altruism and Morality*, London: Routledge and Kegan Paul.

Cannon, W. (1927) 'The James-Lange theory of emotion: a critical examination and an alternative theory', *American Journal of Psychology* 39: 106–124.

Dancy, J. (1993) *Moral Reasons*, Oxford and Cambridge, Mass.: Blackwell.

Darwin, C. (1872) 'The expression of emotion in man and animals', in C. Calhoun and R. Solomon (eds) *What is an Emotion?* Oxford: Oxford University Press, 1984.

De Sousa, R. (1987) *The Rationality of Emotion*, Cambridge, Mass.: MIT Press.

Descartes, R. [1649] (1955) *The Passions of the Soul*, in R. M. Eaton (ed.) *Descartes Selections*, New York: Scribners.

Ekman, P. (ed.) (1973) *Darwin and Facial Expression*, New York: Academic Press.

—— (1982) *Emotion in the Human Face*, 2nd edition, Cambridge: Cambridge University Press.

Frijda, N. (1986) *The Emotions*, Cambridge: Cambridge University Press.

Greenspan, S.I. (1989) *The Development of the Ego*, Madison CT: International Universities Press.

Herman, B. (1993) *The Practice of Moral Judgment*, Cambridge, Mass. and London: Harvard University Press.

Hursthouse, R. (1991) 'Virtue Theory and Abortion', *Philosophy and Public Affairs*, 20: 223–46. Reprinted in R. Crisp and M. Slote (eds) (1997) *Virtue Ethics*, New York: Oxford University Press.

—— (1997) 'Virtue Ethics and the Emotions', in D. Statman (ed.) *Virtue Ethics*, Washington, DC: Georgetown University Press.

James, W. and Lange C. G. (1884) 'What is an emotion', *Mind* 19: 188–205. Reprinted in C. Calhoun and R. Solomon (eds) (1984) *What is an Emotion?* Oxford: Oxford University Press, 1984.

Kant, I [1785] (1964) *The Groundwork of the Mataphysic of Morals*, trans. H. J. Paton, New York: Harper and Row.

McDowell, J. (1979) 'Virtue and reason', *Monist* 62: 331–50.

Murdoch, I. (1970) *The Sovereignty of the Good*, London: Routledge, Kegan and Paul.

Nussbaum, M. (1986) *The Fragility of Goodness: Luck and ethics in Greek tragedy and philosophy*, Cambridge: Cambridge University Press.

Oakley, J. (1992) *Morality and the Emotions*, New York: Routledge.

Piper, A. (1990) 'Higher-order discrimination', in O. Flanagan and A. O. Rorty (eds) *Character, Psychology, and Morality*, Cambridge, Mass.: MIT Press.

Schachter, S. and Singer, J (1962) 'Cognitive, social and physiological determinants of emotional states', *Psychological Review* 69: 379–99. Reprinted in C. Calhoun and R. Solomon (eds) *What is an Emotion?* Oxford: Oxford University Press, 1984.

Shay, J. (1994) *Achilles in Vietnam: Combat trauma and the undoing of character*, New York: Atheneum.

Sherman, N. (1989) *The Fabric of Character: Aristotle's theory of virtue*, Oxford: Oxford University Press.

—— (1997) *Making a Necessity of Virtue: Aristotle and Kant on virtue*, Cambridge: Cambridge University Press.

—— (ed.) (1999) *Aristotle's Ethics: Critical Essays*, Lanham, N. J.: Rowman and Littlefield.

Skinner, B. F. (1953) *Science and Human Behavior*, New York: Free Press.

Stern, D. (1985) *The Interpersonal World of the Infant*, New York: Basic Books.

Stocker, M. (1996) *Valuing Emotions*, Cambridge: Cambridge University Press.

# 4

# VIRTUE, *PHRONESIS* AND LEARNING

## *Joseph Dunne*

In the first part of this chapter, I introduce phronesis (practical wisdom) in the context of Aristotle's characterisation of it as an intellectual virtue. In the second part I analyse its relation to the ethical virtues, and in the third part I elaborate conceptions of learning and of teaching with which it is bound up. Throughout, my account is framed by the convictions that *phronesis* remains philosophically sustainable and that it has considerable light to shed on the contemporary practice of education. But justification of this conviction yields ground to the primarily exegetical intention of the chapter, apart from a statement of characteristically modern objections to *phronesis* at the end of part II and a brief response to them at the end of part III.

## I

*Phronesis* occupies a central place in Aristotle's ethical-political thought and yet remains, in important respects, eccentric. Its centrality lies in the fact that while it names a particular virtue, and so takes its place in the catalogue of distinct virtues that are successively introduced and analysed in the *Nicomachean Ethics* (*NE*, from Book III, 6 through Book VI), it is not just one virtue among others but is rather a necessary ingredient in all the others. A person otherwise well endowed with fear-subduing qualities, for example, but lacking the capacity for sound judgement in actual situations of danger, cannot be said to possess the *virtue* of courage; and it is *phronesis* that supplies the necessary component of judgement. It is this very centrality that accounts for what I call the eccentricity of *phronesis*. It is eccentric first of all in not lying comfortably on either side of the division that Aristotle himself makes between 'intellectual' and 'ethical' virtues. It is officially designated an intellectual virtue, but its deep involvement with the other side of the divide is evident from the fact that not only is it required to complete each ethical virtue by providing the element of judgement indispensable to the concrete exercise of the latter, but conversely (as we shall see presently), ethical virtue is itself required for *phronesis*. If a clever person is not good, neither will he be a *phronimos* (practically wise person).

This complication of *phronesis* as a mode of knowledge leads to awkwardness when Aristotle is formally considering the intellectual virtues: or rather it leads to *absence*, for in his classic analysis of different knowledge-states in the first two chapters of the *Metaphysics* (*Meta*), whereas other intellectual virtues find their place in a hierarchical scheme there is no room for *phronesis*.[1] Clearly, *phronesis* lies athwart the progression marked there from unsystematic sense-perception to the highest achievable level of universality and explanatory power, a progression in terms of which the other intellectual virtues identified alongside *phronesis* in Book VI of the *NE* (*sophia, episteme, nous*, and *techne*)[2] can be both distinguished and rank-ordered. The absence of phronesis from this classic discussion of the intellectual virtues is made conspicuous by the presence of *techne* (since the latter is its companion-virtue of the practical intellect)[3] and considerable illumination about *phronesis* can be gleaned indirectly from the treatment of *techne*. A key role is played in the discussion by the concept of 'experience' (*empeiria*): the epistemic status of different intellectual virtues is related to the degree to which they go beyond mere experience. On this score, *techne* has much to recommend it. For it

> arises when, from many notions gained by experience, one universal judgment about similar objects is produced. For to have a judgment that when Callias was ill of this disease this did him good, and similarly in the case of Socrates and in many individual cases, is a matter of experience; but to judge that it has done good to all persons of a certain constitution, marked off in one class . . . this is a matter of *techne*
>
> (*Meta* I 1 981a5–12).[4]

What is curious about *techne* in Aristotle's treatment of it here is not that it hews so closely to the theoretical ideal (by the universality and causal grasp of its apprehensions) but rather that, in doing so, it can apparently be cut loose from the proper efficacy of the practical. For 'with a view to action', he goes on,

> experience seems in no respect inferior to *techne*, and we even see men of experience succeeding more than those who have theory without experience. (The reason is that experience is knowledge of individuals, *techne* of universals, and actions and productions are all concerned with the individual . . . If, then, a man . . . knows the universal but does not know the individual included in this, he will often fail to cure; for it is the individual that is to be cured.)
>
> (*Meta* I 1 981a12–24)

It seems to be conceivable here that a *techne* might involve 'theory without experience' or that a person might possess it when 'he knows the universal but does not know the individual included in this'. It is all the more striking, then, that in the book in which *phronesis* is most extensively considered (*NE* Book VI), we are given an example of just this divorce between theory and experience, or between the universal and the individuals included in it, in an analysis which both clearly echoes the discussion from the early chapters of the *Metaphysics and* makes it plain that in the case of *phronesis* no such divorce is admissible:

> Some who do not know, and especially those who have experience, are more practical than others who know; for if a man knew that light meats are digestible and wholesome, but did not know which sorts of meat are light, he would not produce health, but the man who knows that chicken is wholesome is more likely to produce health. Now *phronesis* is concerned with action; therefore one needs both kinds of knowledge, but particularly the latter.
>
> (*NE* VI 7 1141b16–22).

Here the proper bias of *phronesis* towards particulars is affirmed, in the context of a correlative affirmation of its *practical* character. It is misleading, however, to speak here of both kinds of knowledge. For if the two kinds are characterised as the major premise ('light foods are wholesome') and the conclusion ('chicken is wholesome') of a practical syllogism, there is in fact a *third* kind of knowledge noticed by Aristotle a little earlier in the passage: that which (merely) experienced people are ignorant of, in this case, 'what sorts of meat are light'. This kind of knowledge is inscribed in minor premises that connect major premises to conclusions, and it is in the capacity for generating it that *phronesis* most essentially resides. *Phronesis* then is at once a deliberative excellence (*euboulia*) and a disposition for perceiving, or having insight (*aisthesis*):[5] it is deliberative in so far as it helps one to mediate between more generic, habitual knowledge and the particularities of any given action-situation, and it involves perceptiveness in so far as its apprehensions are not deductively derived, but are freshly generated in response precisely to the particularity of *this* situation and the individual's involvement in it now.

Aristotle's analysis here must be refigured to take account of the fact that the universals which *phronesis* is concerned with are virtues (subsumed under, though also constitutive of, the ultimate universal of 'living well' [*eu zen*]) and that the nutritional example (wholesome/light food/chicken) only grossly reflects the type of proximately practical knowledge which it is the task of *phronesis* to generate. To know that, for example, courage is a virtue is to possess a type of universal knowledge (analogous to knowing that light food is wholesome). When one knows what courage is, one also possesses a type of universal knowledge (analogous to knowing what sorts of meat are light). The real nerve of moral knowledge, however, is to know the latter in such a way that one knows what *counts as* courage in the variety of situations in which one finds oneself as an agent. The range of candidates that might so count across that whole

51

variety has none of the compactness-for-recognition (conferred by clear-cut criteria of membership) of a natural kind such as 'chicken': so that coming to recognise that a given action or response is indeed courageous may not be at all as straightforward as learning that chicken is a light food. It is all too easy, then, in this case, to have the 'theory without the experience' or to be a person who 'knows the universal but does not know the individual included in this'. In fact 'included' is in many cases too firm a term because, in the process of moral experience, by being 'applied' to particular situations universals are at the same time being refined and enriched: in coming to recognise what courage requires here, I may be learning not only about this new situation but also about courage itself.[6]

There are of course some absolute prohibitions – for example, about murder or malice – that, as Aristotle makes clear, do not bring discriminating judgement into play. But important as these are, they lie outside the frame of his depiction of ethical life as the pursuit of virtue. For they do not admit of a 'mean', a concept that he places at the heart of his notion of virtue ('from the point of view of its essence and the definition of its real nature virtue is a mean'). Far from connoting mediocrity or safe compromise, the mean marks the utmost exigency of virtue, which, 'in respect of what is right and best, is an *extreme*'. It (the 'mean') was already in currency as the hallmark of master-works of craft (*techne*) about which it could be said that 'nothing can be added to them or taken away'; and virtue 'is more exact . . . than any craft'. Failure, then, is possible in endless ways – Aristotle here relates evil to the Pythagorean category of the unlimited – while success is single: 'it is easy to miss the target and difficult to hit it'. It is just in so far as finding the virtuous thing to do requires fixing on a mean that it entails the exercise of *phronesis*: 'So virtue is a purposive disposition, lying in a mean that is relative to us and determined by principle (*logos*), or whatever we like to call that by which a *phronimos* would determine it' (*NE* II 6 1106b11–1107a8). *Phronesis* is seen here in relation to other virtues, but of course *phronesis* is itself a virtue and so, as well as being *logos*-bearing in relation to other dispositions, it too *is* a disposition. Aristotle's image of the archer captures this well and is a salutary corrective to any tendency to set the *phronimos* off against a mechanistic morality of principle as an existentialist hero, or virtuoso of 'undecideability', forever coming up with new and creative moral responses. There is often an element of 'creativity' in finding where virtue lies. But – quite apart from the fact that for Aristotle it lies in any case within the universal and not outside it, and is moreover a definite target that we can more readily miss than hit – we are capable of this creativity only in so far as we have developed that 'eye of the soul' which resides in *phronesis* as a painstakingly acquired disposition.

## II

A great question here is the precise relationship between *phronesis* as an intellectual disposition and those other dispositions that constitute the ethical virtues. One might say (following the archer image) that it sets their aim or direction: that on each occasion of action it must take the lead by determining what is to be done. In so far as one has the resource within oneself readily to accomplish the specified deed, one might then be said to possess the relevant ethical virtue. This would seem both to make sense of what transpires episodically on each occasion of action, and to be confirmed at a more general level by Aristotle's setting of the distinction between intellectual and ethical virtues in the context of his partitioning of the soul in the last chapter of Book I of *NE*. He speaks there of the rational part of the soul which is defined by its possession of *logos* and of another part (the seat of appetite and desire, moved by pleasure and pain) which, although in itself non-rational, can become 'amenable', or 'receptive', or 'submissive and obedient' to the rational part.

This kind of dualistic formulation, however, is more appropriately used of the merely moral (perhaps a happier rendering of *enkrates* than 'continent') than of the properly virtuous person; for the former does the right thing only while actively subduing an element in himself which still 'fights and strains against *logos*', while in the latter this element and *logos* are 'in complete harmony'. The harmony is expressed not only in a lack of recalcitrance but more positively in the fact that a virtuous person in acting rightly is also acting '*gladly*', or '*enjoys* the very fact of so doing*'. This positive inclination is a capital point for Aristotle: there is no virtue without an integral reordering of pleasures and pains, which must indeed be 'the whole concern of both ethics and political science'. But this point introduces a different perspective from that of single acts episodically performed, or of formal analysis of the structure of the soul: what Aristotle himself recognises as a developmental or pedagogical perspective. 'Hence the importance (as Plato says) of having been trained in some way from infancy to feel joy and grief at the right things: true education is precisely this' (*NE* II 3 1104b11–13).

Perhaps we will consider this perspective to be *only* pedagogical or, as we might say, motivational. It would then indicate Aristotle's very lively sense of the kind of challenge faced by those charged with getting other people (especially the young) to become virtuous, a sense made all the more realistic by his depth-psychology. (In his discussion of the non-rational part of the soul he comments on 'what makes the dreams of decent people better than those of the ordinary man.') However we might still take it to be quite extrinsic to the epistemological question, that is to say, to the issue of how or on what basis anyone, whether moral neophyte or sage, knows what is truly good or bad action, either in general terms or in particular situations. Indeed we might want to give priority to this epistemological issue even – perhaps especially – in education.

It cannot be argued that Aristotle is *not* concerned with moral knowledge. But for him this knowledge is inextricably linked to virtuous action; and both can be treated adequately only within the developmental perspective framing his consideration of character (which, as etymology attests, is more or less coterminous with his whole ethical inquiry). This is partly a matter of his regarding moral knowledge as being for the sake of action – its whole point and purpose is to help one to act well and, by doing so recurrently, to become good – and of his impatience with, almost incomprehension of, any concern with such knowledge unmoored from moral practice.

Even of ethical theory – of the kind imparted by himself as a teacher – he can say that it will be 'vain and unprofitable' to the unpractised, precisely because 'the end aimed at is not knowledge but action' (*NE* I 3 1095a5–6); and *a fortiori* of course this is the case for the more concrete kind of knowledge delivered by *phronesis*. Indeed virtuous action is so internal to the latter as its end that it is a necessary condition and even partly constitutive of it: 'merely knowing what is right does not give a person *phronesis*; he must be disposed to do it too' (*NE* VII 10 1152a8–9). Knowing and being disposed to act, then, are co-constitutive of *phronesis*. But in fact Aristotle goes further, suggesting that if a person is not properly disposed to act then neither will he even *know* in the relevant ('phronetic') sense. Thus, they are not independent co-constituents of *phronesis*; rather, the very knowledge is conditional upon having the right disposition.

This thesis is uncongenial to much modern thought, though perhaps it finds some modern parallels, for example in various theories of ideology or false consciousness which interpret and criticise knowledge claims in terms not of their manifest credentials but of the 'interests' that they covertly express, or psychoanalytic theories about both 'resistance' and the kind of insight that is genuinely healing. In an attempt to protect the epistemological integrity of *phronesis* one might ask, does Aristotle hold that, one, in order to have the kind of knowledge he takes to be essential to living a good life one must already have acquired certain dispositions, or that two, these dispositions are, as it were, active in the knowledge, shaping its actual content?

The first proposition will seem unexceptionable because, though it specifies psychological preconditions (and not just environmental ones such as gaining a college place), it may be accepted that all knowledge has such preconditions. A mathematician, for example, is unlikely to progress into the more recondite spheres of this discipline without some considerable discipline of his or her own. Still, it might be insisted that such personal discipline is not unlike that which would be required to become adept in any exacting field, and so is extrinsic to mathematics as such; thus, one is saved from embracing the second proposition, with its apparently unacceptable non-cognitivism. But while Aristotle may have countenanced this extrinsicist position with respect to mathematics, it is clearly not his position on the kind of ethical knowledge conferred by *phronesis*.

*Phronesis* is after all an excellence of the calculative (or deliberative) part of the rational soul, the state best enabling the latter to fulfil its proper function which, no less than that of the scientific part, is to attain truth (*NE* VI 2 1139b11–13). Aristotle believes that true knowledge is possible only because of 'a certain similarity and affinity' between knower and known, or because the soul is 'naturally adapted to the cognition of . . . (its) object' (*NE* VI 1 1139a9–11). If the object of *phronesis*, then, is the good, the soul of the *phronimos* must be somehow attuned or predisposed to this good. It is through the ordering of appetition or desires that one is thus predisposed; and so 'desire must follow the same things that reasoning asserts', or 'the function of practical intellect is to arrive at the truth that corresponds to right appetition'. We may sense an unsatisfactory ambiguity here. The first of these propositions seems to accord priority to reasoning – which desire is to 'follow' – while the second one reverses the priority by requiring practical intellect to 'correspond' to right appetition. In fact Aristotle seems much less concerned to assign priority between intellect and appetition than to stress their close integration, as is evident for instance in the relaxed reversibility of his characterisation of choice (*prohairesis*) as 'either appetitive intellect or intellectual appetition' and his immediately adding that 'man is a principle of this kind' (*NE* VI 2 1139b5–6).

The rub here, once again, is that *phronesis* cannot be simply equated with intellect and thus conveniently separated from appetite or desire. The connaturality posited between knower and known carries the strong consequence that to know the good one must already *be* good. This position is bound up with Aristole's sense that 'good' lies in the neighbourhood not only of the noble (*to kalon*) but also of the pleasurable. There is for each of us a broad horizon – formed by what he calls our first principles (*archai*) or ends (*ton heneka*) – within which our feelings, actions and ethical appraisals occur. And this horizon itself, as well as what occurs within it, is subject to distortion by pleasure and pain, consciousness of which 'has grown up with all of us from our infancy, and . . . (with which) our life is so deeply imbued' (*NE* II 3 1105a1–3). Aristotle exempts some knowledge from susceptibility to such distortion – he explicitly mentions geometrical propositions – but knowledge with regard to our own actions and feelings has a potential for being distorted that puts it in need of protection by the ethical virtue of temperance. (He offers an etymology for the Greek term for temperance [*sophrosune*] as 'preserver of *phronesis*'.) It is preservation of the horizon-forming 'ends' that Aristotle mainly sees as depending on a temperate character; and he can give the impression that *phronesis* is only a cognitive capacity to devise 'means' towards these ends.[7] But in fact we can no more separate ends from means than we can separate character from phronesis; each is internal to the other and both, as it were, go all the way down.[8] Every disposition has its own appreciation of what is fine and pleasant; and probably what makes the man of good character stand out furthest is the fact that he sees the truth in every kind of situation; he is a sort of standard and yardstick of what is fine and pleasant' (*NE* III 4 1113a31–34).

Again, some modern readers are likely to be uneasy with all this. To point to a particular kind of person as the yardstick of virtuous action (they will urge) is surely to beg the question, unless there are prior, independently formulable criteria for identifying such a person. If there are no such criteria, then Aristotle's position can only seem dogmatic; and if there *are*, then it is in these criteria themselves – and no longer in any kind of person – that normativity resides. But, besides, the very notion of making one kind of person paradigmatic in our estimations of moral worth flies in the face of the moral diversity and conflict which are such palpable features of modern experience.

Aristotle's approach seems not only to occlude serious moral disagreement as a fact but, more ominously, to disable us from dealing rationally with it even when we are forced to acknowledge it. For, on his terms, it would seem that a *phronimos*, when confronted with anyone offering a rival view, would have no alternative but to impugn the character of his interlocutor; and this of course must seem altogether subversive of the kind of reciprocity and respect presupposed by moral debate in a democratic society.[9]

Moreover, a modern reader may baulk at the notion of a *phronimos* because of its apparent failure to do justice not only to divisions among members of a moral community but also to division within any individual moral agent. A person not only without error or fault but even beyond conflict in all the interweaving of thoughts, feelings and actions may seem impossible in reality, and unattractive in very conception. Even on his own ground, then – as a phenomenologist of the moral life, and not an epistemologist – Aristotle's account may seem to fail, so that, for example, Iris Murdoch – a philosopher by no means hostile to the kind of ethical project he espouses – may be taken to offer a truer, more recognisably human picture when she depicts the moral agent as fated to 'live and travel between truth and falsehood, good and evil, appearance and reality' (Murdoch 1992: 166).

These objections may be best dealt with on educational ground. For, if it is true that in Aristotle's writing the *phronimos* appears as a dauntingly – even incredibly – formed character, we need all the more to examine the process of *formation* through which he must have passed. In the next section, then, I turn to issues of teaching and of learning.

## III

'Intellectual virtue', we are told in the opening lines of *NE* II, 'owes both its inception and its growth chiefly to teaching, and for this very reason needs time and experience. Moral goodness, on the other hand, is the result of habit'. What is the force of the contrast here between 'teaching' and 'habit'? This question is surely sharpened by the qualification of 'teaching' by a need for 'time and experience'.

A habit differs from a purely natural propensity (which has a determined, invariant directionality, as for example of smoke to rise or of heavy bodies to fall) and from a faculty (which we do not need to acquire but can simply exercise as an already established endowment, such as sight) in that it must be acquired. It can be acquired only through performing, regularly and recurrently, the very activities in terms of which it will then — after suffcient repetition and consolidation — be specified. Aristotle puts this point with disarming straightforwardness:

> 'Anything that we have to learn to do we learn by the actual doing of it: people become builders by building and instrumentalists by playing instruments. Similarly we become just by performing just acts, temperate by performing temperate ones, brave by performing brave ones.'
>
> (*NE* II 1 1103a33–1103b2)

What kind of process, then, is *teaching*? Aristotle has nothing to say on this until he comes to discuss the intellectual virtues in *NE* VI. There, in the context of analysing scientific knowing (*episteme*), he tells us that this intellectual virtue can be taught and that 'all teaching starts from what is already known . . . because it proceeds either by induction or by deduction' (*NE* VI 3 1139b26–28). With regard to those intellectual virtues whose orientation is theoretical, it seems right to suppose that teaching can take a primarily deductive path. Mathematics is the paradigm example: from a few axioms and definitions further knowledge can be derived by a purely apodictic process. Significantly, when Aristotle is discussing *phronesis* a little later, mathematics — which, as he puts it, 'deals with abstractions' — provides a foil; and it is precisely with respect to learning that he notes the difference between mathematics and *phronesis*:

> Although the young develop ability in geometry and mathematics and become wise in such matters, they are not thought to develop *phronesis*. The reason for this is that *phronesis* also involves knowledge of particulars, which become known from experience; and a young man is not experienced, because experience takes some time to acquire.'
>
> (NE VI 8 1142a12–17)

We find here again just those two factors which had been associated with teaching at the beginning of *NE* II, that is, time and experience. But we are still none the wiser about just what kind of teaching is appropriate to the cultivation of *phronesis*, other than that it is *not* the kind of instruction that can be expedited just in so far as the pupils' minds, unimpeded by messy experiential attachments, can be directed to abstract properties and the formal relations between them. If the latter is a deductive style of teaching and if (as we saw in the previous paragraph) all teaching 'proceeds either by induction or deduction', we are clearly left with the question as to what constitutes the *inductive* mode. In the last chapter of the *Posterior Analytics*, Aristotle depicts it as a process that begins with acts of perception or discrimination (*aisthesis*), some of which persist and are repeated so that they produce a coherent memory, only for further repetition at the level of memory to yield (in the midst of multiplicity) a grasp of universals. This in turn not only inaugurates the level of experience but provides the materials that can be then further systematised (non-inductively) by *techne* and *episteme* at the highest level of operation which is that of the intellectual virtues.

Experience and – given the emphasis on repetition – time are clearly bound up in this inductive process, and since the whole movement is consummated at the level of the intellectual virtues, we can now see how it would make sense for Aristotle to suggest that *phronesis* is learned through a mode of teaching that is patterned on this process. The question then recurs as to how different this mode of teaching (proper to the intellectual virtues) is from the process of habituation (proper to the virtues of character) that is distinguished from it at the beginning of *NE* II.

To answer this question, let us look more closely at habituation. Aristotle himself notices a difficulty in saying that people become just and temperate by doing just and temperate acts 'because if they do what is just and temperate, they *already are* just and temperate' (*NE* II 4 1105a19–20).[10] He answers this difficulty by pointing out that 'just' and 'temperate' are not predicated in the same sense of, first, the actions that lead to virtue and second, the actions that characterize the achieved state of the temperate and just person. In the latter case strong criteria are introduced pertaining not to the acts themselves but to the quality of agency through which they are accomplished: it must be the case that the agent 'knows what he is doing . . . chooses it for its own sake and . . . does it from a fixed and permanent disposition' (*NE* II 4 1105a32–35). It is striking that although Aristotle introduces these conditions by way of indicating the qualitative gap between the actions that lead to virtue and the actions that characterize the achieved state, he leaves us quite in the dark as to how this gap is to be bridged (as on his account it *is* bridged) by habituation. For all his insistence that the latter is 'of supreme importance' and 'makes all the difference' (*NE* II 1 1103b25), he has remarkably little to tell us about just what kind of process it is.

From the strength of the conditions introduced by way of marking its *terminus ad quem*, it is clear that habituation cannot be a matter of mindless repetition or simple-minded drill. To make sense of how it can be *more* than this – without Aristotle's direct guidance but also without departing from him – let us assimilate it to the process of induction that we have just seen. The transition to be effected by the latter is from percepts to concepts (for induction in Aristotle's sense is the process of concept-formation), and this seems commensurate with the transition from naïve acts (perhaps only complying with the directions of a parent or teacher) to acts that give expression to a formed character.

Induction involves repetition no less than habituation does, but in its case Aristotle makes it clearer how the retentive power of memory allows for that gathering and sifting that he calls *experience*; it is in and through experience that there emerges 'the whole universal that has come to rest in the soul (the one beside the many, whatever is one and the same in all those things)' (*Post. An.* II 19 100a6–8). I take Aristotle to be indicating in this dense passage that experience is a matter not of exposure to 'one damned thing after another' but rather of particulars giving rise to, and then being perceived in the light of, universals; but also of universals neither cancelling the particularity of the percepts from which they have arisen nor becoming invulnerable to modification by new percepts. Just as, in the case of induction, the accumulation of percepts leads beyond mere aggregation to a kind of organization in the soul that yields a disposition (*hexis*) to 'perceive as', so, in the case of habituation, the accumulation of repeated acts leads to a kind of stabilization in the soul that yields a disposition to 'act as'. Surely this 'acting as' (acting, in Aristotle's own formulation, 'as just and temperate men act') not only parallels but actually includes 'perceiving as'. For by performing actions repeatedly one comes to get a taste of them and indeed to acquire a taste *for* them.[11] The delight in noble actions characteristic of a virtuous person is not then an unattached pleasure; it is a delight in certain actions *as* noble and so must already contain within itself an element of heightened discrimination.

I have been trying to show that cognition is not added to character *ab extra* but is already inscribed in it qua character. But if character-development is itself an 'inductive' process, what is the specific role in this process of *phronesis*? In Aristotle's account in the *Posterior Analytics*, induction culminates in the 'ultimate universals' that bring into play the intellectual virtues of *episteme* and *techne*; but, as in the case of the parallel text in the opening chapter of the *Metaphysics* that we met earlier, *phronesis* does not appear. Despite this absence, however, *phronesis* finds a natural home in the context of this account. The 'ultimate universal' that it is concerned with is a flourishing life (*eudaimonia*), under the sign of the noble (*to kalon*), realized through acting well (*eupraxia*); and this of course encompasses the more specific universals (that is, the virtues) which give substance to this life.

Where then are we to locate the *difference* between *episteme* and *techne* on the one hand and *phronesis* on the other? When Aristotle says that 'experience . . . provides the starting point (*arche*) of *techne* and *episteme*' (*Post. An.* II 19 100a6–8), he means the starting point for subsequent processes of deduction (the structure of which he has already laid out in earlier sections of the *Analytics*). The characteristic feature of *phronesis*, I suggest, lies in the fact that it remains irremediably inductive (or, synonymously, experiential. To repeat the point made earlier in my commentary on *Metaphysics* I 1, one does not possess *phronesis* if one has the 'theory without the experience' or 'knows the universal but does not know the particular included in this'. The decisive upshot of this is that ethical knowledge of the kind possessed by the *phronimos* is not contained in a set of formulable premises which are then applied to, or from which conclusions are derived in, particular situations. It lies rather in an acquired resourcefulness whereby one can recurrently discern what is to be done – that is, what counts as noble – in each situation as one meets it.

Put syllogistically, what *phronesis* gives one is an ability in each case to discover the proximate minor premise; the conclusion, which is reliably drawn by the *phronimos*, then, is simply doing the deed specified in this 'premise'. The reliability here – that is, the disposition to do – is ensured just in so far as the inductive process through which the *phronimos* has been formed is also (as I have suggested) a process of habituation. To reinforce the point that it is indeed a habituating or character-forming process, here is the stunning image that Aristotle introduces in the midst of his difficult chapter on induction: 'It is like a rout in battle stopped by first one man making a stand and then another, until the original formation has been restored; the soul is so constituted as to be capable of this process' (*Post. An.* II 19 100a12–14). If for Aristotle himself this image gestures to the growth in coherence achieved through concept-formation, its suggestion of resistance to dispersion through repeatedly taking a stand is surely no less effective in capturing the growing consistency and stabilization in the soul (which for Aristotle of course includes the body) that takes place in character-formation.[12]

It may now be easier to respond to the charge that Aristotle's position undermines rational argument about ethical issues. From his perspective it is a matter not of rejecting but of defining what is to count as rationality in this sphere. He does not believe that beings such as ourselves can hold a rational stance outside a certain kind of patterning of emotion, nor that the universals implicit in our moral deliberations are specifiable in abstraction from our ability to read situations, or to determine how to act, in their light. It follows from this that if two people disagree about whether a particular action should be done, there are no independent criteria, accessible in principle to both of them, that can be appealed to – by themselves or by a third party – to resolve their dispute. Must we conclude from this, however, either that such criteria are indeed available or that, in their absence, genuine argument is impossible, and not only (as experience surely tells us is the case) very difficult?

The case here against Aristotle might be turned back on his critics. Perhaps what really cripples ethical argumentation is the expectation that it can be conducted on some neutral ground between competing 'principles'. Its failure to meet this external (and anyhow impossible) standard is then taken as the basis of a quite pervasive moral scepticism (which, it might be claimed, is simply assumed in versions of political liberalism that exclude substantive moral discussion *ab initio* from the public domain). If it is not ethical argumentation as such that fails, but rather the apodictic mode inappropriately imposed on it, we can derive from Aristotle an alternative *ad hominem* mode in which to conduct such argument.[13] This latter would not exclude the possibility of genuine persuasion, that is to say, that one person, through exchange with another, might be moved to a 'change of mind' on the matter in question. However, such persuasion would occur not by the force of new principles pressed upon one by the interlocutor but rather by the opportunity afforded by the exchange to refigure one's existing convictions. If this reconfiguring is to be more than merely notional, it must latch into what Aristotle calls one's character, which might roughly be translated as one's 'self-understanding'.[14] Nor need we suppose – to answer another part of the charge levelled earlier at Aristotle – that on his view one cannot, just by attentiveness to one's own experience, come to change some of one's moral perceptions.[15] To be sure, on his account of it induction can seem an inexorable process: anomalies do not feature in the smooth march towards the universal. Yet in the image we have seen this movement is precisely not a march: it is by *reversing* a general retreat that a particular perception eventually recomposes our experience differently. And from Aristotle's recurrent emphasis on the particular perception, perhaps the possibility of such disconfirmation remains a permanent feature of experience.[16]

## Notes

1 The same is also true, as we shall see later, of the parallel passage in *Posterior Analytics* (*Post. An.*) II 19.

2 *Sophia* (philosophical wisdom) is the highest and most comprehensive intellectual excellence, combining in itself the more specialised and mutually complementary virtues of *nous* (intuitive reason) and *episteme* (science). These three virtues fall on one side of a further division within the intellectual virtues themselves, between those of the theoretical (or 'scientific') and those of the practical (or 'calculative') intellect, the latter comprising *techne* and *phronesis*. This division is ontologically based: it points to two quite distinct object-domains, the former being amenable *only* to theoretical knowledge (since it comprises necessary and unchangeable realities) and the latter (since it has to do with the contingent and inherently variable) inviting not only our – non-theoretical – understanding but also our active regulation.

3 See the previous note.

4 All quotation from Aristotle are from Barnes (1985) or Thompson and Frederick (1976).

5 Even in its most basic meaning, as designating the sense perception of animals, Aristotle already credits a 'critical' function to *aisthesis* (*Post. An.* II 19 99b35). But the sense of discrimination is more marked when it is used in ethical contexts, where it has been well rendered as 'situational appreciation' (Wiggins 1980) and 'discernment of particulars' (Nussbaum 1985).

6 Aristotle provides the classic analysis of this point, in his consideration of the equitable judgement required 'when a case arises . . . which is not covered by the universal statement'. It is thus 'a correction of law where the latter is defective owing to its universality', though the defect, as he points out, so far from being culpable or avoidable, simply 'goes with the territory': it 'is not in the law nor in the legislator but in the nature of the thing, since the matter of practical affairs is of this kind from the start' (*NE* V 10 1137b15–20).

7 For example at 1144a7–9, 'virtue ensures the correctness of the end at which we aim, and *phronesis* that of the means towards it'.

8 This non-separation is clearest in his discussion of resourcefulness (*euboulia*) and 'cleverness' (*deinotes*) in *NE* VI 9 and 10.

61

9 Characteristically, this criticism of Aristotle is made by thinkers with Kantian sympathies; see e.g. Habermas (1993) and Schneewind (1997).

10 This is a variant of the 'paradox of learning' which Aristotle himself refers to at the beginning of *Posterior Analytics* and which had already been given classic expression in Plato's *Meno*.

11 Aristotle himself uses the term 'taste' – in a context congruent with the thrust of my analysis here – when he ascribes people's lack of receptivity to arguments about the merits of virtue to the fact that they have never tasted it (*NE* X 9 1179b16).

12 My reading of Aristotle in this chapter (which is more fully developed in Dunne (1993)) converges closely with that of McDowell (1996). In this part, however, I find a different way from his of explaining how (in his words) '(t)he relevant habituation includes the imparting of conceptual apparatus' (p. 28).

13 I take the terms 'apodictic' and 'ad hominem' (used non-pejoratively) from Taylor (1995), which – albeit that he makes no reference to Aristotle – I take to be congruent with my argument here.

14 The significance of 'self-understanding' here is elucidated, with crucial strategic significance accorded to Aristotelian *phronesis*, in Gadamer (1975).

15 In *NE* I 4 Aristotle quotes with approval lines from Hesiod urging that while it is better to listen to the wise counsel of others it is best to be able to see things for oneself.

16 I argue more fully for this view, setting *phronesis* in an explicitly narrative context, in Dunne (1996).

# References

Barnes, J. (ed.) (1985) *The Complete Works of Aristotle: The Revised Oxford Translation*, Princeton: Princeton University Press.

Dunne, J. (1993) *Back To the Rough Ground: Phronesis and techne in modern philosophy and in Aristotle*, Notre Dame: University of Notre Dame Press.

Dunne, J. (1996) 'Beyond sovereignty and deconstruction: The storied self', in R. Kearney (ed.) *Paul Ricoeur: The hermeneutics of action*, London: Sage.

Gadamer, H.-G. (1975) *Truth and Method*, trans. G. Barden and J. Cumming, London: Sheed and Ward.

Habermas, J. (1993) 'Lawrence Kohlberg and Neo-Aristotelianism', in *Justification and Application: Remarks on discourse ethics*, trans. Ciaran Cronin, Cambridge, Mass: MIT Press.

McDowell, J. (1996) 'Deliberation and moral development in Aristotle's Ethics', in S. Engstrom and J. Whiting (eds) *Aristotle, Kant and the Stoics*, Cambridge: Cambridge University Press.

Murdoch, I. (1992) *Metaphysics as a Guide to Morals*, London: Chatto and Windus.

Nussbaum, M. (1985) 'The discernment of perception: An Aristotelian conception of private and public rationality', in J. Cleary (ed.) *Proceedings of the Boston Area Colloquium in Ancient Philosophy*, Vol. I.

Schneewind, J. B. (1997) 'The misfortunes of virtue', in R. Crisp and M. Slote (eds) *Virtue Ethics*, Oxford: Oxford University Press.

Taylor, C. (1995) 'Explanation and practical reason', *in Philosophical Arguments*, Cambridge Mass: Harvard University Press.

Thompson, J. A. K. and Treddenick H. (1976) *The Ethics of Aristotle*, Harmondsworth: Penguin.

Wiggins, D. (1980) 'Deliberation and practical reason', in A. O. Rorty (ed.) *Essays on Aristotle's Ethics*, Berkeley: University of California Press.

# Part 3

# VARIETIES OF VIRTUE

# 5

# CULTIVATING THE INTELLECTUAL AND MORAL VIRTUES

*Randall Curren*

## I

One of the most familiar aspects of Aristotle's account of virtue is the distinction he draws between the intellectual and moral virtues at the end of Book I of the *Nicomachean Ethics*:

> some kinds of virtue are said to be intellectual and others moral, contemplative wisdom (*sophia*) and understanding (*sunesis*) and practical wisdom (*phronēsis*) being intellectual, generosity (*eleutheriotēs*) and temperance (*sōphrosunē*) moral.
>
> (I 13 1103a5–7)[1]

This division of the virtues follows the pattern of his division of the soul or psyche. 'By human virtue (*anthropine aretē*) we mean not that of the body, but that of the soul', he says (I 13 1102a16). Understanding the soul to be the source and cause of growth and movement, he divides it into rational and irrational elements, and divides the irrational part itself into the desiring part responsible for initiating movement and the nutritive part responsible for growth. Setting aside the nutritive part of the soul, and having implicitly identified the rational and desiring elements as the parts of the soul that contribute to action, Aristotle then says that 'virtue is distinguished into kinds in accordance with' the difference between the rational and desiring parts of the soul (I 13 1103a4). That is to say, he identifies the moral virtues as states of the desiring part of the soul, and intellectual virtues as states of the rational part of the soul.

Moral virtues thus come to be defined as dispositions to feel and be moved by our various desires or emotions neither too weakly nor too strongly, but in a way that moves us to choose and act as reason would dictate, and allows us to take pleasure in doing so (II 5, 6). Intellectual virtues are later defined as capacities or powers of understanding, judgement, and reasoning which

67

enable the rational parts of the soul to attain truth (VI 2 1139b11–13), the attainment of truth being the function of the calculative or practical part no less than the scientific or contemplative one.

Having drawn this distinction between the intellectual and moral virtues at the end of Book I, Aristotle opens Book II with a remark about the origins and development of virtue, which contrasts these forms of virtue in a way that would seem quite significant for the enterprise of moral education:

> Virtue, then, being of two kinds, intellectual and moral, intellectual virtue in the main owes both its birth and its growth to teaching . . . while moral virtue comes about as a result of habit, . . . none of the moral virtues arises in us by nature
>
> (II 1 1103a14–20)

The obvious implication of this for the moral upbringing and education of children is that moral virtue is not something that can be taught or engendered through verbal instruction alone, but is rather something that can only be brought about by ensuring that children consistently act in the right ways. The development of habit presumably requires consistency of conduct, or conduct that is consistently shaped in all its details toward what is desirable, and Aristotle's claim here is that habit is the proximate origin of moral virtue. The development of good habits is thus the target at which moral instruction should aim:

> by doing the acts that we do in our transactions with other men we become just or unjust, and by doing the acts that we do in the presence of danger, and being habituated to feel fear or confidence, we become brave or cowardly. The same is true of appetites and feelings of anger; . . . Thus, in one word, states arise out of like activities . . . It makes no small difference, then, whether we form habits of one kind or of another from our very youth; it makes a very great difference, or rather *all* the difference.
>
> (II 1 1103b17–25)

As interest in Aristotle has spread beyond the universities to the larger educational community, what has received the most attention is this idea that moral learning is properly concerned with developing virtues of character and requires supervised practice of the right kinds.[2] Yet Aristotle's account of the development of moral virtue is not as simple as it may appear to be from these opening passages. Although he distinguishes the moral and intellectual virtues, he also holds that no one is fully virtuous or has true moral virtue without having the intellectual virtue of practical wisdom (VI 13 1144b7–17, 1144b30–32), and he holds that no one can become practically wise without first possessing natural or habitual moral virtue (VI 12 1144a29–37; VII 13 1144b20).

These interdependencies are grounded in the premise that human agents are a union of intellect and desire (VI 2 1139a32–1139b5). They are explained more specifically by a conception of goodness or virtue as not merely a form of moral innocence, but rather what enables its possessor to achieve outward success in pursuing the proper ends of action (I 12 1101b2–3; II 9 1109a24–29), and by the view that although it is the function of thought to identify the proper ends of action, its capacity to do so is limited by the fact that people tend to regard what they are accustomed to taking pleasure in as good (III 4; VI 5 1140b7–19)[3]. Since virtue is what enables one to perform actions that *successfully* pursue good ends, it will require success in the intellectual tasks of discerning what is salient in the circumstances of action and thinking through what it is best to do. Good habits formed under the guidance of *others'* good judgement will not fully equip one to face life's complexities. On the other hand, to the extent that one's conception of the proper ends of action and perception of the circumstances of action is formed and limited by one's emotional dispositions, one can only have the intellectual virtue of practical wisdom or *phronēsis* if one is morally virtuous.

These interdependencies between the intellectual and moral virtues are exceedingly important to Aristotle's theory of virtue and the human good, and my purpose here will be to explore their significance for moral education. I shall begin by saying a few words about their role in Aristotle's ethical theory, and then shift my attention to their bearing on current curricular developments. Aristotle's account of the relationships between the moral and intellectual virtues suggests the importance of integrating what is now promoted under the rubrics of character education and instruction in critical thinking, and it provides a useful starting point for thinking about how to succeed in integrating these pedagogical enterprises. If his account is correct, then neither can be complete without the other, although they are popularly perceived to be in conflict and little theoretical attention is devoted toward a synthesis.[4] I shall devote much of my attention here to examining some philosophical obstacles which seem to stand in the way of a synthesis, and I shall do so in a way that sets the issues on a larger historical stage, in order to see better what is at stake and to appreciate better what is distinctive in the Aristotelian view.

## II

Aristotle distinguishes the moral and intellectual virtues but he also asserts the double-edged thesis that practical wisdom both presupposes and completes moral virtue. In taking this position he follows Plato in rejecting the moral intellectualism of Socrates, while also preserving the doctrine of the unity of virtue. Virtue 'in the strict sense' involves practical wisdom, and this explains, he says, why:

> some say that all the virtues are forms of practical wisdom, and why Socrates in one respect was on the right track while in another he went

astray; in thinking that all the virtues were forms of practical wisdom
he was wrong, but in saying they implied practical wisdom he was
right . . . [I]t is . . . the state that implies the *presence* of right reason,
that is virtue; and practical wisdom is right reason about such matters. Socrates, then, thought the virtues were forms of reason (for he
thought they were, all of them, forms of knowledge), while we think
they *involve* reason.

It is clear, then . . . that it is not possible to be good in the strict sense
without practical wisdom, nor practically wise without moral virtue.
But in this way we may also refute the dialectical argument whereby
it might be contended that the virtues exist in separation from each
other; the same man, it might be said, is not best equipped by nature
for all the virtues, so that he will have already acquired one when he
has not yet acquired another. This is possible in respect of the natural
virtues, but not in respect of those in respect of which a man is called
without qualification good; for with the presence of the one quality,
practical wisdom, will be given all the virtues.

(VI 13 1144b16–1145a2)

Practical wisdom entails the presence of all the virtues because although one may
have some natural or habituated virtues in some degree without having them all,
if one lacks the perceptions associated with even one form of virtue, then one's
perception of moral particulars, conception of the proper ends of action, and
deliberations about what to do will all be corrupted in at least that one respect.
There will be situations in which the emotions associated with the missing form
of virtue will be felt too strongly or weakly and will lead one astray. It is in this
way that practical wisdom entails the presence of all the virtues, and since true
virtue requires practical wisdom this implies that one cannot have any one virtue
fully without having all the others.

This unity of virtue thesis is a centrepiece of Aristotle's ethical theory in as
much as it grounds his central thesis about the essential place of virtue in a
happy life. He holds that happy lives require activity of the rational soul in
accordance with rational principle (I 7 1098a3–9), and it follows from his
views on the unity of virtue that such activity is impossible without moral
virtue (see Kraut 1989; Korsgaard 1986).

For our purposes, however, what has most immediate importance is
Aristotle's distinction between habituated virtue and full or true virtue, and
his conception of the consummation of virtue in phronesis (practical wisdom,
good judgement, or practical intelligence). There are several reasons to accept
the idea that true virtue is the proper object of moral instruction.

First, only a true virtue is good without qualification, and it is surely
better for people to acquire traits that are good without qualification than ones
that are not. On the one hand, supposing that it is possible to have moral

knowledge without having a settled disposition to do what one knows is right, it is not unreasonable for us to prefer that our fellow human beings acquire not only the knowledge but the disposition to act on it. On the other hand, a moral disposition that is not guided by understanding and good judgement can have avoidably bad consequences for both its possessor and others. Loyalty *in due measure* is a good and fine thing, for instance, but conceived as a disposition that is not accompanied by good judgement it exposes its possessors to risks of manipulation and betrayal, and may induce them to inflict wrongful harm in the service of their affiliations.[5] The disadvantages of blind loyalty are significant enough that one may reasonably doubt whether it is a good thing to inculcate it, but the same cannot be said of loyalty that is judicious.

A second reason for regarding true virtue as the appropriate object of moral instruction is that liberal democracy is a form of government which widely distributes the responsibility for exercising judgement in matters of public interest. It thus invites, and in some sense demands, a public which exhibits moral intelligence, rather than simple obedience or habitual virtue. If liberal democracy is the most desirable form of government which we may succeed in establishing, or any equally good or better form of government stands in a comparable relation to virtue, then this is a reason to want true virtue to be very widespread.

Finally, the very idea of an open and progressive moral order involves the idea that the various functions of moral life, including exercises of moral judgement, are more or less universally distributed. This is a conception of social existence which demands widely distributed moral intelligence, and it is arguably a desirable form of social existence, quite apart from any political ramifications that this idea of a moral order might have.

### III

Let us suppose, then, that it is clear that true virtue in Aristotle's sense is the appropriate aim of moral instruction, and that this entails cultivation of both the moral and the intellectual virtues. The popular perception of an opposition between inculcation of 'community values' and encouragement of critical thinking suggests there are at least prima facie tensions in this project of instructional synthesis, arising from the objections that may be lodged against each side of this instructional divide by the other. It will be useful to enumerate these objections, identify the tensions which this enumeration yields, and take stock of the moral tradition's attempts to grapple with them.

The objections or problems which I shall survey here I shall call the problem of *indoctrination*, the problem of *foreclosed options*, the problem of *force*, the problem of *skepticism*, the problem of *local variation*, and the problem of *free-riding*. The problems of indoctrination and free-riding together give rise to a bind or paradox, which I shall call the *paradox of public morality*.

## *Indoctrination*

A common fear about moral education is that it will inevitably be indoctrina-
tive, in the sense that it will establish beliefs which are not all evidently true,
and will do so in such a way that those beliefs are not easily dislodged at any
later time. The spectre of Plato's *Republic* looms in the background of this fear,
and Aristotle's moral psychology inherits some of the *Republic's* fundamental
assumptions. It is commonly assumed now, as then, that the powers of reason
take time to develop in children, and that until those powers have developed
their beliefs remain vulnerable to manipulation. Another Aristotelian (and
Platonic) assumption with broad contemporary currency is that what we have
been habituated to in our youth tends to exercise an enduring influence on
what we desire and perceive to be good. A third assumption, also evident in
Aristotle's thought and derived from Plato's, is that children become neither
good nor responsive to reason without an upbringing that surrounds them
with good models and guides them toward good habits. On these assumptions, moral habituation may be supposed both a prerequisite for critical
thought, as Aristotle held, and an obstacle to its unfettered employment. Will
it not be generally true that one is not in as good a position to judge the
conception of the good in which one has been raised as others, since one will
tend to see what one has grown accustomed to as good?

## *Foreclosed options*

A second and related objection is that in suppressing alternative conceptions of
the good, moral habituation restricts life options. The child's so-called 'right to
an open future' is breached.

## *Force*

A third objection is that moral habituation necessarily involves force, and is
thus morally suspect, particularly in government schools. If moral habits must
be cultivated without the benefit of children being antecedently reasonable,
then a substantial reliance on force may seem inevitable. Peter Simpson's work
on Aristotelian educational theory exemplifies exactly this line of thinking, in
insisting that in the Aristotelian account of becoming good, habits of good
conduct can only be established by force, since they cannot be established by
rational persuasion (Simpson 1990).

## *Skepticism*

Coming at this from the other side, one might worry that children are all too
easily initiated into the deadly game of logic, and that once immersed in its
culture of criticism, they can all too effectively wash themselves and each other

in a 'cynical acid' which eats away even the sturdiest moral fibres, denuding them of the sheltering fabric of culture, community and tradition.[6] One need only imagine that the attitude of the critical thinker is to believe just what there is adequate reason to believe, and that there are no rational foundations for morality, or none that can be easily discovered.

## Local variation

A fifth problem is that even if there are rational foundations for morality generally, there will almost certainly be legitimate local variations, since some problems of social coordination will have no uniquely best solution. Different interests may be balanced somewhat differently, leaving the members of each of the various moral communities pained in one way here, in another way there. What is local in this way appears, and is in some sense, arbitrary. This renders it vulnerable to critical scrutiny, however valuable and irreplaceable it may be.

## Free-riding

Even if there were easily discernible foundational arguments for morality generally, and for any merely local rules, one might fear that instruction in critical thinking will embolden children in their embrace of self-interested arguments to free-ride on public morality, to take advantage of the self-restraint of those who accept the demands of morality. The idea of morality as a system of conduct-guiding norms is that it provides reasons for action that take precedence over all others. Its norms are solutions to problems of social coordination which yield mutual advantage when complied with, and this mutual advantage provides us all with reasons of prudence to prefer life in a community constrained by such norms. Some people may understand how this provides a rational foundation for morality, but not fully accept what it demands, namely that we all accept the reasons of morality as compelling reasons, even when the reasons of prudence counsel a different course. The price of morality's benefits is accepting *limits on our liberty to govern ourselves by our own reason*, but how rational will this seem to one who is encouraged by instruction in critical thinking to think for herself?

The situation in which 'everyone is governed by his own reason' is inevitably 'a condition of war', says Hobbes (1994 [1651]: xvi, 4), but the 'fool', without denying the existence of a social covenant, 'questioneth whether injustice . . . may not sometimes stand with that reason which dictateth to every man his own good. [He questions whether] it be not against reason [to violate the covenant]' (ibid.: xv, 4). 'The force of words being . . . too weak to hold men to the performance of their covenants', and virtue being too rare, we must authorize a sovereign to establish moral law by force of arms and the suppression of academic freedom, says Hobbes (ibid.: xiv, 31; xviii, 9; xlvi, 23 (OL)).

If we are to find some principled grounds on which to resist the repugnantly illiberal aspects of this Hobbesian solution, we need to show either that habits of virtue, and the sentiments, perceptions, and inclinations that comprise them, are robust and resistant to any corrupting influence that critical reason might have, or that critical reason can be counted on to counsel fair play and adherence to moral norms.

Surveying this list, we find three forms of the concern that moral training compromises individual freedom, and three forms of the concern that the liberating capacity of critical reason undermines fidelity to common morality. At least four of these concerns were on the philosophical agenda at its outset, and have been perennially at the heart of philosophical concern with education, the problems of *local variation* and *foreclosed options* being the exceptions. I will set these exceptions aside in what follows, and begin my discussion of the others with some brief remarks on their place in the philosophical tradition.

## IV

When Thrasymachus argues in Book I of Plato's *Republic* that laws aim at the advantage of the rulers alone, while those who have made the laws 'declare what they have made – what is to their own advantage – to be just for their subjects' (Grube and Reeve 1992: 338e), he confronts Socrates with a problem of indoctrination which the Socratic *elenchus* cannot answer, but which Plato hopes to. The *elenchus* is a mode of dialectical reasoning which can drive out the contradictions in a set of beliefs, but it offers no hope of arriving at a consistent set of *true* beliefs unless one has begun with beliefs which are weighted toward the truth to begin with. In the face of systematic error, which could arise from systematic deception, it is powerless, and this points up the desirability of having some basis for judging a society which is independent of what is taught in it.

Thrasymachus's consistent disdain for conventional morality may also be considered an expression of moral skepticism, to be answered by Plato's theory of moral knowledge, while the challenge from Glaucon that follows in Book II shows how the free-rider problem arises even among those who accept the rationality of entering into a social covenant to create and enforce a common morality. It is in hopes of answering this free-rider problem that Plato spends the better part of Books II–IX trying to show that virtue is not simply an instrumental good, related to happiness only unreliably through external sanctions, but an internal good of the psyche, without which no one can have any prospect of happiness. It is, at least in part, in hopes of answering this problem that Rousseau later undertakes to convince us that Emile can *without benefit of instruction* discover natural moral law (along with the laws of physics), and the existence of God and the afterlife (i.e., the essential elements of 'natural religion') Rousseau 1979 [1762]).

Thrasymachus represents the problem of force, no less than the problem of indoctrination, and Plato affirms in response that in the best kind of city children are educated by 'persuasion' embodied in music and poetry, and not by 'force', as they are in deficient cities (401b–402a; 548c). In the *Republic* (401b–402a, 548c, 590c–d) as in the works of Locke (1996 [1693]: sect. 31–85), the resistance to using force in education rests in the idea that reliance on force tends to undermine the development of responsiveness to reason, and the idea that force need be used only sparingly, since children are quite ready to imitate those who are praised and admired, and quite inclined to adopt the standards and way of life of those who take care of them.

What this brief historical introduction begins to reveal is that the problems of indoctrination and free-riding are the most challenging. The problem of force depends upon failing to recognize the ways in which children are drawn to the good, without force or rationally compelling argument. Plato, Aristotle, and Locke all had a reasonably good understanding of how this occurs. On Aristotle's account, what is lacking in most children without moral training is specifically an attachment to what is *praiseworthy* or *admirable* (*kalon*) (*NE* 1179b4–26), and argument alone will not engender such an attachment, but this does not mean that children are without other motives that can be relied upon to persuade them, often without force, to engage in conduct that will allow them to develop a taste for what is good and admirable and a devotion to it for its own sake.[7] They thereby become responsive to reasons of a distinctively moral kind, which Aristotle regards as practical reasons of the highest order.

By contrast, what may seem the obvious adequate response to the problem of indoctrination is not adequate. That response would note the reference, in my statement of the problem of indoctrination, to establishing 'beliefs which are not all evidently true', and hold that there is no problem if we take care to inculcate only beliefs which are evidently true. I think there is a lot of good sense in this response, and that school districts typically do attempt to exercise such care when they pursue initiatives in character education. Non-violence and mutual respect are on the list, but beliefs about sexual orientation, gender roles, and what constitutes a family are not. When the various constituencies in a district are brought to the table, their initial apprehensions about 'whose values' are to be taught give way to a consensus that is remarkably stable across districts.

As gratifying as such success may be, however, we have to make some allowance for our collective fallibility. Recognizing our fallibility, and making allowance for the possibility of moral progress, should lead us to embrace the ideal of a moral community that is held together by norms which are open to public evaluation and revision, a community that chooses fundamental law for itself and makes moral progress by revising it over time. Even if we take care to find common ground in what we teach, if we teach it in a way that precludes any possibility of thinking beyond it, then the ideal of a progressive common morality is compromised, and a form of the problem of indoctrination remains.

The problem of skepticism is also an easier one than the free-rider problem. Although it is periodically fashionable to profess moral skepticism, the contractarian view that it is mutually advantageous and therefore rational to impose on ourselves duties of mutual respect, or at least self-restraint, is not only an attractive fall-back position in theory, but one which is easily grasped as self-evident in practice. Although there may be specific provisions of particular moral codes that are not mutually advantageous, the general proposition that moral order is mutually advantageous seems true. On the other hand, the free-rider problem would remain unsolved even if the problem of skepticism were solved.

Taken together, the problems of indoctrination and free-riding create something of a bind or dilemma, a paradox of public morality, if you will:

1 Either one's capacity to critically evaluate the morality one is habituated into is limited by the perceptions and sentiments one acquires in that habituation, or it is not.
2 If it is limited in this way, then no consistent system of morality is open to internal public scrutiny, and no one brought up in it has any rational assurance that it is not deficient.
3 If it is not limited in this way, then the perceptions and sentiments which incline us to give the reasons of morality priority over others can be undermined by critical thinking, resulting in moral free-riding.

The problem, in short, is how morality can both command our fidelity and be open to effective public scrutiny and appropriate revision. It would seem that it can only have one of these properties at the expense of the other.

The classical and modern traditions share a common aspiration to solve the free-rider problem by means of a theoretical demonstration that it is rational to be moral, but they divide on the questions of whether the requisite moral knowledge can be easily acquired, and whether it can be acquired independently of one's prior moral beliefs. To the extent that it can be acquired easily and independently of one's prior moral beliefs and perceptions, a solution to our paradox may be found in the possibility of our all having moral knowledge.

The Platonic and Aristotelian view is that moral habituation and true moral belief are an essential foundation for becoming reasonable and acquiring moral insight, and that such insight is a rare achievement. Thus, few people become fully virtuous, on their view. Those who do will understand why a happy life requires virtue, and their reason will confirm the perceptions of what is good with which they have grown comfortable (Rep. 402a). But most people will never have the capacity or knowledge to judge the moral code of their city, and the preservation of their incomplete virtue will require some modest enforcement of laws which embody divine reason or natural moral law (NE X 9 1180a1–4). Though the texts are less clear on this point, the view of Aristotle and the later Plato may be that even the moral insight of the practically wise might not obviate the need for such external assistance.[8]

By contrast, the view that emerges in the early modern period is that faith and reason converge, but may do so quite independently of one another. According to the doctrines of 'natural reason' and 'natural religion', human beings possess as a gift of nature a faculty of reason by which they can easily discover within themselves a knowledge of God, moral law, and the afterlife. Such knowledge of the moral law and its divine enforcement would provide us all with assurance that virtue pays, and provide an independent measure of human laws and customs. This doctrine provides Rousseau with a solution to the tension he sees between domestic and public education, between education in the interests of the child and education in the interests of society. On a proper understanding of natural law, which the child will allegedly discover for himself, these interests coincide.

I am not sanguine about the prospects for making good on this idea that there is easily, and thus widely, attainable moral knowledge which not only provides an independent measure of the soundness of whatever moral code one has grown up with, but also a compelling motive to be moral. The Aristotelian account of virtue and reason seems more plausible in this respect. If such knowledge is not widely attainable, however, what possibilities for escaping the *paradox of public morality* remain? I can think of four which may warrant some consideration.

First, one might hypothesize that reason can outstrip the sentiments, that what one rationally judges to be best will not always be possible for one emotionally. If this is true, then critical reason may be able to provide evaluations of one's moral mother-tongue sufficient for moral progress, even as it remains the language of one's heart. Progress would be intergenerational, not intragenerational, and the sentiments of each generation would bind its actions, if not its tongue. A difficulty with this suggestion is that if the advances in moral judgement are not put into practice in any way, it is not clear how intergenerational progress can proceed. Inconsistencies between speech and conduct are as likely to engender cynicism as progress, especially on Aristotelian assumptions about how moral virtues are cultivated.

Second, one might argue that allowance for fallibility in our identification of fundamental moral principles is misplaced, that what we think of as moral progress, and wish to leave room for, is progress in the consistency and sensitivity of application of the same fundamental principles which have been transmitted already through many generations. On this line of argument, there is no harm in people being forever bound in their sentiments, conduct, and perception of the good by the correct fundamental morality they are brought up in. That will prevent them from exploiting opportunities to free-ride, while a training in critical thinking and moral case analysis will develop their capacity for advancing moral progress through sensitive and creative application of the fundamental principles they have learned. This is a solution quite consistent with the moral finality of Plato's *Republic* and *Laws*, but not obviously compatible with Aristotle's conception of *phronēsis*. The idea that moral insight is tied up with the discernment of particulars and is aggregative (Sherman 1989: 13–55) does not lend itself to this suggested partitioning of principle and application.

Third, a suggestion which is more authentically Aristotelian than either of the preceding is that as a body of citizens reaches better collective judgements about matters of moral concern, it can and should bind itself under new laws, thereby creating for itself the motivation to act in a more enlightened way. This is possible, by Aristotle's lights, even if people who have been brought up well, and have acquired a conception of what is good and admirable and a seriousness about it, remain in some danger of backsliding. Given the advancement of moral insight and judgement which they can attain when they bring their somewhat different perspectives together in conversation, they will at least be in a position to advance enlightened legal reform, and will wish to do so. They will thereby bind themselves, while both instructing and binding those who have not achieved the same progress of understanding. Aristotle stakes a great deal of his political theory on the idea that legal reform can be an effective instrument of moral progress, provided the instructional and motivating force of law is not undermined by changing it too much or too frequently (*Pol.* I 2 1253a30–39; II 8 1269a14–23).

A final possibility is that if children are initiated into habitual practices of giving and taking reasons, including moral reasons, they will become both morally serious and committed critical thinkers, motivated by conceptions of themselves as both moral and devoted to the truth. Being motivated in this way will preclude free-riding, since selfishness and making an exception of oneself will be incompatible with a desire to be moral, but if thoughtfulness about what counts as a reason has been cultivated, it is hard to see how the perceptions and sentiments formed by such an upbringing would preclude an examination of fundamental morality and a potential for moral progress.

On this alternative one pictures the intellectual virtues as themselves originating in training or habituation in accordance with norms of reason, as much as in teaching, and one pictures training in the habits of virtue as also including a training in the practice of giving adequate reasons for what one does, and respecting the adequate reasons that others give. This is not a straightforwardly Aristotelian view to the extent that it rejects the idea that reason emerges late, identifies a stage of habituation in norms of reason, and sees habits of giving and taking reasons as part of the habituation of ethical virtue. In these ways it is a more obviously Lockean view than Aristotelian, but the differences may be more apparent than real. What is evident in Locke is that he regards children as able to grasp reasons, though not the deepest reasons, and that he thinks it a good thing to initiate children from the earliest possible age in the practices of reason-giving. I am not sure that Aristotle's conception of moral habituation precludes any of this, since it must surely promote the development of rational and self-critical capacities if it is to promote true virtue (Sherman 1989: 157–99). What *is* precluded on

Aristotle's account is the view that children are responsive to reason in the sense of grasping and being moved by appeals to what is good and admirable, but this is not to say that they are incapable of reasoning or unresponsive to other kinds of reasons.

This final solution is in some ways the most attractive, but a great deal remains to be examined. Having provided some indication of the agenda for educational theory and practice which the Aristotelian view of the relation between the moral and intellectual virtues seems to entail, I must close now and commend the difficulties that remain for further investigation.

# Notes

1 The translations of passages from the *Nicomachean Ethics* that I provide here follow most closely the Urmson revision of Ross's Oxford translation, appearing in Barnes (1984), though my departures from it are occasionally substantial. If the context does not make it clear which work of Aristotle's I am referring to I will use *NE* and *Pol.* to indicate the *Nicomachean Ethics* and *Politics* respectively.

2 Two examples of the use being made of the Aristotelian dictum that we learn justice and lyre-playing alike 'by doing' (1103a31–1103b2), are the arguments currently being given for public service requirements for high school graduation in the United States ('service learning'), and a recent variant of 'control theory'. Harris Woffard, former director of the Peace Corps and current director of the Corporation for National Service, has recently cited Aristotle in defence of service learning requirements in a speech given at the White House/ Congressional Conference on 'Character Building' (Washington, DC, 7 June 1996). His argument is that if children are to become generous or benevolent they must devote some of their energies to helping others. Gregory Bodenhamer, a former juvenile probation officer who now trains parents, teachers, and school administrators in techniques for managing difficult adolescents, has developed a self-consciously Aristotelian account of parenting (Bodenhamer 1995). One illustration of his Aristotelianism is his insistence that children should not be told that it is their choice to do the right thing or something else, with a reminder of the consequences of bad choices. Many children will care more about doing what they want to do at the moment than about future consequences, and will soon grow accustomed to choosing the worse over the better. The better and more Aristotelian approach is to insist on acceptable conduct and provide supervision sufficient to induce it.

3 Rackham (1934) renders I 12 110162–3 'praise belongs to goodness, since it is this which makes men capable of accomplishing noble deeds', a translation which captures better than the alternatives the background notion, pervasive in Aristotelian ethics, that virtue is what enables a person or thing to do well what is appropriate to it.

4 The idea that there is a direct opposition between inculcation of morality and instruction in critical thinking is evident, among other places, in the criticisms levelled at the US courts for endorsing the view that state and local authorities have a legitimate interest in inculcating 'community values' through the public schools. See, e.g., Van Geel (1983) and Roe (1991).

5  It was for such reasons, offered by a community representative who had served in the Vietnam War, that loyalty and patriotism were recently struck from a tentative list of 'core values' to be taught in a public school district in New York state. Courage and honesty remained on the list, although similar objections could be made to them. This inconsistency could be attributed to a failure to consider consistently the traits under discussion, as entailing the good judgement needed to 'hit the mean' between different kinds of error. My observations from the trenches of the character education movement suggest that unrecognized vacillations between true and merely habitual virtue are common.

6  The phrase 'cynical acid' is Oliver Wendell Holmes's.

7  Note Aristotle's references to children being moved by affection (*NE* X 9 1180b4–7) and to social instincts which create some natural tendency to cooperation (*Pol.* I 2 1253a30).

8  See e.g., *Laws* 653c–d, where Plato describes the religious festivals of a city as restoring the virtue which people tend to lose over the course of their lives, and Lord (1982) which argues that Aristotle develops a similar view through the idea that public performances of tragedies induce a cathartic purging of emotions which tend to accumulate and corrupt practical wisdom.

# References

Portions of this paper will appear in (Curren forthcoming-a) and (Curren forthcoming-b).

Barnes, J. (ed.) (1984) *The Complete Works of Aristotle: The Revised Oxford Translation*, Princeton: Princeton University Press.

Bodenhamer, G. (1995) *Parent in Control*, New York: Simon and Schuster.

Curren, R. (forthcoming-a) *Aristotle on the Necessity of Public Education*, Savage, Md.: Rowman and Littlefield.

Curren, R. (forthcoming-b) 'Critical thinking and the unity of virtue', in S. Tozer (ed.) *Philosophy of Education 1998*, Urbana, IL: Philosophy of Education Society.

Grube, G. M. A. and Reeve, C. D. C. (trans.) (1992) *Plato: Republic*, Indianapolis: Hackett Publishing Company.

Hobbes, T. [1651] (1994) *Leviathan: Or the matter, form, and power of a commonwealth ecclesiastical and civil*, ed., intro. and notes E. Curley, Indianapolis: Hackett Publishing Company.

Korsgaard, C. (1986) 'Aristotle on function and virtue', *History of Philosophy Quarterly* 3, 3: 259–79.

Kraut, R. (1989) *Aristotle on the Human Good*, Princeton: Princeton University Press.

Locke, J. [1693] (1996) *Some Thoughts Concerning Education*, in R. W. Grant and N. Tarcov (eds) *Some Thoughts Concerning Education and Of the Conduct of the Understanding*, Indianapolis: Hackett Publishing Company.

Lord, C. (1982) *Education and Culture in the Political Thought of Aristotle*, Ithaca: Cornell University Press.

Rackham, H. (trans.) (1934) *Aristotle: The Nicomachean Ethics*, Cambridge, Mass.: Harvard University Press.

Roe, R. (1991) 'Valuing student speech: The work of schools as cognition and conceptual development', *California Law Review* 79, 4: 1269–1345.

Rousseau, J.J. [1762] (1979) *Emile*, trans. A. Bloom, New York: Basic Books.

Sherman, N. (1989) *The Fabric of Character*, Oxford: Clarendon Press.

Simpson, P. (1990) 'Making the city good: Aristotle's city and its contemporary relevance', *The Philosophical Forum* 22, 1: 149–166.

Van Geel, T. (1983) 'The search for constitutional limits on governmental authority to inculcate youth', *Texas Law Review* 62, 4: 197–297.

# 6

# VIRTUES OF BENEVOLENCE
# AND JUSTICE

*James D. Wallace*

Character is the interpenetration of habits.
John Dewey, *Human Nature and Conduct*

## I

People are sometimes moved to act by a familiar and distinctive motive: direct concern for the welfare of another. They care about others. Sometimes this concern flows from deep affection for another, as with lovers, friends, and family members. People care also, however, about people whom they know only slightly or not at all. They care about and feel sympathy sometimes for the suffering and grief of casual acquaintances and strangers and are moved to aid and comfort them. The special character of this concern for others that all these phenomena exemplify is captured by Aristotle's description in the *Nicomachean Ethics* (NE) of one aspect of the attitude of friends towards one another. 'The decent person . . . is related to his friend as he is to himself, since the friend is another himself' (NE 1166a30–31). Kind, sympathetic, compassionate people – those who possess virtues of benevolence – tend in their feelings and actions, in varying degrees, to respond to others' fortunes as they do to their own.

The central cases of virtues of benevolence involve a tendency to act from a direct concern for the welfare of others. There are, of course, variants and peripheral cases (Brandt 1976: 430–3; Sidgwick 1907: 238–63). Someone who is not particularly sympathetic might make it a policy to act as kind people act, out of a desire to be good and to act well. In so far as such a person cares about being good rather than the welfare of another, the person's motive is not the direct concern for another that is characteristic of paradigmatic kindness. This exemplifies one of the variants (the peripheral forms) of virtues of benevolence. In what follows, the discussion will focus on the central cases of virtues of benevolence.

People are also influenced in their actions by a desire to get something right according to a certain standard or norm. Their concern in such actions may be the necessity of observing the norm in order to produce a certain desired result, as when surgeons perform prescribed scrubbing routines in order to promote antisepsis. Architects, scholars, musicians, and many others, however, when they are engaged in complex activities that they value, are sometimes concerned simply to do things right. Their love of the activity, their appreciation of it, is expressed in their concern to do it in accordance with the highest standards they know. The phenomenon of being guided by norms extends to all areas of human life, embracing a wide variety of activities and concerns. Being guided by moral norms is an instance of this general phenomenon.

Kindness, generosity, sympathy, and compassion are prominent virtues of character that are forms of benevolence. Honesty, truthfulness, and fairness are among the virtues of character that evince a commitment to certain norms of social ethics. Let us call these forms of justice. It is widely thought that in order to be a person of good character, it is necessary to possess both kinds of virtues, benevolence and justice. It is not always easy, however, to combine these qualities in a single character. Sometimes, one cannot avoid hurting someone without failing in some important obligation. Such situations can be painful for people who are both conscientious and sympathetic. The conflict is a common one in many areas of life: judges, members of university tenure committees, loan officers, teachers and many others are painfully familiar with it. Benevolence and justice may seem incompatible character traits. 'Justice, rigorous justice, is for some people an absolute value, but it is not compatible with what may be no less ultimate values for them – mercy, compassion – as arises in concrete cases' (Berlin 1992: 12).

Consider the tender-hearted teachers. They are unable to give students failing grades for truly poor work; they don't want to hurt the students' feelings. Giving these students passing grades, however, is bad pedagogical practice. It is, moreover, unfair to better students and to those who rely on accurate evaluations of students' work for important decisions. Many tender-hearted teachers know this, but they cannot bring themselves to hurt and disappoint weak students. Their sympathy leads them to act contrary to pedagogical and ethical norms. They fail the practice they are engaged in by insufficient commitment to its norms. They are deficient in justice.

On the other hand, teachers who grade students' work solely on the basis of the quality of the work, undeterred by the knowledge that some students will as a result be deeply disappointed, even wounded, are just, though not necessarily unkind. Here, it appears, the fact that an act that hurts someone is required by a relevant norm can turn aside the charge that in hurting someone, the agent was being unkind.

## II

Immanuel Kant noted that sympathy and benevolence sometimes lead people to act contrary to a moral norm, and thus to act wrongly. Benevolence, therefore, he said, is not good 'without qualification'. The firm determination to act in accordance with moral norms, however, the trait of character that Kant called 'a good will', is sufficient to motivate people to do what they should do (Kant 1948 [1785]: 61–71). Benevolence can motivate people to act contrary to norms, including moral norms, whereas the conscientious determination to be guided by moral norms is not an incentive to violate such norms. It would seem to follow, then, that moral character is simply a matter of commitment to the relevant norms. Benevolence is, at best, an unreliable ally of Kantian good will. Kant did not draw the conclusion that benevolence is a dispensable element in good character, although his view of benevolence was ambivalent. (For a discussion of the vexed question of Kant's view of the place of benevolence in good character see Baron 1995: 207–26.) The view that a person might lack benevolence and still be of good character is not plausible. Why, though, is it not enough in order to be a good person to be firmly determined to be guided by the relevant norms of action, the norms that determine what is right? Just people are committed to acting as they should in moral matters. Why do we suppose that it is important as well to be moved by sympathetic concern for others, especially in view of the frequency with which sympathetic impulses conflict with the indications of norms? What is the particular contribution of benevolence to good character?

David Hume went some distance in explaining the presence of both benevolence and justice in good character. His ethical theory also provides an explanation why these virtues tend to conflict. Morality, Hume claimed, is internally connected with our deepest concerns, with matters that are central to needs and interests that we all have:

> The social virtues of humanity and benevolence exert their influence immediately, by a direct tendency or instinct, which chiefly keeps in view the simple object, moving the affections, and comprehends not any scheme or system, nor the consequences resulting from the concurrence, imitation or example of others.
>
> (Hume 1751: 93)

Acting because so doing fulfills an important need of another or advances the interest of another, simply because one cares about another's welfare, is acting in a way that expresses the trait of benevolence. The act is aimed by the agent directly at another's good. We tend to value benevolent acts; we identify with the people who are the beneficiaries of such acts. In the absence of interfering considerations, we tend to be glad for the recipient and pleased with the agent. That the trait benevolence is a virtue, Hume says, is explained by the fact that it is found universally to be both useful (in promoting our important needs and interests) and agreeable (ibid.:16–20, 66–8).

Hume contrasts benevolent acts with acts that express 'the social virtues of justice and fidelity'. The latter virtues are 'absolutely necessary to the well-being of mankind', he says, but the benefit of them 'is not the consequence of every individual single act'. A single act of justice may have pernicious consequences. Rather, the benefit 'arises from the whole scheme or system, concurred in by the whole, or the greater part of society'. There is no way, Hume claims, to realize the benefit of the 'whole scheme' without bad consequences in some cases:

> General inflexible rules [are] necessary to support general peace and order in society. . . . Though such rules are adopted as best serve the same end of public utility, it is impossible for them to prevent all particular hardships, or make beneficial consequences result from every individual case.
>
> (Hume 1751: 93–4)

The rules of justice are artefacts, on Hume's view. They are instruments we employ for certain purposes, which are connected with needs and interests central to our well-being. They are useful. The virtue justice involves an acceptance of and a willingness to observe certain of these rules: his examples are the norms of property, promising, and government. Since the rules in question are artefacts, the creations of human beings, Hume calls justice an 'artificial' virtue (Hume 1739–40: 477, 496–7). The virtue is essentially an individual's disposition toward certain artefacts – an acceptance of the authority of the rules and a commitment to follow them. Without the artefacts, this virtue could not exist. These are special artefacts, however. They consist of rules, and their existence depends entirely upon the fact that there is general understanding of them and an acknowledgment of their authority. These are, in this sense, social artefacts. Benevolence, on the other hand, is a 'natural' virtue. It is based upon a tendency that people have by nature, and it requires no particular social artefacts for its existence as justice does.

On Hume's account, justice and benevolence will conflict on some occasions. When a rule of justice requires an act that has 'pernicious consequences' for some individual(s), justice will prompt the action but, presumably, benevolence will oppose it. One might suppose that the existence of such conflicts shows that the rules of justice require revision, but this is not Hume's view. The need for the system of rules that define the institution of property, Hume argues, is the need for a peaceful way to resolve the conflicts of interest between people when more than one individual wants the same material good. Because of the moderate scarcity of the material things people need and desire, such conflicts are inevitable, and a generally accepted scheme for resolving such conflicts of interest promotes security and social harmony. The resulting peace and security of possession provides incentives for production of goods and fruitful co-operation among people. Because of the nature of the circumstances that call for such a scheme, however, no scheme could guarantee that every party's desires will be satisfied on every occasion. It is not possible to satisfy fully every particular claim based upon need or interest. The resolution of a particular conflict of interest in a way that satisfies the interest of one party would likely frustrate and disappoint another party. Because of the nature of the rules and the purpose that it is their function to serve, those who accept the rules must be willing sometimes to forgo their own interests when the rules so indicate, and to see others from time to time lose under the rules as well (Hume 1739–40: 497–8).

Notice, though, that on Hume's account, the whole point of the practice composed of rules which sometimes indicate acts that will harm people is '"the public interest". . . . Public utility is the *sole* origin of justice, and . . . reflections on the beneficial consequences of this virtue are the *sole* foundation of its merit' (Hume 1751: 20). People who were not keenly interested in the welfare of people generally would not have such artefacts.[1]

Hume's account explains in a plausible way why a person who is both just and benevolent is likely to encounter circumstances in which one virtue prompts the person to one course of action and the other virtue to a contrary action. If Hume is right, such conflicts between benevolence and justice are not eliminable. What Hume thinks one should do in circumstances where justice and benevolence are in conflict is not clear. Sometimes, he seems to endorse the position that one should in every such case follow the rules of justice. He does allow, however, that the rules of justice are properly suspended in an emergency: in times of famine, the granaries are thrown open; in a shipwreck, one seizes any object that will keep one afloat without worrying about the rights of the owner of the object, and so on (Hume 1751: 22–3). Would Hume accept the possibility, though, that justice might on occasion properly be tempered with mercy even though no catastrophe threatened? This part of Hume's account is not developed.

Hume conceived the norms of justice as rules that constitute property, promising, and government. He explained why these rules regularly require people to act contrary to their own interests and contrary to the interests of others, thus accounting for the conflicts of justice with self-interest and with benevolence. This is plausible, as far as it goes. It is important to notice, however, that the rules of property, promising, and government are not the only norms which conflict in this way with benevolence. Remember the tender-hearted teachers and the tenure committee members. Think of parents who must punish a beloved child and referees in competitions. A wide variety of rules, precepts, and instructions – some clear candidates for the category 'moral' and others not – occasion such conflicts.

## III

Another classical philosophical text offers a useful perspective on these matters. Plato argued in the *Republic* that a human community is properly organized on the basis of a division of labour and specialization (369a–374e). People's needs and interests are many and varied, and few individuals are able by themselves to provide for the satisfaction of all or even most of their own needs. Although solitary individuals are not self-sufficient, the various talents and abilities of a large enough group of people are likely to provide for all or most needs and interests. The most efficient way to effect this broad provision is to ensure that those who are well suited to certain useful tasks work full time at their tasks to develop their abilities through experience.

Plato's view provides the basis for an illuminating view of community as we understand it. Communities so organized properly foster the development of bodies of practical knowledge based upon the experience of practitioners with specific useful tasks. People who specialize in building, agriculture, inquiry, law, healing, teaching, and so on master a body of practical knowledge which contains the distillation of the experience of many others who have practised the activity. They receive this shared knowledge, practise it, add their bit to it, and communicate it to other practitioners.

These bodies of practical knowledge that we practise as specialists are social artefacts too. They are also complexes of norms. What a specialist knows and practises is how to proceed so that tasks are done well rather than badly. The norms themselves, of course, reflect the experience of many individual practitioners: what they have learned about how to proceed in various circumstances, so that the activity will actually serve the particular interest that is its reason for being. Among the norms that guide the participants in a particular practice are technical instructions that pertain to the task of producing such and such a result: a durable pot, a habitable shelter, an illuminating explanation, the reduction of a fever. Some of the relevant norms, however, can be classified as ethical: certain tasks cannot go forward unless workers communicate truthfully with one another, unless individuals can be trusted to do what they say they will do, unless they trust one another not to harm them, and so on. Among the norms that constitute a body of practical knowledge such as medicine or agriculture are both technical norms and ethical norms (Wallace 1996: 9–39, 85–108).

Plato was concerned that a community organized according to the principle of division of labour and specialization should be so structured that it promoted the simultaneous harmonious pursuit of these various specialized activities. A community that succeeds to an appreciable extent in fostering these activities and promoting their harmonious and effective practice Plato called a just community (433a–434c). The aim, here, is the simultaneous effective practice of many different activities that contribute in various important ways to the satisfaction of people's needs and interests with a minimum of conflict and interference with one another. It would be even better, of course, if the activities were practised in ways that sustained and advanced the effective practice of other activities. The community would then be a system of harmonious and mutually reinforcing activities which served an expanding variety of important needs and interests. The different activities would be practised in a way that reflected their adjustment to one another. To realize this aim, the practitioners of the various special activities would not only have to be guided by norms that indicated how the purpose of their particular activity was to be attained, but they would as well have to practise their activities in ways that did not interfere with, and preferably fostered the practise of, other important activities.

Among the norms that constitute bodies of practical knowledge such as agriculture, sculpture, and navigation, then, are norms that indicate the right way to proceed in order to attain the purpose that defines the practice, and other norms that indicate how the practice is to be performed in such a way that it harmonizes with and supports other important practices. The norms of various activities will reflect the current knowledge of how things should be done in order to realize the activities' own purpose, but they will also reflect the presence of other activities in their adaptation and adjustment to them. The activities pursued simultaneously in the same community in varying degrees 'interpenetrate' (Dewey's term). It is worth noting too that among the norms of an activity that serve to harmonize its practice with the practice of other activities are some Humean 'rules' of justice: rules of property, promising, and government.

## IV

Plato's description of the *kallipolis* (the good community) in the *Republic*, used in that work as a theoretical model for the individual human psyche, provides a brilliantly transparent account of something that is extraordinarily complicated: community. The account can be appropriated for the exposition of a view of practical norms generally, including ethical norms, that is straightforwardly empirical and naturalistic. This view of norms is most un-Platonic.[2] Plato's account of the *kallipolis*, though, helps to make the complexity of community intellectually manageable. At the same time, the account is most useful and plausible if it is modified in a particular way.

At the beginning of the *Politics*, Aristotle announced that the way to study community is to go back to its beginnings and trace its growth (1252a25–6). People live together because individuals are not self-sufficient, they cannot on their own provide even the bare necessities of life. Community, Aristotle says, 'comes to be for the sake of living, but remains in being for the sake of living well' (*Politics* 1252b30–2). This remark is made, presumably, with Plato's account of community organized on the principle of division of labour and specialization in mind. Good living for human beings, according to Aristotle, is activity that exhibits excellences of thought and character: virtues, *aretai* (*NE* 1097b23 –1098a21). The activity that exhibits excellences, of course, is activity that is done well in accordance with the appropriate standards or norms. (I am going to ignore Aristotle's attempt to rank excellences and the activities that exhibit them according to which is 'best and most perfect'.)

Community, conceived in Plato's way as a means for making human beings more self-sufficient by providing them with food, shelter and security, is also the occasion, the matrix, for creating complex activities rich with norms and standards. These activities and the standards for doing them well are related to people's needs and desires for food, shelter, security, and so on, but once the activities develop in a complex community, the interests that occasioned them develop and multiply (Dewey 1922: 56–57; MacIntyre 1981: 189–190). The developed activities become in themselves objects of intense interest and appreciation. A good life is not merely a life of subsistence; it involves absorption in useful complex activities that require practical knowledge for their performance. The acquired, refined capacities and dispositions that individuals need in order to participate successfully in these activities are excellences of thought and character: skills, know-how, and virtues of character. Community is necessary, then, not only for providing the necessities for human existence, but because sociality is a necessary condition for developed practical knowledge, cultivated know-how, and technical and ethical norms. Living well, as Aristotle said, is more than merely securing the necessities for sustaining life; it is a matter of doing well in accordance with such standards.

Complex activities that obviously serve the purposes of various cultivated human needs and interests are themselves objects of intense interest and cultivation: they themselves are central constituents in living well. Fortunate people are able to flourish in activities they love. Obviously, we do not value such things only instrumentally. Community, which repairs our lack of individual self-sufficiency, makes possible the knowledge of good and bad and, of course, activity in accordance with such knowledge. Central to such activity is observing standards, following technical and moral norms. Community is in these and other ways the *sine qua non* of living well and doing well.

The sociality, the living together and sharing a highly structured way of life, is obviously necessary for all these things, and in that sense it is a means to survival *and* to good living. This indicates its importance. At the same time, sociality, like cultivated complex activities, is itself a focus of intense interest and appreciation. As we participate together in many activities, we value our associates and our association with them, and we do not value them merely as instruments. Such associations are, in themselves, a possible source of deep satisfaction and, as Aristotle saw (*NE* 1097b10), an important component of living well. Friendship, affection, love, and fellow-feeling are refinements of this appreciation, this valuing, of those with whom we share our lives. People are associates, actual and potential. Benevolence can be viewed as the perfection of the appreciation of *us*, we who are together in a community a *sine qua non* of good human life and of satisfaction in living it. It is an appreciation that is expressed in an active concern for that association and for other individuals who are our partners in living such a life. It belongs, though, to a form of life that is at the same time thoroughly structured by technical and ethical norms.

It is *our* needs and interests that are so obviously served by the existence of the community; *we* are the beneficiaries of the division of labour and the cultivation of bodies of practical knowledge, and the efforts to co-ordinate and harmonize the simultaneous pursuit of these myriad activities. We benefit from the 'utility' (in Hume's sense) of a variety of social artefacts, including the social artefacts Hume called justice. For our benefit, the norms that guide these matters are shaped.

There are worthwhile things that we are unable to do, and problems that we have been unable to solve. Our activities and practices, obviously, are imperfect; nor will they be adequate as they stand for the unprecedented problems that continually confront us in a changing world. The improvement, refinement, reformation and adaptation of practices is a continuing project of first importance. Improvement is possible only with an eye in the end to our many and varied needs and interests. We are quite right to reject the idea that justice without benevolence might suffice for good character. We would not see the point of justice without the concern and fellow-feeling of which benevolence is the perfection; we could not think critically and constructively about issues of justice and norm-governed action generally without an appreciation of our stake in the matter, without an appreciation of *us*.

The specialized activities resulting from the division of labour in our community are the actualization of highly complex bodies of practical knowledge in which technical and moral norms are more or less adjusted to one another so that a practitioner can, with difficulty, strive to observe all pertaining to one activity simultaneously. These various bodies of practical knowledge are more or less adjusted to one another so that the activities they govern can, with varying degrees of difficulty, all be pursued harmoniously in our community. This harmony, at least, is one thing we strive to attain, with varying degrees of success. This adjustment of one activity to another is reflected in the norms that guide the activities. Because the world, the social and physical environment, changes so rapidly, this must be a moving adjustment. Dislocation, conflict and controversy are continual accompaniments of change and the community's efforts to readjust, readapt its practices (Will 1988: 147–52; Will 1997a: 165–8). Practical knowledge and morality change in the process. To the extent that efforts to readjust and adapt are successful, they will be guided by, among many other things, a lively appreciation of the importance of the welfare and happiness of people.

## V

As individuals, we encounter with some frequency situations in which benevolence indicates one course of action and justice a contrary one. What help can the foregoing reflections offer to an individual confronted by such a problem? Following a central insight of Plato's *Republic*, we can think of such problems as reflections in the psyches of individual human beings of the problems of a community in harmonizing the simultaneous cultivation and pursuit of a great variety of activities. Activities and the norms that guide people in their practice exist only in so far as individuals master the requisite shared practical knowledge and practise it. The locus of these norms is to be found in the skills, know-how, dispositions, and concerns of individuals. An individual can practise a complex activity only if these capacities and dispositions are so adjusted to one another that they operate harmoniously and express themselves in a unified course of action. 'Interpenetration of habits' was Dewey's term for this adjustment to one another of individuals' psychical dispositions, in the manner needed to practise effectively complex activities. This is character (Dewey 1922: 29). In their cultivation of just a few activities, people encounter the problem of following simultaneously the many technical and moral norms that constitute their activities in accordance with their many concerns. These matters conflict again and again, because of their nature. In so far as individuals are able to find ways to follow these norms simultaneously in ways that advance their concerns, they mirror the community's mission of harmonization, and they may contribute to the mission. Whatever success individuals attain in harmonizing their many skills and concerns in a unified character must be understood as a temporary achievement. The changing physical and social world will require continual readjustments.

One thing an individual properly strives to do is to pursue a complex activity in a way that reflects a proper concern for the happiness and welfare of others. At first glance, it seems hopeless: for example, teachers must disappoint certain students with stringent criticism of their work or they must give undeserved praise, which is unfair and bad pedagogy. One cannot, it seems, be both just and benevolent. This account, however, is superficial. If the pedagogy is well conceived and properly executed, the teachers' criticism can in the end benefit the students. This is a matter of the health of the practice of teaching and the mastery of it by individual teachers. Nor are teachers required to harden their hearts in criticizing students and forget about the students' immediate discomfort. Criticism can often be delivered in a way that says convincingly, I want you to improve because I care about you, and I am going to help you. A teacher who offers pedagogically well conceived criticism in this manner and then delivers on the promise of help is effectively harmonizing benevolence, justice, and pedagogical art. The adverse criticism, properly delivered, can effectively express concern for students' welfare. Every teacher recognizes that this is good pedagogy and realizes, too, that this is often very difficult to do. There are, of course, circumstances where it is just not possible to harmonize these things very well. The art of teaching, however, involves dealing with all of these matters. These patterns recur with variations in other activities (Dewey 1922: 132–53).

The ways in which benevolence may conflict with moral and technical norms for individuals in particular situations are uncountable. The aim of harmonizing these norms and values in conflict will have to be sought in every case with an eye to what the particular circumstances will permit. Tuition in this sort of task – harmonizing conflicting norms and values – is best conceived as a part of instruction in one or more of the activities that make up our lives. The observance of ethical norms is indispensable to the proper performance of the activities that constitute our lives. The shape and the purpose of these norms is determined by their place in these activities. The norms themselves reflect their role in activities. Understanding them is properly a matter of understanding how they, together with other norms, contribute to the practice of these activities. The effort to teach ethics as an autonomous subject, abstracted from the particular complex activities that constitute our lives, actually distorts the ideas of these values and norms. It contributes to the idea that ethics in real life is optional, an embellishment on our practice that, while it might be nice, is really dispensable.

The virtues of justice and benevolence are the perfection of capacities and dispositions that are indispensable to the sorts of activities to which people dedicate their lives. The activities are inconceivable without them. Technical considerations, moral norms, and a complex recognition of the importance of needs and interests of people 'interpenetrate' in complex practices. The corresponding dispositions in individuals who have mastered these activities, their skills, know-how, valuings, and commitments likewise interpenetrate, and this, Dewey points out, is what we call character. These traits in a well integrated character are so related that they can, in a wide range of circumstances, be expressed simultaneously. They even support and reinforce one another, as a skilled teacher's benevolent concern for the welfare of students and cultivated ability to impart effective criticism are mutually reinforcing. Character is best inculcated by properly learning the activities of daily life.

Plato's ideal of the unity of the virtues is well expressed by a contemporary philosopher.

> We cannot disentangle genuine possession of kindness from the sensitivity which constitutes fairness. And since there are obviously no limits on the possibilities for compresence, in the same situation, of circumstances of the sorts proper sensitivities to which constitute all the virtues, the argument can be generalized: no one virtue can be fully possessed except by a possessor of all of them, that is, a possessor of virtue in general.
>
> (McDowell 1979: 333)

This is not a description that applies only to the saints in heaven. An appreciable degree of this unity, this interpenetration of good habits, is an indispensable condition of living well as a human being. Such a life is possible only in a community, and community is possible only with a sufficient number of individual members who have achieved sufficient unity of character. Achieving and maintaining such unity in a changing world is a never-ending struggle.

# Notes

I am grateful to my colleague Robert McKim for comments that were helpful in revising this essay.

1 Hume is sometimes thought to be defending a version of 'rule utilitarianism' in his account of justice. The word 'utility' figures prominently in Hume's argument, but it does not have the meaning that Bentham later gave it, where it is thought of as a single, homogeneous, quantifiable thing that enlightened people strive always to maximize. In Hume, utility is a synonym for usefulness. When Hume speaks of the utility of rules, he means their usefulness to people for quite specific purposes. Rules, norms, have utility for Hume in exactly the sense that the tools in a tool box do. It helps in understanding and appreciating his account of justice not to think of him as any sort of utilitarian. For a discussion of Hume and utilitarianism, see Mackie 1980: 151–4.

2 Plato, of course, held that the norms that properly guide our activities are radically independent of the activities themselves. I am defending the view that our resources for determining the right way of doing things are internal to the activities themselves. For more on the idea that activities are self-regulating, that norms are constituents of practices, see Dewey 1922: 43–62; Will 1997b: 63–83; Wallace 1996.

# References

Aristotle (1985) *Nicomachean Ethics* (Ethica Nicomachea), trans. T. Irwin, Indianapolis: Hackett.

Aristotle (1995) *Politics*, in *Aristotle: Selections*, trans. T. Irwin and G. Fine, Indianapolis: Hackett.

Baron, M. (1995) *Kantian Ethics Almost Without Apology*, Ithaca, NY: Cornell University Press.

Berlin, I. (1992) 'The pursuit of the ideal', in H. Hardy (ed.) *The Crooked Timber of Humanity*, New York: Vintage Books.

Brandt, R. (1976) 'The psychology of benevolence', *Journal of Philosophy* 73: 429–53.

Dewey, J. (1922) *Human Nature and Conduct*, in *John Dewey: The Middle Works, 1899–1924*, vol. 14, ed. J. A. Boydston, Carbondale: Southern Illinois University Press.

Hume, D. [1739–40] (1978) *A Treatise of Human Nature*, ed. L. A. Selby-Bigge, rev. 1978 by P. H. Nidditch, Oxford: Clarendon Press.

—— [1751] (1983) *An Enquiry Concerning the Principles of Morals*, ed. J. B. Schneewind, Indianapolis: Hackett.

Kant, I. [1785] (1948) *Groundwork of the Metaphysic of Morals*, trans. H. J. Paton, under the title *The Moral Law*, London: Hutchinson University Library.

MacIntyre, A. (1981) *After Virtue*, 2nd edn., Notre Dame: University of Notre Dame Press.

Mackie, J. L. (1980) *Hume's Moral Theory*, London: Routledge and Kegan Paul.

McDowell, J. (1979) 'Virtue and reason', *The Monist* 62: 331–50.

Plato (1992) *Republic*, trans. G. M. A. Grube, rev. by C. D. C. Reeve, Indianapolis: Hackett.

Sidgwick, H. (1907) *The Methods of Ethics*, Chicago: The University of Chicago Press.

Wallace, J. (1996) *Ethical Norms, Particular Cases*, Ithaca, New York: Cornell University Press.

Will, F. L. (1988) *Beyond Deduction: Ampliative aspects of philosophical reflection*, New York: Routledge.

—— (1997a) 'Philosophic governance of norms', in F. L. Will, *Pragmatism and Realism*, ed. K. R. Westphal, Lanham, Md. Rowman and Littlefield Publishers.

—— (1997b) 'The Rational Governance of Practice', in F. L. Will, *Pragmatism and Realism*, ed. K. R. Westphal, Lanham, Md. Rowman and Littlefield Publishers.

# 7

# SELF-REGARDING AND OTHER-REGARDING VIRTUES

*Michael Slote*

## I

When someone speaks of virtue or of a virtuous person, we are most likely to think of people who are kind or fair to other people. That is because it is natural to connect being a virtuous person with being moral, and in our ordinary thinking about morality, being moral is primarily a matter of doing the right thing by others. But the focus on our relations with other people leaves out of the account an extremely important dimension of our ethical thought. We can admire and deplore what people do to or for *themselves*, and such self-regarding considerations need to be taken just as seriously as the other-regarding factors in morality narrowly conceived.

In the narrow sense I have in mind, we ordinarily do not find *moral* fault with someone who neglects his or her own interests. Or, if we do, it is because we fear that such neglect will somehow lead to problems and worse for others. But in contrast with the moralistic notions of a virtuous person and of virtue *tout court*, the notion of *a virtue* casts its net more widely. Prudence and resourcefulness on one's own behalf are definitely considered virtues; and a lack of prudence and a tendency to blunder when dealing with one's personal affairs are both considered vices, though it perhaps seems less accusatory and oldfashioned to call them (as philosophers do) antivirtues. So what we think well or badly of in people, what we admire or deplore in them, is not just how they treat others, but also how they lead their own lives and promote their own interests. Yet, if we focus on 'morality' in some intuitively narrow sense or confine our thinking to what makes someone a virtuous person, the self-regarding factors of ethical thought tend to get short shrift.

Recent virtue ethics, under the inspiration mainly of Aristotle, has done something to right the balance between the self- and other-regarding. Kantian, utilitarian, and ordinary intuitive morality in their differing ways all treat concern for the well-being of others as more important than concern for one's own welfare or interests, but Aristotle in the *Nicomachean Ethics* is different. His account of virtues and vices lays stress on other-regarding virtues like justice, but also, for example, on the self-regarding virtue of moderate appetite. For Aristotle, it is as deplorable to take too little pleasure in food, drink, and sex as it is to overdo those things, and this stands in stark contrast especially with Kantian and ordinary moral thinking, where it would be said that, even if it is foolish not to satisfy one's appetites at all, there is no moral fault in abstemiousness or asceticism.

But why should we focus more on immorality than on foolishness? Do we think less well of the immoral person than of the foolish or stupid one? Not necessarily. But that fact, if it is one, goes against the entire spirit of Kantian ethics at least, and one real advantage of Aristotelian over Kantian ethics may well lie in its ability to balance concern for one's own happiness with concern with the happiness of others.

In addition, however, there are structural difficulties with Kantian ethics and with our ordinary thinking about (narrowly conceived) morality. Both deny that we have any obligations to promote our own well-being (except to the extent such well-being is necessary for us to fulfill our other obligations); and both explain that supposed fact by reference to the 'inevitability' and/or 'naturalness' of the pursuit of self-interest. How, they ask, can what we do inevitably or naturally be an 'obligation'?

But this explanation falls into difficulty in relation to other things Kant and ordinary morality wish to say. Both hold that we have obligations to our friends and families that we lack toward others, yet some of those obligations precisely are, again, obligations to do what comes naturally between friends or loved ones. So by the previous reasoning, we actually *should not* have these sorts of special obligations to family and friends. (To be sure, we do not inevitably help family members in need in the way we are supposed to, but by the same token we do not inevitably or invariably pursue self-interest: lots of people act, sometimes intentionally, in ways that defy and undermine their own happiness.) Kantian and ordinary morality are in fact incoherent or inconsistent, therefore, and that fact gives us a reason to (re)consider Aristotelian virtue ethics, which is not inconsistent in the way just mentioned precisely because of the central, though hardly exclusive, ethical significance it gives to the well-being or happiness of the agent.

But still, we cannot simply go back to Aristotle. Aristotle does not leave significant room for truthfulness, for promisekeeping and for *general* concern for the fate of other human beings, within his ethical scheme of things; and so there are factors in contemporary ethical thought that are simply not dreamt of in Aristotle's moral philosophy. However, the emphasis on both self-regarding and other-regarding virtues that is the hallmark of Aristotelian virtue ethics can be turned into an overarching, explicit, practical principle or rule that allows us to do greater justice than either Kant or utilitarianism to the complex character of our deepest values.

What if we say, for example, that an ideal ethical life requires a balance between self-concern (concern for one's own interests) and concern for the interests or well-being of others? This would allow us to give significance to both self-regarding and other-regarding virtues, but it would have crucial added significance because it would tell us we cannot live well if we merely 'specialize' in self-regarding or in other-regarding virtue(s). A person who is prudent and resourceful merely on behalf of his or her own interests, is, we say, selfish: and we do not think it is good or admirable to be selfish. But neither, nowadays, do we think that it is good or admirable to be self*less*. The person who prefers the least interests of other people to his or her own vital interests is certainly self- sacrificing, but here self-sacrifice is carried to a suspect extreme. If others always count more than you do, then there is something wrong with you, we think: you must be masochistic or subject to inordinate, misdirected guilt or simply lacking in self-respect. The Victorians loved and idealized selflessness and self-denial, but most of us think we are more psychologically sophisticated than they, and we tend to think that one should be self-assertive and self-interested, at least to an extent that does not overwhelm reasonable concern for other people.

This sounds precisely like the ideal of balanced concern, as between self and other, that I briefly enunciated above. Self-concern should not dwarf concern for others, but neither should the latter dwarf self-concern. (Another way to put this would be to say that no one should be concerned mostly about him- or herself rather than others, but that neither should anyone be concerned mostly about others rather than about him- or herself.) However, it is important to see the implications of this.

Because it gives such a significant place to self-concern, the general ideal or principle I am proposing does not tell us to give away most of our money and abandon our comfortable lives in order to do what we can to relieve poverty and disease in the world. Utilitarianism effectively does tell us to make this enormous sacrifice, because it tells us we ought to treat our own well-being as of no more concern to us than the well-being of any other given person, and this means that self-interest can be swallowed up in the huge sea of all the interests of humanity. But the ideal of balance between self-concern and other-concern balances the former against concern for others *considered as a class or category*. Someone who is concerned about his or her own welfare and also concerned about the suffering of so many others need not *impoverish* him- or herself or *give up* most of his or her own goals in an effort to help those others. Rather, he or she will work on behalf of others, expending substantial energy and time in doing so, but will *also* work hard to make his or her own life reasonably comfortable and successful. There is simply less he or she can do to raise the general well-being than to raise or maintain his or her own well-being, and so, given comparable efforts in both directions, the result of balanced concern is likely to be a life that is more comfortable for the individual than for those whose poverty or sickness he or she should (a good deal, but not most, of the time) aim to relieve.

The ideal of balance tells us, then, that we do not have to be absorbed (almost) totally in the fate of others simply because, given all the suffering in the world, we can do more total or aggregate good for others than we can for ourselves. That is what utilitarianism commits us to, but many, even most moral philosophers have argued that utilitarianism is just too demanding to be a credible moral theory. The ideal of balance that emerges (and is extrapolated) from Aristotle is less demanding and to a large degree, fairer to the agent's natural concern with his or her own self-interest. It is an ideal or standard of excellence that quite unashamedly tells the individual to be somewhat self-assertive in behalf of his or her own interests, plans and life. But it also demands more of us than most of us are inclined to do or give, because most of us, far from making extreme sacrifices for others, do not even make *substantial* sacrifices of time or money for those who are badly off. (That is why, despite the Aristotelian 'realism', we can still talk here of an *ideal* of balance.)

## II

Once we see the attractions of viewing ethical lives as involving and requiring a balance between self-interest and practical concern for the interests of others (in order to simplify, I am leaving out of account here the greater concern we naturally have for those near and dear to us over and against strangers and people we do not know personally), it makes sense to take another look at 'the virtues', that is, at the qualities of character (or intellect) we admire or think well of. For it turns out that the primary emphasis most philosophers have put on helping others has led to a general neglect both of self-regarding virtues and of the self-regarding side of what most philosophers at least regard as (primarily) other-regarding virtues.

I once kept a list of all the self-regarding virtues I could think of, and, to the surprise of the philosophers I told about it, the list eventually grew to include forty different named items. Think of it: perseverance, sagacity, moderation, prudence, discretion, resourcefulness, decisiveness, carefulness, far-sightedness, toughmindedness, patience, fortitude, tact, and circumspection (to name just a few that spring to mind) are all primarily valued or admired for the way they enhance the lives of those possessing the traits, not other people. But this rich lode of self-regarding virtues tends to be neglected by any moral philosophy that puts primary or exclusive emphasis on (concern for) the interests or rights of other people. It is time, at least to the extent that the neo-Aristotelian ideal of balanced concern is found attractive, to explore that lode and, of course, also to place it in relation to all the other-regarding virtues that have received so much attention from ethicists.

This leads to another point that deserves some stressing. Many of the virtues philosophers talk about are misconceived by them as other-regarding, when in fact, they can also be thought of as having a self-regarding side or aspect, one which (especially if one believes in self–other balance) can easily be just as important in our lives as the other-regarding side of those virtues. Thus consider lying to or deceiving others. Not doing such things is normally and quite properly regarded as important to the moral life, and honesty or truthfulness is certainly considered a virtue. But honesty with oneself, non-self-deception, is treated by most moral philosophers as a virtue of honesty only in a derivative, truncated or degenerate sense. The real ethical issues involving deception, it is thought, concern how we do or do not deceive others; self-deception and its opposite are simply not central to our lives in quite the same way.

Once we think in a self–other–symmetric fashion about activities and virtues concerned with human well-being, it makes sense to wonder whether a virtue like honesty is not also best portrayed in a self–other symmetric fashion. Honesty, to be sure, is normally regarded as valuable to some extent independently of concerns for human well-being. (That is why it is often thought to be all right to tell the truth even at some cost to people's feelings or interests.) It does, none the less, have two sides, and it is hardly as clear as proponents of (chiefly) other-regarding morality have thought that it is only marginally important to avoid self-deception. Deceiving others can sometimes be a trivial matter (as in lying to someone who has just purchased a new tie), but of course it can also be a very bad and deplorable thing to do. However, self-deception can also be a terrible thing, and literature, if not most moral philosophy, is replete with examples of debilitating, pathetic, cowardly, or even tragic self-deception.

Who do we have more contempt or distaste for: the person who deceives his wife with other women in flagrant fashion or the wife who turns a blind eye to all the deception and does not (at least consciously) acknowledge to herself how she is being devalued and traduced? If a lack of concern for one's own well-being is a sign of a lack of self-respect (or self-esteem) and as such deplorable and anti-virtuous, can we not say the same about the wife who persists in self-deception about her husband? Even if we would not call the self-deceived wife evil or cruel in the way we might be tempted to speak of the husband who deceives her, still we want to say, or have to admit, she is pathetic. What tells us that it is more deplorable, further from our human ideals, if someone is cruel rather than pathetic? Again, once we have signed on to an ideal of balanced concern for self and other, we may end up sympathetic to or at least willing seriously to consider the idea that there may be no very great difference in how badly we should think of someone who is pathetic and someone who is cruel. Both may simply be horrible, deplorable ways to be.

But deception/honesty is not the only example of a virtue or anti-virtue whose self-regarding side has been obscured or devalued by moral thinking that puts the chief emphasis on concern for others. Consider (un)trustworthiness. A person can be considered untrustworthy not only for deception in regard to the truth or falsity of certain claims, but for being unreliable or untrustworthy in ways that do not focus centrally on the issue of truthfulness. A person can blow hot and cold toward his friends or be erratic in the performance of other-regarding duties, and these are examples of other-regarding untrustworthiness that do not hinge primarily on issues of truthfulness. However, there are also various self-regarding analogues of such unreliability and untrustworthiness toward other people, and one nice example emerges from considering frequent or repeated weakness of will.

A person who, as a result of anger or lust or pressure from others, often fails to act on his or her intentions displays a kind of self-regarding untrustworthiness or unreliability that does not exactly amount to self-deception or a disregard for truth; and he or she may appropriately criticize him- or herself and be criticized by others for (acting from) such weakness of will. Indeed, a person who has vowed to stop drinking may be deeply chagrined and shaken by his or her own frequent backslidings, and he or she may deplore this self-regarding untrustworthiness (or unreliability) in terms as bitter as those with which he or she would castigate instances of other-regarding untrustworthiness either on his or her own part or on the part of others.

Take another example. We have reason to be highly critical of the disloyalty of someone who betrays his or her friend or lover's secrets (as, for example, the poet Robert Lowell apparently did with things Elizabeth Hardwick had revealed to him in letters), or who betrays his or her friend or lover to the Gestapo, or who refuses to help a friend or lover when that person most needs help. Such people would normally be considered to have behaved badly or deplorably toward other people. But it is interesting to note that self-regarding betrayal or disloyalty can also easily give rise in us to the belief that someone has acted badly or deplorably.

When Wordsworth, later in life, said that he would be willing to give up his life for the established Church of England, many people regarded him as having betrayed his earlier social and political ideals. Such betrayal is also naturally regarded as a kind of disloyalty to the person one once, so desirably, was; to one's better, but earlier, self. Is such self-betrayal or 'selling out' really a less serious matter than the betrayal, say, of another person's secrets? It is not clear, in the light of all we have said, why it should be, and in that case we see once again how an almost exclusive focus on the other-regarding yields an impoverished and, as we might say, unbalanced conception of what is important in human life and desire and action.

Thus once one focuses on and sees the importance of self-regarding examples of dishonesty, disloyalty, and untrustworthiness, it seems reasonable to think of these virtues as single virtues each with a self-regarding and an other-regarding side or aspect. One will be more inclined toward a self–other symmetric conception of how one should live, and will certainly no longer be tempted to treat self-regarding trustworthiness and the like as merely degenerate or idiosyncratic examples of the (general) virtues that lend them their names. So in focusing more on self-regarding virtues than other approaches to ethics encourage, we bring the self-regarding and other-regarding instances of any given virtue together and make them seem more of a piece than is possible under the assumptions to which other approaches to morality/ethics subscribe. That means, in addition, that a neo-Aristotelian approach to ethics has implications for moral education.

## III

In the wake of John Rawls's *A Theory of Justice* (1971), educational psychologists like Lawrence Kohlberg have attempted to apply Rawlsian ideas and categories to the exploration of personality development. (See, for example, Kohlberg 1976.) Among other things, it has been argued that children go through a number of moral stages which culminate in a highest level (to the extent any particular individual develops this far) at which their understanding of morality is Rawlsian or quasi-Rawlsian. This is neither the time nor the place to enter into a discussion of this literature and of the objections that have been made to this enshrining of Rawlsian views at the pinnacle of human moral development. But if the reader thinks about the matter, it should be clear that educational-psychological issues concerning the acquisition of various virtues can be raised along somewhat parallel lines, and I think such issues are well worth pursuing both conceptually and in their empirical ramifications.

For example, both altruism and a (largely) self-regarding virtue like prudence require cultivation within the individual, and even if young children display elements of both these traits, parents, teachers and others have a difficult task on their hands when they attempt to overcome or mitigate children's selfishness or their tendencies to heedless or shortsighted behaviour. In that case, and as an analogy with what Kohlberg and others have done, it may well be worthwhile to study the ways in which both self-regarding and other-regarding virtues develop within individuals. There may or may not turn out to be a relatively fixed series of stages, for example, through which a given virtue like altruism or prudence or honesty or discretion develops, and there could well be interesting differences to uncover in the multiplicity and order of the stages of development for particular virtues. But at this point I think we know relatively little and I think much less than we should about these matters.

Of course, since some virtues are other-regarding, previous empirical and conceptual studies of individual moral development may have already in some measure, and at least implicitly, taken them into account. But I none the less think – in fact, it seems obvious – that one might well learn interesting new things if one were to study the other-regarding virtues one by one and as virtues. In any case – this really is the most important point – previous studies of moral development have had a bias or slant toward the other-regarding that we have seen to be characteristic of our ordinary moral thinking (and of Kantian ethics, which tends to follow the lines of ordinary moral thought). So work done previously on moral development has largely ignored the development of desirable/admirable traits like fortitude, prudence, perseverance, and circumspection. But these traits of character are, after all and by our common lights, virtues, and if it is worth our while to study other-regarding desirable/admirable moral development, then one will presumably also have reason to study the development of self-regardingly admirable traits of character or personality.

Such studies have been fewer and farther between than they should be, and certainly any validity one may see in the neo-Aristotelian approach to ethics outlined above should simply add to the reason one has to hope for or encourage the empirical and conceptual study of self-regarding and other particular virtues, along lines already familiar from the literature of moral development. The lacuna in our understanding is presently enormous, and even if we cannot say that the study of moral development has led to results as firm and as plausible as one might hope for, the study of particular virtues (and, given what was said above, this should include studying the similarities and connections between the self-regarding and other-regarding 'sides' of a single virtue like trustworthiness) has much in and of itself to recommend it. It may even have useful things to teach those working specifically on childhood and adolescent (other-regarding) moral development.

If, for example, moral development can, among other things, be divided into preconventional, conventional, and post-conventional phases or stages, then the development of various particular virtues may well turn out also to be chartable (though perhaps with different timing for different virtues) into three such stages. However, the particular contours discovered in the state-by-stage development of various virtues may also serve to clarify, support, or undermine received or disputed ideas about specifically moral development. I would think those already engaged in studying the latter have reason to pursue, or at least encourage, the kind of virtue-by-virtue developmental study that, as far as I am aware, has been so largely neglected in the recent literature of both psychology and education. To give you some initial sense of how rich and interesting the studies I am suggesting might prove to be, let me now mention in no particular or meaningful order some of the questions that it might occur to one to investigate if one were going to approach the development of the virtues along the above general lines.

With regard to a self-regarding virtue like fortitude, for example, one might be interested in knowing the aspects of family background and individual temperament with which it correlates positively or negatively. One might also seek crosscultural and/or historical information regarding the development of this trait. For example, are peoples who have been persecuted like the Jews and Armenians more or less likely to develop this trait? From a conceptual standpoint, can we make sense of the idea of a preconventional or of a conventional stage in the development of fortitude? Clearly such questions, and many others, could be applied to other primarily self-regarding traits as well as to other-regarding traits (and to traits like self-control and courage that philosophers regard as 'mixed' of self-regarding and other-regarding elements in fairly equal measure).

If studies of the kind just recommended were eventually to accumulate and give us a sense of knowing more about how various virtues develop, those studies might also turn out to be relevant to educational theory and practice. At present, there is much controversy about, and interest in, questions about the proper division of labour between home and school in relation to the teaching of moral ideals and standards. That issue, in the light of what has just been suggested, might well be profitably opened up to include issues concerning the teaching of various virtues, including self-regarding ones. If it is urged against this suggestion that self-regarding virtues mainly benefit their possessors only, so that there is less need to teach them than to teach other-regarding standards and habits that serve to make everyone better off, then the immediate answer ought to be that we can also improve the lot of everyone by making each person better off in self-regarding terms. If one benefits, for example, from being prudent or having fortitude in trying circumstances, then teaching students, or children in general, to have these traits will also tend toward the general good, though it will do so more atomistically, less relationally, than the instilling of moral standards, or of other-regarding virtues, would tend to do.

None the less, one might think that the absence of other-regarding virtues makes life, or community life, impossible, while we can at least get by in the absence of self-regarding virtue. But I wonder. If, for instance, the explosion of crime in the ghetto is partly a function of failure to respect the property and lives of other people, is it not also partly a result of a breakdown in normal prudence and planning on the part of (many of) those growing up there? Where people feel a sense of hopelessness about their own lives, habits of thinking about and planning for the (distant) future never develop properly, and in the short or blighted lives of those who go in for drug-trafficking or prostitution, the influence of personal hopelessness seems just as prominent as any lack of respect or concern for others (though obviously the two are also related in both conceptual and psychological ways).

In any event, because of our presentday emphasis – not just in moral philosophy but in society at large – on moral education and moral standards and ideals, most of us tend not to dwell on the self-regarding virtues and on the particular ways in which they are desirable and admirable. Virtue ethics (re)awakens us to the importance of self-regarding virtues and also makes us aware, probably for the first time, of the number and variety, the sheer exuberance, of such virtues. Virtue ethics can also lead us to ask and to investigate whether children are best led into ethical behaviour by being taught the importance of particular virtues, or whether it is better to teach them moral rules or standards in what I take to be the more usual way.

If inculcation of (all the) individual virtues turned out to be an easier or more efficient way to teach people to act in ways we admire, or at least do not want to criticize, this would not necessarily demonstrate the superiority of neo-Aristotelian virtue ethics to other approaches. But for obvious practical purposes and as a matter, I think, of general interest, such studies of the comparative effects of the two forms of teaching – whether at home or at school – would be worth having.

Am I therefore saying that we should turn children into guinea pigs and ask or bribe schools or parents to focus on the virtues so that we can learn what we might all profit from knowing? Not in the least. There may already, within our society or perhaps among different societies, be relevant differences in parental and school practices in regard to the inculcation of ethical standards. Without in the least tampering with human lives, we might find parents (in different segments of societies or with ethnically different backgrounds) differing in regard to their emphasis on nameable virtues, and these differences might well be enough to give us a better empirical understanding of the relative usefulness or efficiency of virtue-ethical versus standardly moral modes of moral/ethical education.

Also, there may be the possibility of shorter studies that tamper only in the mildest way with people's personalities or lives, and that can tell us interesting and important things about the efficacy of teaching particular virtues. At a given school, for example, a civics class might be taught about, and given illustrations of, the virtue of fortitude; then suddenly, on a pretext that did not imply any connection with the content of the class, be subjected one day to a deprivation such as going lunchless or having to stay several hours after school. Another control group might be given irrelevant information in class over a similar period of time, before being subjected to the same deprivation. The focus of the psychological study is of course any perceivable difference in the patience/ fortitude with which the deprivation is faced.

Such studies might teach us a good deal about the teachability (at least in a school setting and at a certain age) of various particular virtues. They could help, therefore, to answer the question whether or how best to teach ethics in school or at home. Clearly I have been very impressionistic and incomplete in discussing the psychological and educational issues that may be raised by attempts to revive a form of ethics in which the (self-regarding and other-regarding) virtues assume an importance they have typically lacked in modern philosophical ethics. Still, the practical implications of what I have been saying are very real and arguably deserve further attention.

In addition, I have given only the briefest kind of defence of the neo-Aristotelian approach I favour. A lengthier treatment occurs in my book *From Morality To Virtue* (1992). But one further point about virtue ethics needs to be made before I conclude.

By treating self-regarding and other-regarding virtues in the more balanced or evenhanded way I have described above, neo-Aristotelianism avoids what I take to be a very serious further problem with both Kantian ethics and intuitive or commonsense morality conceived in a narrow or moralistic fashion: that they devalue or depreciate *the moral agent*. (This cannot so easily be said about utilitarianism, but the latter appears to have quite enough difficulties of its own.) After all, Kantian ethics tells the moral agent that he or she must seek the well-being, the good, of other people, but that no such imperative exists in regard to his or her own well-being. As far as rational morality is concerned, he or she does not absolutely have to worry about that (except in so far as it bears on other duties). What this seems to mean is that *from the agent's standpoint* his or her well-being counts less than that of other people.

This, I think, devalues the person as an agent, and it is no use to protest that Kant shows the high valuation he places on moral agents by morally demanding so much from them. That is as may be: in this one respect Kant does appear to value agents highly. But in another and crucial respect, he takes away from or deprecates the well-being of the moral agent, and that is what I find objectionable in the self–other asymmetry of Kantian duty: that we have duties to promote the happiness of others but not of ourselves. Nor does it help Kantian ethics to point out that if everyone is performing their duties, then even if I do not (have to) seek my own happiness directly, *others will*. This does not seem to be enough. What if others are not doing their duty, what if they do not help me? Even in such circumstances, according to Kant, I do not have the strong or overriding reason to pursue my own welfare that I have to pursue that of others, and this, I submit, is invidious as between myself as agent and those others.

So I think Kantian ethics devalues (the role of) the moral agent in an unacceptable way. (Is Kant not also in a measure inconsistent in saying, as he does, that we should respect humanity both in our own person and in the person of others, but then denying any immediate obligation of concern with one's own, as opposed to others', happiness?) In fairly similar fashion, ordinary non-theoretical moralism also downgrades or devalues the moral agent by claiming that there is nothing morally wrong or bad about denying oneself good things. For if, as moralistic thinking tends to hold, being moral is more important than being intelligent or happy or beautiful or rich, then (such moralism is saying) in the most important area of our thought and action, self-interest in no way is or ought to be our (immediate) concern. This too devalues or depreciates (the well-being of) the moral agent, and in much the same way as Kantianism.

By contrast, the neo-Aristotelian emphasis on both self-regarding and other-regarding virtues, and the principle of balanced concern that we saw earlier emerge out of that emphasis, puts the agent in a prominent place within (his or her own) moral or ethical concern, and is clearly not subject to the above criticisms. Whether that, together with everything else we have said in its defence, is sufficient to prove the superiority of the present approach to other ways of conceiving and living an ethical life is a question, however, that at this point must be left to the further reflection and judgement of the reader.

# References

Kohlberg, L. (1976) 'Moral stages and Moralization: The cognitive-developmental approach', in Th. Lickona (ed.) *Moral Development and Behavior: Theory, research, and social issues*, New York: Holt, Rinehart & Wilson.

Rawls, J. (1971) *A Theory of Justice*, Oxford: Oxford University Press.

Slote, M. (1992) *From Morality To Virtue*, Oxford: Oxford University Press, 1992 (paperback, 1995).

# Part 4

# WEAKNESS AND INTEGRITY

# 8

# MORAL GROWTH AND THE UNITY OF THE VIRTUES

*Bonnie Kent*

## I

Recent philosophical works on virtue often fault Kant and the utilitarians for ethical theories that no ordinary person would be likely to endorse, much less live by. Much of the same literature praises Aristotle for an ethical theory far more practical and appealing to common sense. However reasonable this picture may be in broad outline, it falls down in detail, for Aristotle and every other major ancient philosopher defended several important theses widely rejected by ordinary people (Irwin 1996). One such thesis, commonly dubbed 'the unity of the virtues', says that no one can truly have justice, courage, temperance or any other moral virtue without practical wisdom (*phronesis*), nor can one truly have practical wisdom without *all* the moral virtues. This all-or-nothing conception of moral character jibes no better with common opinion now than it did in antiquity. Even in philosophical studies of the virtues, enthusiastic support for the unity thesis is hard to find.

Consider, for example, Alasdair MacIntyre's pioneering work, *After Virtue* (1981). Though much of the book goes toward urging the superiority of pre-modern ethics, MacIntyre draws the line at the unity of the virtues. He criticizes Aquinas for defending the unity thesis and Peter Geach for following suit:

> Suppose it is claimed that someone whose aims and purposes were generally evil, a devoted and intelligent Nazi, for example, possessed the virtue of courage. We ought to reply, says Geach, that either it was not courage that he possessed or that in that kind of case courage is not a virtue. . . . But it is crucial that he would not have to unlearn or relearn what he knew about avoiding both cowardice and intemperate rashness in the face of harm and danger. Moreover it was precisely because such a Nazi was not devoid of the virtues that there was a point of moral contact between him and those who had the task of re-educating him, that there was something on which to build. To deny that that kind of Nazi was courageous or that his courage was a virtue

obliterates the distinction between what required moral re-education in
such a person and what did not.

MacIntyre (1981: 179–80).

A closer reading of Geach (1977: 164) reveals that he himself scorns the unity
thesis as 'both odious and preposterous'. Michael Slote (1983: 77) goes even
farther in the anti-unity vein, arguing for immoral but admirable traits of
character, for virtues that run counter to morality. Stanley Hauerwas and Charles
Pinches (1997) urge Christians to affirm at most an eschatological unity of the
virtues, one rooted in God-given charity, not some naturally acquired pagan
wisdom. Amelie Rorty (1988) attacks the unity thesis on strictly philosophical
grounds, while Philippa Foot (1978), David Norton (1991), and Roland Beiner
(1992) all propose carefully hedged, democratic versions rather far from what
the ancients had in mind. The days when philosophers joined in proclaiming
the unity of the virtues are plainly long past.

If persons concerned mainly with moral and political theory have little use
for the unity thesis, those concerned with the practice of moral education
might reasonably conclude that it has nothing to offer. It might seem at best
an inspiring ideal with little practical value, at worst a failure even as an ideal.
The unity thesis, however, cannot be so lightly dismissed. While it does
indeed raise practical problems – problems all the greater in large, modern,
pluralistic democracies – it also forces us to think more clearly about exactly
what a virtue is, how we should judge people's characters, which persons
we should present to students as moral exemplars, what deserves to be considered moral growth, and, not least, how moral growth relates to psychological
development.

The case of the Nazi could serve as an example, but since Nazi examples
often prove better at engaging passions than clarifying moral intuitions,
suppose that we choose a drug dealer instead. Do we really want to claim that
a drug dealer with the trait commonly called 'courage' is better, all other
things being equal, than one without it? Someone sufficiently daring to eliminate competitors by gunning them down on the street surely is not better for
society than a person whose timidity limits him to occasional sales at suburban parties. Is the brave drug dealer even likely to lead a happier life? Is he
better off than his more fearful counterpart? Weighing his higher profits
against the likelihood of disabling injuries or an early death, we might
conclude that his own life would be better if he were more averse to danger.
Even if one believes the brave dealer better off, we might still ask whether he
deserves to be regarded as a better human being, or better from the moral
standpoint. Is courage without justice truly a virtue, so that someone with this
trait of character should be considered farther along in moral development
than someone with neither courage nor justice?

Any programme of moral education concerned with the virtues must
inevitably face such questions. No longer do movies and television favour

pistol-packing heroes who kill only attacking Indians and villains in black hats. From early childhood on, students see a host of violent characters impressive for their fearlessness but with no discernible concern for morality. A daring bank robber now wins rousing applause in movie theatres when he succeeds at outsmarting the police. In inner-city neighbourhoods, the local drug trade provides many real-world exemplars of what looks to be courage unconstrained by either justice or temperance. If one asks students to list persons, real or fictional, whose courage they admire, how should one respond when a successful bank robber or drug dealer appears on the list?

Merely *ad hoc* answers tend to overlook deeper theoretical problems for virtue-centered moral education. MacIntyre was hardly the first to notice that the ancient unity thesis offers no account of how virtue develops, little by little and unevenly, over the course of many years. It suggests, as the paradox-loving Stoics enjoyed pointing out, that the individual moves in an instant from having no genuine virtues to having them all. But what happens if we scrap the ancient conception of virtue as an indivisible organic whole and speak instead of a plurality of freestanding virtues? While we gain by acknowledging character as often a morally mixed bag – really mixed, not just apparently so – we encounter problems on the other end of the spectrum. Virtuous character threatens to dissolve into a hodgepodge of admirable traits, leaving moral development to look like nothing more than a matter of acquiring *more* such traits, no matter which combination or in which order.

We might respond by simply refusing to talk about, much less evaluate, moral character. We could focus on the wide range of admirable traits that human beings might acquire, emphasizing their rich diversity and having nothing to say about how they might combine to constitute virtuous character (e.g. Slote 1992). This approach enables one to avoid the charges of conservativism that virtue-centered moral education sometimes triggers. Alas, it invites some of the same criticisms made of programmes in 'values clarification' born in the 1960s, now mostly deceased and little lamented. It also raises doubts whether virtue theory lives up to its own advertising as a vast improvement on Kantianism and utilitarianism. (Can one rightly complain that rival theorists reduce moral persons to performers-of-actions when one's own theory apparently reduces them to bearers-of-traits?) On the other hand, if we evaluate moral character but do it strictly in quantitative terms, so that a collection of more freestanding 'virtues' is automatically better than a collection of fewer, we seem pressed to judge the pistol-packing drug dealer morally superior to his jittery suburban counterpart. A professor of philosophy might have no great reservations about promoting such a view in his or her classes, but primary- and secondary-school teachers would justifiably cringe at the prospect.

In sum, virtue-centered moral education seems to require something more than the anything-goes view but something less than the all-or-nothing view. In what follows I shall accordingly try to explain why ancient philosophers argued for the unity of the virtues, some of the lessons we might learn from their teachings, and some of the lessons we might do best to revise or ignore.

## II

Virtually every leading specialist in ancient philosophy has written about the unity of the virtues, often at considerable length (e.g. Annas 1993; Broadie 1991; Cooper 1998; Irwin 1988, 1996; Kraut 1989; Schofield 1984). Readers should consult this wealth of scholarly literature for detailed discussion of who taught what and why. Here we shall consider only the main lines of argument and some of the related issues in moral education.

Aristotle's version of the unity thesis acknowedges a plurality of virtues, both moral and intellectual, but denies any necessary connection for intellectual virtues, whether among themselves or with the moral virtues. A good mathematician need not be just, nor a just person a good mathematician; a good artist need not be brave, nor a brave person a good artist; and of course, someone might well be a brilliant painter or pianist while remaining a mathematical moron. As intellectual virtues (which include what people now would probably call 'skills') have no necessary connection with virtues of character (alias 'moral' virtues), neither do they have any necessary connection with each other. This much accords with common sense. Practical wisdom represents the sole but crucial exception to the rule of freestanding intellectual virtues. According to Aristotle, nobody can have any moral virtue without practical wisdom, nor can somebody have practical wisdom without all of the moral virtues (NE 1144b1–1145a6).

A more radical version of the unity thesis claims that there really is no plurality of virtues: there is only a single unified condition of virtue which expresses itself in various ways. While Aristotle's position can accurately be called 'the unity of the virtues', the more extreme position – defended by Socrates, and apparently by Zeno, founder of the Stoic school, and certainly by Zeno's follower, Ariston of Chios – would more appropriately be labelled 'the unity of virtue' (Cooper 1998). The difference between the plural and the singular merits consideration, especially in the context of developmental psychology and moral education, for the singular form of the thesis resembles the position of Lawrence Kohlberg.

While Kohlberg's thinking was most heavily influenced by Kant and Kant's follower, John Rawls, it does have some claim to ancient precedents. One of his earliest attacks on the 'bag-of-virtues' approach to moral education was framed not as a rejection of ancient ethics in general but rather as an attack on Aristotle and, at the same time, a defense of what Kohlberg dubs 'the Platonic view':

> First, virtue is ultimately one, not many, and it is always the same ideal
> form regardless of climate or culture. Second, the name of this ideal

form is justice. Third, not only is the good one, but virtue is knowledge of the good. Fourth, the kind of knowledge of the good which is virtue is philosophical knowledge or intuition of the ideal form of the good, not correct opinion or acceptance of conventional beliefs.

(Kohlberg 1970: 58)

No matter that all this comes far closer to the view of Socrates than the view of Plato. The intended contrast with Aristotle's teachings is more important. According to Kohlberg, Aristotle erred in dividing virtue into moral and intellectual, in claiming that we learn only by doing in the moral sphere, and in treating character as the bag of virtues that his own society, or maybe just his own social class, happened to prize. Citing the 1928 study by Hartshorne and May – which suggested that people's behaviour fails to reflect their stated commitment to honesty, and that honest behaviour in one situation has no connection with honest behaviour in another – Kohlberg denies that the generalized traits of character posited by virtue theory even exist (1970: 63–4).

Let us set aside for the moment Kohlberg's objection about the rational foundation for choosing one particular 'bag' of virtues rather than another. His other objections to Aristotle leave ample room for reply on both philosophical and psychological grounds. Most philosophers – indeed, most ordinary people – favour Aristotle's version of the unity thesis over either the Socratic or the Platonic version, in part because it clearly distinguishes theoretical from practical wisdom. That theoretical wisdom has no necessary connection with moral character seems obvious from experience. If it did have such a connection, would we not expect university faculties to have a good share of moral paragons? Would the ranks of the arrogant, the gutless, the selfish and the indolent not be much thinner than they actually are?

This certainly appears a weighty objection to arguments for a necessary connection between theoretical wisdom and morally virtuous character. It is indeed a fair objection, though less decisive than it looks. Appeals to empirical observation can never entirely defeat any kind of claim regarding the unity of the virtues, because such claims are themselves never simple empirical assertions. To say that someone cannot have justice without courage or courage without wisdom is not like saying that two blue-eyed parents cannot produce a brown-eyed child. Reasonable persons with the same knowledge of someone's behaviour, even making the same assumptions about the individual's reasoning, intentions and emotional responses, may none the less disagree about whether he or she has a given virtue. Ascriptions of virtue always reflect normative ethical theories, theories about how people *should* be, even though the speakers may have given little thought to what their own theoretical commitments amount to.

At the same time, ancient arguments for the unity thesis should not be reduced to the uninteresting claim that the best possible person must have all the virtues, since lack of any one virtue would make the person less than ideal.

They are not purely conceptual arguments, as arguments in modern ethics often are, but instead rest on views about human psychological development. The ancient conception of virtue represents what philosophers considered normal human psychology developed to perfection (Annas 1993: 84; Cooper 1998: 234). While such perfection might seldom, if ever, be attained, the ideal always remains rooted in reality to the extent that the best human beings are thought to develop greater and greater integration over time. Empirical evidence about psychological development accordingly has a legitimate place in this debate, and it does tend to cast doubt on claims for some connection between moral virtue and theoretical wisdom.

In arguing for a necessary connection between moral virtue and *practical* wisdom, Aristotle aims to preserve the very cognitive element that Kohlberg (strangely) believes Aristotle's theory lacks. Perhaps Kohlberg failed to notice that Aristotle regards appropriate habituation, beginning in early childhood, as only a necessary condition for good moral character in later life. Far from presenting mindless drill as sufficient for true moral virtue, Aristotle insists that one must know *why* certain actions in given circumstances are just and noble, not merely *that* they are (*NE* 1095b2–13, 1098a33–b4; Burnyeat 1980). Practical wisdom is thought to unify the virtues precisely because the intellectual requirements for genuine virtue are so high. While rejecting Plato's view that moral virtue demands a grasp of mathematics or other such theoretical knowledge, Aristotle preserves a distinction between the practical wisdom necessary for moral virtue and mere correct opinion.

To be truly brave, the argument goes, one needs to know not only what courage requires but also what justice requires, what temperance requires, and so on for all the other moral virtues. Virtue requires a correct grasp of one's life *as a whole*. One's life as a whole, in turn, cannot be considered a mere aggregate of so many specialized domains (the area of justice, the area of courage, and so on), as if sound moral judgement in one area were possible without sound moral judgement in others. Consider the case of a career soldier famous for bravery in combat but sadly lacking in temperance. Such a person would be inclined to overvalue honour: when he returns home on leave, the most trifling slight in a bar could easily lead him into a fist-fight. In Aristotle's view, the soldier lacks true courage, for true courage requires not only moderation in appetite (so that drinking does not impair one's judgement), but also understanding of the value of honour in a complete human life. Is it worth coming to blows over every perceived slight? Is it worth even launching into vituperative debate? (No, but someone who cares too much about honour often becomes like the proverbial man with a hammer, to whom every problem looks like a nail.)

Aristotle is right to suggest that an individual's life cannot be neatly comparmentalized into so many 'areas', with virtue in one easily coexisting with vices in others. Nor can human character be neatly compartmentalized, with a firm commitment to justice easily coexisting with cowardice, greed, or other serious character flaws. Perhaps the most important benefit of the unity thesis is simply its challenge to common tendencies toward thinking compartmentally. Justice, for example, supposedly has to do with the good of others, temperance and courage with the agent's own good; justice supposedly has to do with actions, temperance and courage with emotions; virtue in private life is supposedly one thing, virtue in professional life quite another: all widely held opinions in our own day. For Aristotle, however, the good of others cannot be separated so neatly from the agent's own good. Instead of the modern conception of justice as some altruistic, 'artifical' virtue needed to offset the natural human penchant for self-ishness, we find a conception of justice as the perfection of a natural human capacity for partnership. The Aristotelian approach to education in justice is accordingly not to give children lessons in altruism or impartiality, but rather to work on changing their conception of their own goods, so that they come to understand the need for partnership and value it. Team sports, where someone can win only by co-operating with others, provide a more appropriate model than contract negotiations between individuals (O'Connor 1988).

As Aristotle would challenge the self/other dichotomy, so too would he challenge the private/professional dichotomy and the action/emotion dichotomy. How can the 'area' of justice be regarded as only its little compart-ment when temptations to *in*justice routinely arise from excessive fears or appetites of various kinds, the supposed 'areas' of other virtues? According to Aristotle, unjust behaviour towards others always finds its source in an emotional disorder inclining the individual to overweight or underweight some particular good or goods. This ancient insight has rather frightening twentieth-century corroboration. If Hannah Arendt's conclusions about 'the banality of evil' are at all justified, one need not be an idiot, a lunatic, or some monster of evil to participate actively in genocide. It suffices to be a no-holds-barred careerist, ambitious for advancement, unwilling to acknowledge that superiors can make demands that no morally decent person would meet, and generally expert in regarding professional life as its own little compartment with its own rules (Arendt 1977). One might even display impressive intellectual sophistication in rationalizing genocide. So even though moral development requires some level of cognitive development, cognitive development alone looks to be no guarantee of moral development (Noam 1993).

Aristotle's distinction between theoretical and practical wisdom helps to avoid making the moral a simple function of the cognitive. So, too, does Aristotle's distinction between practical wisdom and mere 'cleverness', that is, expertise in achieving one's ends, however base one's ends might be (*NE* 1144a23–b18). The ends may even be admirable in their own right, genuine elements in a good, flourishing human life, objectionable only when they acquire greater importance in the individual's mind than they deserve and thereby tend to undermine all-round flourishing. In this respect, Aristotle's account seems superior to any that tends to equate moral goodness with knowledge, theoretical reasoning, or some other purely cognitive ability.

Kohlberg's objection that there simply are no general traits of character corresponding to what Aristotle calls 'virtues' remains to be considered. Here, however, Kohlberg's own theory stands on rather shaky ground, since there is no firm evidence that what he considers improvement in moral reasoning produces improvements in actual behaviour. Analyses of reasoning about real-life dilemmas prove to be far better at predicting how individuals actually behave than analyses of reasoning about Kohlbergian hypothetical dilemmas, which tend to minimize emotional involvement and require students to report what they would do in situations they have never experienced and might have difficulty even imagining. As one undergraduate test subject blandly observed, 'It's a lot easier to be moral when you have nothing to lose' (Walker et al. 1995: 381–2). When explaining their reasoning about dilemmas they actually have experienced, not only students but adults routinely appeal to expected consequences (versus principles or intentions alone), to personal relationships (versus only impartial universal norms), and to religious values, all of which Kohlberg treats as symptomatic of suboptimal moral development. Aristotle excludes religious values as well, but at least his account of moral reasoning is sufficiently complex to approximate normal moral thinking.

Equally important, recent research suggests that Hartshorne and May were hasty in concluding that there are no general traits such as 'honesty' related to how someone actually behaves. Experimental design has gradually shifted from regarding traits as merely what people *have* – or worse, merely say that they have ('Yes, I'm honest and proud of it!') – to including consideration of what people *do*, and what they 'do' not just physically but cognitively and emotionally. The reconceptualization of traits accompanies a more general trend towards expanding the notion of intelligence beyond IQ scores, so that social behaviour, coping skills, and emotional responses increasingly figure in the overall assessment (Goleman 1995; Mischel 1990). Aristotle would probably be pleased that modern psychologists, struggling to make sense of 'personality' and to predict how individuals will behave, have moved closer and closer to something roughly approximating his own conception of practical wisdom.

# III

We turn now to some objections that one might raise against incorporating Aristotle's teachings on the unity of the virtues into a programme of moral education for the twenty-first century. The first objection is by far the most sweeping. The others, however related, are more specific.

## *The first objection*

*Perhaps human character and human life should not be seen as a collection of compartments, but neither should they be seen as the complete organic unities Aristotle suggests. His ideal of virtue fails to capture common-or-garden goodness, so that the crucial distinction between bad persons and good-but-flawed persons tends, disastrously, to disappear.*

This sort of objection has quite a distinguished pedigree. One of its most famous proponents was Augustine, who worried that ordinary Christians, lacking some virtue or other, would receive credit for no genuine virtues at all. Our ordinary use of moral language and everyday moral judgements would likewise require a radical overhaul to bring it into conformity with the supposed philosophical Truth (Augustine, Epist. 167).

Taken strictly, the unity thesis does indeed imply that any vice, even any notable moral weakness, is as fatal to moral character as a cholera germ in a glass of water. Lack of any one virtue automatically proves spurious all the other virtues an individual appears to possess. If, for example, someone we have long admired for justice and courage should demonstrate an unfortunate penchant for getting tiddly at parties, we would have to judge him or her lacking not only in temperance and practical wisdom but also in justice, courage, and every other genuine moral virtue. The practice of moral education encounters a good many difficulties when the standards of genuine virtue are set so high. Consider only the problem of finding individuals that might appropriately be regarded as moral exemplars. Since real people scarcely ever demonstrate equal virtue, or even moral strength, in all areas, exemplars could not be sought in real life or in history books. Fiction would prove an equally barren field, because the most admirable characters invented by novelists and playwrights typically display weaknesses. Educators would therefore seem to be left with only philosophical treatises, such as the *Nicomachean Ethics*, as a useful source of moral exemplars.

Sarah Broadie praises the practicality of this approach:

> The morally mixed character need not be an incoherent personality, and the mixed ethical description is only too often true. But in Aristotle, the various characters and their kinds of action are models of what ought or ought not to be . . . It makes sense in a work of practical ethics to shape the logic of the terms in such a way that they cannot send mixed messages. Thus the action will not be treated as brave if it is also unjust, or if it is done for a wager of beer, or if we know that the person who risked his life for his country on the battlefield was one month later selling secrets to a foreign power.
>
> (Broadie 1991: 259)

Having myself argued against casting drug dealers and bank robbers as exemplars of the virtue of courage, I certainly would not want to denigrate Broadie's wish to avoid sending children 'mixed messages'. At the same time, I seriously doubt the practical efficacy of any programme of moral education so obsessed with purity of message that only the tiresome figures sketched by philosophers may serve as role models. This restriction itself seems to deliver the message that real people are too flawed to deserve such status, a view much in keeping with Kant's (1993 [1797]: 148), but something of an insult to the family members and friends whom the vast majority of test subjects name when asked who they regard as moral exemplars (Walker *et al.* 1995: 392). The more moral education comes to resemble a thinly disguised version of some intro. philosophy course, the more it risks being received as some intro. philosophy course – which is to say, as an academic game having nothing to do with what students themselves care about, how they normally reason, and how they actually live.

Even at the level of theory, one might question whether unattainable ideals are as potent in motivating as philosophers sometimes assume (e.g. Norton 1988). Watching the gorgeous Jane Fonda bouncing and sweating on some no-pain, no-gain exercise video, while banishing from my mind any cynical thoughts about the benefits of plastic surgery and a life luxurious enough to allow plenty of time and energy for muscle-toning, I *might* be inspired to bounce and sweat along with Jane. Then again, the depressing realization that I can never be so fit, no matter how hard I try, might leave me more inclined to wrap my hand around a double martini than a barbell. Perhaps an exercise video showing Oprah in her continuing battle to keep her weight down might actually do more to motivate me. By the same token, perhaps various friends and family members who are well short of flawless, but at least demonstrate what real people can attain in the way of virtue, actually prove more effective in motivating moral growth than the paragons invented by philosophers.

Aristotle's idea that people *should* aim to become better integrated, and will lead happier, more admirable lives if they succeed, has much to recommend it. Conflicts between what an individual believes to be good and what he or she longs to do are so distressing that people normally do strive for greater self-consistency (Blasi 1993). Ironically, this very striving for internal harmony raises doubts about both moral weakness (*akrasia*) and moral strength, the only two dispositions between vice and true virtue that Aristotle discusses. Can such dispositions be psychologically stable over time, or do they inevitably tend to develop into virtue or degenerate into vice? Is moral weakness even supposed to be a disposition properly speaking – that is, a steady pattern of failing to act as one habitually believes that one should – or is it more like an epileptic seizure: an occasional succumbing to temptation quite compatible with a generally admirable pattern of behaviour? (*NE* 1150b31–35.)

Ancient philosophy's consistent focus on the ideal tells us a great deal about excellence but little about ordinary goodness. The guidelines for distinguishing between the moral characters we most often encounter in everyday life are relatively crude. Even serious analysis of moral character as a genuinely mixed bag turns out to be rare. Small wonder, then, that Aristotle's discussion of moral weakness should have triggered such a flood of late twentieth-century philosophical commentary. The vast majority of authors probably identify far more with Aristotle's *akrates* than they do with either his ideal hero or his ideal villain. (No slight intended: I do, too.)

In sum, I recommend that present-day virtue theorists join in working to refine Aristotle's theory. Because most people do demonstrate striking inconsistencies – because our characters and lives are less like seamless organic unities and more like patchwork quilts straining at the seams, which we are chronically working (or at least hoping) to remake in order to reduce the tension – we need a more fine-grained analysis of ordinary people. One refinement might be a distinction between persons who consistently pursue bad ends, or so consistently overweight a single end, however good in itself, that their whole characters and lives are seriously distorted, and persons who only go wrong now and then, or go wrong only in comparatively minor ways (Foot 1978; Geach 1977). The idea that 'nobody can make bad use of a virtue' is too perfectionistic, or perhaps merely too misleading, to be helpful in the practice of moral education. It would be more plausible to claim that no virtue aims at bad ends or is habitually put to bad use, though *the person having the virtue*, owing to weakness in some other virtue, might sometimes put it to bad use (Duns Scotus 1986 [c. 1300]: 389).

Another refinement might be some distinction between virtues in general – which, by their very nature are admirable – and the subset of virtues, the lack of which tends to make a person blameworthy or reprehensible (Brandt 1988). Are not some virtues more *important* than others? Are some not more crucial not only to good relations with family, friends and fellow citizens but also to the individual's own prospects for a flourishing life? Here today's virtue theorists themselves divide, with some wanting to expand what they deem narrow, modern conceptions of 'morality' in order to retrieve something closer to the Aristotelian understanding of moral character (e.g. Norton 1988, 1991), and others seeking to eliminate any distinction whatsoever between moral and non moral virtues (e.g. Slote 1992). But whatever the details of a suitably refined theory, I see no way that it can avoid considering moral character as a whole, and settle for discussing only a cafeteria selection of freestanding virtues or admirable traits, without leaving it utterly unclear what constitutes moral growth. The anything-goes approach, like the values-clarification approach, purchases diversity at too high a price.

### The second objection

*Aristotle's intellectual requirements for virtue are far too high. One does not need to be nearly so 'intellectual' to be morally good.*

With all due respect for Aristotle's fans, this certainly looks to be true. Granted, psychological studies suggest that moral growth involves learning how to generalize from one situation to another, gradually developing a better grasp of morally salient features, so that cheating on an exam and stealing money both look like cases of dishonesty, instead of like two unrelated bits of behaviour. Research also suggests that moral developments in action, affect and cognition are best regarded as interdependent (Burton 1963,

1984). The ability to generalize, however, demands no special flair for abstraction. Indeed, a study of persons commonly regarded as morally outstanding shows they do not explain their own behaviour in terms of abstractions or general 'principles'. Far from making explicit such theoretical elements in some putative moral decision procedure, they usually appeal to what they knew in their hearts was right and what they felt they simply 'had to do' (Colby and Damon 1992).

While Aristotle's intellectual requirements for genuine virtue prove more modest than Plato's or Kohlberg's, they remain quite high. Although he never equates virtue with knowledge, he does hold that cognitive development drives moral development. As Cooper (1998: 266) observes, 'The ethical virtues are crucially dependent on practical wisdom – not the other way about'. Today's educators would do best to limit their claims to interdependency, making the affective and the cognitive equal (or at least more equal) partners in moral development. Not only does this approach seem better justified on psychological grounds, it avoids downgrading moral qualities widely admired. For example, when eighty persons from four different age groups, divided about 50:50 between male and female, were asked to list the characteristics of individuals they regard as moral exemplars, 'compassionate/caring' was the trait most often mentioned (Walker et al. 1995). 'Thoughtful/rational' came lower on the list, and 'wise' a great deal lower.

Even if the last finding reflects the fact that 'wise' no longer figures in common speech, it seems safe to conclude that today's students place a much higher value on virtues of the 'heart' than does Aristotle. Many will also resist the suggestion that morality and religion are separate domains (Blasi 1990; Walker et al. 1995). By allowing the affective a greater place in moral development, teachers could leave room for discussion of how charity, love, or compassion might play an important and legitimate role in someone's understanding of good moral character and a fulfilling human life.

### The third objection

*Aristotle thinks that even a weak sense of humour automatically costs one a claim to genuine moral virtue. Not only are his intellectual requirements too high, his emotional and social requirements are too high.*

In fact, the unity thesis does become less plausible and more culturally loaded as one moves beyond such virtues as justice, temperance, courage and honesty into such Aristotelian virtues as wittiness, magnanimity and magnificence. Even the virtue of generosity (or 'liberality'), the pale sister of magnificence, simply does not seem to have the importance that a virtue such as justice does.

There are good reasons for thinking that one cannot be truly generous without justice. (If I do not understand and respect what I owe people, how can I have a stable disposition to give more than I strictly owe?) On the other hand, it is not at all clear that one cannot be truly just without being gener-ous. Even Aquinas, who generally supports the unity of the virtues, declares that justice can exist without generosity (*Aquinas 1969*: Ia-IIae, q. 66, a. 4). Indeed, the whole Thomistic scheme of treating a relatively small number of virtues as central to human life, then discussing other virtues either as different species of these central virtues, or as compatible with and potentially related to them, merits consideration (*Aquinas 1969*: IIa-IIae, q. 48, a. un.). Not only has this scheme been put to effective use in studies of comparative religion (e.g. Yearley 1990), it fits rather well with purely secular philosophical efforts to distinguish culture-specific virtues from virtues that all people need (e.g. Nussbaum 1988).

### The fourth objection

*Aristotle endorses one set of virtues for free, well-born men, another for women, and yet another for slaves. But the only genuine virtues are those of the (male) rulers: all others are 'virtuous' only in so far as they fulfil their functions in the social hierarchy.*

Virtue theorists might reasonably reply that Aristotle's theory has better, more lasting value than his own application of it, much as Kantians argue that Kant's insistence on mutual respect and treating every individual as an end in himself has better, more lasting value than his description of marriage as a contract for the exclusive use of each other's genitals. While this has its merits as an opening sally, it stops well short of ending the debate. For even if one rejects Aristotle's views on slavery and insists that both sexes be equally valued, it remains open to question whether boys and girls should be encour-aged to acquire different virtues.

Belief in sex-specific virtues continues to be quite common. John Gray's *Men Are From Mars, Women Are From Venus* (1992) not only won a long stint on Western best-seller lists but has recently triumphed as one of the few popular American books approved by government censors in Iran. Even in strictly Anglo-American educational circles, Carol Gilligan (1982) has persuaded a good many people that women value 'caring' more than men and reason differently about moral issues. No matter that further psychological research has repeatedly failed to find any empirical basis for the kind of sex differences Gilligan claimed to discover (e.g. Mednick 1989), her work still enjoys a considerable following.

Try as one might to detach moral education from both religious values and political alignments, I see no way to accomplish this feat. Moral education can never be neutral regarding political reform, just as it can never be neutral about the substantive conceptions of good moral character and a good human life that it embraces. It can at most try to be self-conscious, honest in declaring its own commitments, and willing to offer reasons for them. In this vein, I myself would argue that males and females are a deal less different in their values and actual behaviour than in how they merely describe their values and behaviour (e.g. Burton 1963; Harter *et al.* 1997). Reduce the number of 'tests' based on self-description – a form of measurement favoured by Gilligan and Kohlberg alike – and the similarities between the sexes might well become more impressive than the differences.

The dangers of gender stereotyping are all the greater because they tend to become self-fulfilling prophecies. One group of college women, told that men do better on the math test they were about to take, performed worse on the test than the group of women told that both sexes do roughly the same (Harter *et al.* 1997: 159). The general lesson for moral education was already suggested in 1792, in Mary Wollstonecraft's *A Vindication of the Rights of Woman*. Complaining bitterly about 'prejudices that give a sex to virtue' (1985: 83), she argues that the goal for *all* human beings is the development of their faculties: a goal that will remain elusive as long as boys are encouraged to seek independence and respect, while girls are encouraged to remain dependent and to long for 'love'. Substitute 'caring' for 'love', and the double standard in morals that Wollstonecraft attacked looks to be still very much alive. But given that it was already under attack in the eighteenth century, at least one cannot reasonably be cast as some radical postmodernist for continuing to challenge it.

# References

Annas, J. (1993) *The Morality of Happiness*, New York and Oxford: Oxford University Press.

Aquinas (1969) *Summa Theologiae, vol. 23: Virtue*, trans. W. D. Hughes, London: Blackfriars/Eyre and Spottiswoode.

Arendt, H. (1977) *Eichmann in Jerusalem*, New York: Penguin Books.

Aristotle (1984) *Nichomachean Ethics*, in J. Barnes (ed.) *The Complete Works of Aristotle*, Princeton: Princeton University Press.

Augustine (1955) *Saint Augustine: Letters*, vol. 4, trans. W. Parsons, New York: Fathers of the Church, Inc.

Beiner, R. (1992) *What's the Matter with Liberalism?* Berkeley, Los Angeles and London: University of California Press.

Blasi, A. (1990) 'How should psychologists define morality? Or, the negative side effects of philosophy's influence on psychology', in T. Wren (ed.) *The Moral Domain: Essays in the ongoing discussion between philosophy and the social sciences*, Cambridge: MIT Press.

—— (1993) 'The development of identity: Some implications for moral functioning', in G. Noam and T. Wren (eds) *The Moral Self*, Cambridge and London: MIT Press.

Brandt, R. B. (1988) 'The structure of virtue', in P. A. French *et al.*

Broadie, S. (1991) *Ethics with Aristotle*, New York and Oxford: Oxford University Press.

Burnyeat, M. (1980) 'Aristotle on learning to be good', in A. Rorty (ed.) *Essays on Aristotle's Ethics*, Berkeley and Los Angeles: University of California Press.

Burton, R. (1963) 'Generality of honesty reconsidered', *Psychological Review* 70: 481–99.

—— (1984) 'A paradox in theories and research in moral development', in W. Kurtines and J. Gewirtz (eds) *Morality, Moral Behavior, and Moral Development*, New York: John Wiley and Sons.

Colby, A. and Damon, W. (1992) *Some Do Care*, New York: Free Press.

Cooper, J. M. (1998) 'The unity of virtue', *Social Philosophy and Policy* 15: 233–74.

Duns Scotus [C. 1300] (1986) *Duns Scotus on the Will and Morality*, ed. A. Wolter, Washington, DC: Catholic University of America Press.

Foot, P. (1978) *Virtues and Vices and Other Essays in Moral Philosophy*, Berkeley and Los Angeles: University of California Press.

French, P. A., Uehling, T. E. and Wettstein, H. K. (eds) (1988) *Midwest Studies in Philosophy. Volume XIII. Ethical Theory: Character and virtue*, Notre Dame: University of Notre Dame Press.

Geach, P. (1977) *The Virtues*, Cambridge: Cambridge University Press.

Gilligan, C. *In a Different Voice*, Cambridge Mass.: Harvard University Press.

Goleman, D. (1995) *Emotional Intelligence*, New York: Bantam Books.

Gray, J. (1992) *Men are from Mars, Women are from Venus*, New York: Hatrper Collins.

Harter, S. , Waters, P. and Whitesell, N. (1997) 'Lack of voice as a manifestation of false self-behavior among adolescents: The school setting as a stage upon which the drama of authenticity is enacted', *Educational Psychologist* 32: 153–173.

Hartshorne, H. and May, M. (1928) *Studies in the Nature of Character. Volume I. Studies in Deceit,* New York: MacMillan.

Hauerwas, S. and Pinches, C. (1997) *Christians Among the Virtues*, Notre Dame: University of Notre Dame Press.

Irwin, T. H. (1988) 'Disunity in the Aristotelian virtues', *Oxford Studies in Ancient Philosophy*, supplementary volume: 61–78.

—— (1996) 'The virtues: Theory and common sense in Greek philosophy', in R. Crisp (ed.) *How Should One Live?* Oxford: Clarendon Press.

Kant, I. [1797] (1993) *The Metaphysical Principles of Virtue*, in I. Kant, *Ethical Philosophy*, 2nd ed., trans. J. Ellington, Indianapolis and Cambridge: Hackett Publishing.

Kohlberg, L. (1970) 'Education for justice: A modern statement of the Platonic view', in N.F. and T. R. Sizer (eds) *Moral Education: Five lectures*, Cambridge: Harvard University Press.

Kraut, R. (1989) *Aristotle on the Human Good*, Princeton: Princeton University Press.

MacIntyre, A. (1981) *After Virtue*, Notre Dame: University of Notre Dame Press.

Mednick, M. (1989) 'On the politics of psychological constructs', *American Psychologist*, August: 1118–23.

Mischel, W. (1990) 'Personality dispositions revisited and revised: A view after three decades', in L. Pervin (ed.) *Handbook of Personality: Theory and research*, New York and London: Guilford Press.

Noam, G. (1993) '"Normative vulnerabilities" of self and their transformations in moral action', in G. Noam and T. Wren (eds.) (1993).

Noam, G. and Wren, T. (eds) (1993) *The Moral Self*, Cambridge and London: MIT Press.

Norton, D. L. (1988) 'Moral minimalism and the development of moral character', in P.A. French *et al*.

—— (1991) *Democracy and Moral Development*, Berkeley, Los Angeles and London: University of California Press.

Nussbaum, M. (1988) 'Non-relative virtues', in P. A. French *et al*.

O'Connor, D. K. (1988) 'Aristotelian justice as a personal virtue', in P. A. French *et al*.

Rorty, A. (1988) 'Virtues and their vicissitudes', in P. A. French *et al*.

Schofield, M. (1984) 'Ariston of Chios and the unity of virtue', *Ancient Philosophy* 4: 83–96.

Slote, M. (1983) *Goods and Virtues*, Oxford: Clarendon Press.

—— (1992) *From Morality to Virtue*, New York and Oxford: Oxford University Press.

Walker, L. J., Pitts, R., Hennig, K. and Matsuba, M. (1995) 'Reasoning about morality and real-life moral problems', in M. Killen and D. Hart (eds) *Morality in Everyday Life: Developmental perspectives*, Cambridge: Cambridge University Press.

Wollstonecraft, M. [1792] (1985) *A Vindication of the Rights of Woman*, London and New York: Penguin Books.

Yearley, L. (1990) *Mencius and Aquinas: Theories of virtue and conceptions of courage*, Albany: State University of New York Press.

# 9

# THE VIRTUES OF WILL-POWER: SELF-CONTROL AND DELIBERATION

*Jan Steutel*

## Introduction

In his justly celebrated anthology *Moral Development and Moral Education* (1981: 18, 27–31), R. S. Peters distinguishes three senses of 'character'. First, the term is often employed to denote the sum of a person's traits of character: as when, for example, in response to a request to assess someone's character, we describe him or her as ill-mannered, vigorous, impertinent and outspoken. Secondly, the word is sometimes used to indicate a certain *type* of character: for example, when social scientists speak of oral, psychopathic, altruistic or aesthetic types. In that case the focus is upon a distinctive arrangement of traits, or upon typical exaggerations or distortions of particular traits. A third sense of 'character' is given in the idea of a 'man of character', or of someone 'possessing character'. This sense seems concerned to pick out people who are not at the mercy of their moods and inclinations and who habitually stick to their guns, not least in the face of temptation, intimidation or other social pressure.

According to Peters, people of character in this third sense are primarily characterized by such traits as perseverance, determination, consistency and courage, and he refers to these as 'virtues of a higher order' (1981: 70, 94, 122). In his view, whilst such traits as honesty, politeness, compassion and charity – which may be called 'virtues of a lower order' – relate more to rule observance or the pursuit of particular goals and purposes, higher-order virtues are concerned more with the ways in which rules are followed or purposes pursued: firmly, persistently, courageously, tenaciously or whatever.

In this chaper, I shall be concerned with just these virtues of character, though from here I shall more naturally and less cumbersomely refer to what Peters calls 'virtues of a higher order' as 'virtues of will-power'. From the outset, however, I will construe this term broadly to comprehend not only such core traits of will as persistence, endurance and resoluteness, but also such more loosely related characteristics as patience, diligence and temperance.

I appreciate that it is not entirely consistent with common usage to refer to such traits as patience and diligence as 'virtues of will-power'; but I shall argue that they have enough in common with core virtues of will-power to warrant their inclusion alongside these in a distinctive class of virtues with peculiar and interesting characteristics.

My interest in discussing virtues of will-power, however, is primarily educational. For while my discussion assumes from the outset that most parents would want their children to come to possess such virtues in fair measure, it is by no means clear what should be our focus of attention in promoting their development. Thus, at what exactly should parents or teachers aim if they wish to cultivate virtues of will-power? It will be my main claim in this essay that virtues of will-power are basically comprised of two main characterological components – namely, deliberative capacities and powers of self-control – and I shall attempt in what follows to address the question of how such virtues stand to education by exploring the relationship between them.

## Powers of self-control

It is clear that someone may possess virtues of will-power without being a morally good person, which argues for the not especially moral nature of such traits. By reference to Peters's explanation of what it is to 'have character' in terms of 'virtues of a higher order', one might say that bearers of virtues of will-power have 'strong' characters, but unlike bearers of such typical moral virtues as benevolence, fairness, honesty and forgivingness, they will not necessarily have *good* characters. Indeed, persistence, application and determination in the teeth of hardship are all too often qualities of brute dictators and cunning criminals.

The non-moral status of virtues of will-power can be underlined by attention to the difference between 'wilfully' and 'morally' virtuous behaviour. In practising moral virtues, we are doing what is at least *prima facie* morally right or desirable: if honouring our promises is expressive of the virtue of loyalty, for example, then we are doing the morally right thing by keeping our promises; if giving according to need rather than due is expressive of the virtue of charity, then we are behaving morally by such largesse. But exercising virtues of will-power does not necessarily consist, even on the face of it, in performing actions that are morally right or worthwhile. Witness, for example, the dictator who demonstrates his resolution in marginalizing or even annihilating opposition, or the criminal who demonstrates patience in waiting for the right opportunity to break and enter.

Thus, interesting differences emerge from any comparison of virtues of will-power with typical moral virtues. According to Philippa Foot (1978: 8–14), there is much that is common to both kinds of virtues: amongst other things, that they can equally be construed as corrective of potential defects in human nature. Even with respect to this generalization, however, we may observe that virtues of will-power have a specific corrective function, which does not readily apply to such moral virtues as (say) honesty. Without exception, virtues of will-power can be regarded as corrective of contrary inclinations. The virtue of perseverance, for example, offsets an inclination to backslide in the teeth of setbacks or adversities; diligence serves to counteract an inclination to avoid laborious physical or mental exertion; courage is opposed to a tendency to look after only our own skins in times of danger or threat; temperance is concerned with restraining importunate appetite; patience is a counterweight to the potentially debilitating effects of emotions as diverse as impetuosity, irritation and boredom. Each virtue of will-power has its own inclination(s) to keep in check.[1]

Moreover, as Foot rightly argues, all the inclinations which stand to be corrected by the virtues of will-power are, rather than products of socialization or education, part of natural human make-up, at least in their basic forms. Further, all are connected with phenomena (activities, processes, states of affair) which are in themselves either agreeable or disagreeable. Most, of course, are opposed to what is unpleasant to us: things which are painful or hurtful, strenuous or exacting, boring or dreary, frightening or threatening. Since we are naturally disaffected by such things, have an inbuilt aversion towards them, we are inclined to avoid or withdraw from them. But some virtues of will-power are associated with what is pleasant, delightful, amusing, gratifying and in other senses agreeable to us; since we are attracted by such things, have a natural desire for them, we are inclined to pursue them or to yield to them. However, irrespective of whether the inclinations to be resisted are agreeable or disagreeable, they are all – in one way or another – potentially threatening to the realization of our moral, prudential or other principles, ideals or long-term objectives. The temptations which can be put in our way by our natural aversions and desires are an ever-present source of ruin to our best laid plans and projects.

Given this corrective function of virtues of will-power, one may reasonably refer to them as virtues of *self-control*. However, it is by no means clear what this notion means. On one interpretation it might be said that practising virtues of will-power involves on all occasions the concurrent exercise of self-control: that only by strenuous control of contrary inclinations can we practise temperance, show our patience or demonstrate our firmness. Peters seems to defend such a view, writing in one place, for example, that virtues of will-power 'have to be exercised in the face of counter-inclinations' (1981: 94; cf. Carr 1984/5; 1991: 198–204). But a second interpretation might be that possessing virtues of will-power itself implies capacities of self-control. Since the first interpretation logically implies the second – but not the other way around – the second is less demanding than the first. If practising virtues of will-power invariably involves deliberate control of certain inclinations (the first interpretation), the capacity to control must be a necessary component of such traits (the second interpretation); but if possessing virtues of will-power itself presupposes powers of self-control (the second interpretation), it is not obviously necessary that (concurrently) exercising self-control would be required on each and every occasion of the practice of such virtues (the first interpretation).

Which of these accounts of the relationship of virtues of will-power to self-control – the former (strong) or the latter (weak) explanation – is most plausible? In order to answer this question adequately we need to be clear about the meaning of 'exercising self-control'. It might be suggested that this expression has sense only given the fulfilment of two conditions. First, it must be the case of any person who exercises self-control that he or she experiences some conflict between his or her preference(s) and inclination(s); such a person is motivated simultaneously by a belief that something is over-all the best thing to do, and an inclination which points in the opposite direction. We already indicated two kinds of such conflicts: sometimes we are inclined to avoid or to give up on things that are disagreeable, despite the fact that we would prefer to persist with them; at other times we are inclined to pursue or to proceed with things that are in themselves agreeable, while we would prefer to abstain from them. In the first case, exercising self-control consists in enduring what fatigues or repels us; in the second case, exercising self-control consists in resisting what attracts us (cf. Von Wright 1963: 152; Steutel 1988: 105–6).

Secondly, a person who exercises self-control intervenes in his or her motivational field in order to accomplish that which he or she prefers. Someone who controls him- or herself is therefore clearly *active*. He or she forces him- or herself to work hard; he or she withstands the temptation to jump in with both feet; he or she tempers any feelings of annoyance; he or she suppresses any inclination to admit defeat; he or she breaks out of a bad habit; he or she struggles against his or her appetites. The verb phrases at work here do basic duty for a rich range of overt and covert activities through which we try to influence our destinies as agents. In the light of this, William P. Alston (1977: 76 ff.) refers to such efforts, where successful, as forms of 'self-intervention'. By various strategies, human agents try to influence the courses of their lives – perhaps by weakening the causal force of their inclinations, perhaps by strengthening preferences with powerful supporting desires – all with a view to realizing best preferences.

This account of things, however, suggests that the 'strong' interpretation of the relationship of virtues of will-power to self-control is implausible, and that practising such virtues by no means always involves exercising self-control concurrently. If, for example, our temperance is displayed in moderate conduct during a lavish reception, it need not be that the first condition is fulfilled; on the contrary, it is more than likely that we are not in any way under such circumstances inclined to drink to excess or to eat more than is proper. Moreover, in showing courage in the face of fear, it might also be that the second condition is unfulfilled. To be sure, there may be in that case some conflict between preferences and inclinations – the inclination, for instance, to run away from danger – but because our preferences and possible supporting desires are much more powerful than any contrary inclinations, we may not need self-intervention to do the things which overall we consider to be for the best.

Indeed, it is even arguable that exercising self-control may sometimes be a sign that certain virtues of will-power are lacking, or at any rate that they are significantly underdeveloped. Suppose, for example, that someone is quick-tempered, always needing to control strong feelings of irritation in situations which call for patience. Would that not be a sign that the virtue of patience is not entirely present, even if the person always succeeded in acting as patience requires? Again, imagine someone who lacks powerful commitments and always needs self-control in the teeth of adversity, even in circumstances where the difficulties involved are relatively slight. Would we not have some cause to doubt that such a person really was resolute, even if he or she consistently acted in accordance with his or her commitments because he or she succeeds in controlling any inclinations to give up? In general, then, we might say that on some occasions where virtue-like behaviour is appropriate – in particular on those where the demands made on an agent are not excessive – exercising self-control can be contra-indicative of full possession of virtues of will-power. All this makes the 'strong' interpretation of will-power rather implausible.[2]

In other circumstances, of course, exercising self-control is quite compatible with the virtues of will-power. It cannot be doubted, for example, that there are situations which would provoke strong feelings of annoyance or irritation in most normal people. In such conditions, exercising self-contol to act as patience would require is not at all inconsistent with being a patient person. Likewise, in circumstances in which people would by and large be bitterly disappointed, successful control of one's inclination to throw in the sponge would be more a sign of having, than of lacking, the virtue of persistence. So we need not doubt that there are especially demanding circumstances in which exercising self-control is not at all incompatible with the possession of virtues of will-power. But such possibilities would seem to support the latter, 'weak' interpretation of the relationship of virtues of will-power to self-control; for if a person lacked any capacity to control his or her inclinations, how might he or she then act as virtue required in exceptional circumstances?

At all events, my analysis so far indicates that cultivating virtues of will-power at least involves the promotion of certain capacities for self-control. It also affords some insight into what is needed for the training of such capacities: the child should learn to perform effective acts of self-intervention in cases of conflict between preference and inclination. But what, exactly, does such motivational intervention mean? How are such processes to be understood?

There can be little doubt that the control of inclinations often involves the deployment of crude or subtle, mechanical or reflective, simple or complex, psychological techniques or strategies. Take, for example, the varieties of verbal self-intervention. One simple but effective technique for keeping undesirable impulses under one's thumb – often taught to children by parents – is to count to ten in annoying circumstances. A rather more sophisticated example of verbal self-intervention is described by Robert C. Roberts (1984a: 246). A small boy is trying to delay bedtime by all manner of means, and his father – tired after a long working day – is becoming irritated and losing patience. All the same, he defuses his irritation and succeeds in retaining his patience by telling himself: 'I did the same when I was four', or (better), 'Notice how ingenious his tactics are. What a bright little guy!' A similar example of such 'rationalizational' self-control is offered by Walter Mischel and Harriet N. Mischel (1977: 298) who concluded, on the basis of interviews, that children of nine and ten are able to check aggressive feelings by means of quite complex techniques. One child reported that in order to avoid getting angry and hitting out at others she would remind herself: 'Now, Joanie, do you want to get hurt? No! Do you want to get hit? No! Do you want to get in trouble? No!'

Other interesting self-intervention techniques seem to consist in deliberately acting in ways which run counter to our inclinations (cf. Roberts 1984a: 245–6; 1984b: 400–1). Suppose, for example, that we wish to challenge the impertinence of someone else, although we fear his reaction. One way in which we might try to moderate our fear is to approach him with an upright posture, look him straight in the eye, and address him calmly and deliberately. Roberts offers another example. A teacher repeatedly explains a relatively simple problem to a student, but the student is still in a fog, and the teacher is becoming irritated. All the same, instead of raising her voice, pounding on the desk or making sarcastic remarks, she deliberately behaves in a way which conceals her feelings of irritation, putting her hand gently on the student's shoulder and warmly encouraging him to re-read the relevant chapter at home. By means of this ruse she succeeds in softening the irritation which, if left unchecked, might have had less desirable consequences. In short, by behaving in ways that run contrary to natural negative inclinations, we may well succeed in doing something to assist the transformation of such inclinations into something rather more positive.

Most such techniques of self-intervention involve what might be called 'intentional' changes in attention and/or representation. We know from experience that it is possible to influence the power of motives by shifting or distracting attention from what we feel, or by otherwise representing or re-interpreting the objects of our affective attention. Thus, we can temper the affective force of inclinations by excluding their objects from attention – in short, by putting thoughts of them completely out of our heads – or we can generate powerful disincentives by vividly picturing the disastrous long-term consequences of our current inclinations. Richard B. Brandt (1979: 58–64) gives an interesting account of the apparent efficacy of such techniques. Whereas leading psychologists have defended the view that the strength of our tendency to perform a certain action (TA) is a function of our expectancy (E) of that action's outcome, and the positive or negative valence (V) that such an outcome might have for us (E x V = TA), Brandt suggests that this explanation of intentional behaviour is too simple and that a third factor should be introduced: namely, the adequacy of representation (R) of the belief that performing a certain action will result in a certain outcome (E x V x R = TA). On this model, whether or not something is the focus of attention, or whether or not it is imagined clearly, vividly or realistically, will also influence agency. In short, manipulation of representations can increase or decrease the likelihood of action on inclinations.[3]

In sum, we may conclude that in so far as a wide variety of techniques of self-intervention are available for the purpose of promoting capacities of self-control, helping children to acquire and apply such techniques effectively may contribute significantly to educating the virtues of will-power.[4]

## Deliberative capacities

Clearly, however, there is rather more to virtues of will-power than the possession and exercise of skills of self-intervention. We would not normally credit a person with possession of the virtues of will-power unless they were motivated by a certain sort of *preference*: and the ability to control inclinations says nothing about the nature of one's preferences. More precisely, one might expect a bearer of the virtue of will-power not only to make the transition from preference to appropriate behaviour, but also to be motivated by appropriate preferences for what is right or good. But the formation of such preferences requires capacities other than self-intervention: namely, appropriate deliberative capacities.

This may be made somewhat clearer by reference to Aristotle's well-known doctrine of the mean. In Book II of the *Nicomachean Ethics* (*NE*), Aristotle introduces the doctrine of the mean as part of the definition of virtue (*ethike arete*), Aristotelian definition being a matter of determining first the *genus* and then the *differentiae* of the thing to be defined. According to Aristotle, the genus of virtues is that of settled dispositions or states of character (*hexeis*); but many settled states – such as weakness of will or badness of character – cannot possibly be regarded as virtues. This is why the definition requires to be completed by determining the *differentiae* of the virtues – the characteristics, that is, which distinguish virtues from other settled states. The doctrine of the mean is introduced to perform just this task.

For Aristotle, virtues occupy a logical space between excess and deficit of natural inclination, between the vices of 'too much' and those of 'too little'. Thus, for example, the virtue of temperance (*sophrosune*) is located between the vices or (perhaps better) defects of intemperance or self-indulgence ('too much') and insensibility or imperviousness ('too little'); likewise, the virtue of courage (*andreia*) is the proper mean between cowardice and recklessness. In short, the doctrine of the mean rests on the possibility of tracing a certain tripartite relationship between states of character: 'two of them vices, involving excess and deficiency respectively, and one a virtue, viz. the mean' (*NE* 1108b11–13).

The claim that each virtue is a mean between two defects may be substantiated by reference to both the emotions and the actions of the virtuous person

131

(cf. Urmson 1973). Aristotle (*NE* 1105b21–24) instances anger, fear, envy, confidence, appetite, joy, hatred, pity, longing – and in general, the feelings that are accompanied by pleasure or pain – as examples of emotions (*pathe*). Although he does not seem inclined to regard any of these feelings or inclinations as inherently bad, he points out that they may be inappropriate with respect to either intensity or occasion of exercise. All, then, can fall away – in one direction or the other – from the desired mean: our emotions can be too strong, but also too weak; they may be experienced too often, also too infrequently; on some occasions what is felt is not appropriate, on others we feel nothing where we should feel something; we may be touched by too many things, also by too few; and so on. None of this, however, is true of the virtuous, who feel the right amount of emotion on each occasion and for the right reason; their emotions and inclinations are neither excessive nor deficient, but apposite: they are 'in the mean'.

Take, for example, the virtue of temperance. The *pathe* implicated in this virtue are diverse inclinations to food, drink and sex, as well as the pleasures we derive from exercising such inclinations. To be sure, the temperate will enjoy food and other pleasures of the senses, for, unlike the insensible, they do not suffer any deficit of *pathe* in this respect. But neither are their appetites excessive: unlike the self-indulgent they are not overly inclined towards bodily pleasures, they do not take enjoyment in illicit pleasures, and they are not unduly put out at not getting pleasant things. In Aristotle's words, the temperate person 'craves for the things he ought, as he ought, and when he ought' (*NE* 1119b16–18).

But what is true here of virtuous emotions – that they exist in the mean – is true also of virtuous actions (*praxeis*). In so far as it is proper to regard the activities of the virtuous as outwardly expressive of their inner states – states characterised in terms of mean affectivity – we may also expect virtuous conduct to be a mean between 'too much' and 'too little'. Moreover, it is precisely by reference to this perfect match of emotion and action that we are able, according to Aristotle, to distinguish the virtuous from the self-controlled (the *enkrates*). Like the actions of the virtuous, the activities of the self-controlled are in the mean; unlike the inner life of the virtuous person, however, the encratic person's emotions are not in the mean. As far as their behaviour is not aptly expressive of their affectivity, there would appear to be something basically disordered about the feelings and inclinations of the self-controlled. Unlike the virtuous, the self-controlled cannot simply give vent to their emotions; on the contrary, in order to act properly, they must act – with some internal struggle – against their emotions. (cf. Urmson 1988: 31–2; Sherman 1989: 166–7).

Aristotle's view that virtues are mean dispositions with regard to emotions and actions is undeniably suggestive, but is it also tenable? More to the present purpose: to what extent is his doctrine of the mean adequate to account for virtues of will-power, and are these virtues truly mean traits of character as explained in terms of his theory?

With regard to the affective life of those who possess virtues of will-power we must, I think, return a negative verdict. Indeed, it seems more reasonable to locate the moral life of such persons somewhere between *ethike arete* and *enkrateia*. For, on the one hand, since the feelings and inclinations of the bearer of the virtues of will-power are not necessarily in the mean, the standards laid down by the doctrine of the mean seem too demanding. In the last section we argued that controlling oneself in certain circumstances, particularly in very demanding ones, is not at all incompatible with genuine possession of such traits as temperance, courage and patience. Aristotle's account of the complete harmony of emotion and conduct in the life of the virtuous calls up images of saints rather than people of flesh and blood. For such reasons, some commentators have preferred 'excellence of character' to '(moral) virtue' as a translation of *ethike arete* (cf. Urmson 1988: 27).

On the other hand, it does not seem quite correct to identify the possessor of the virtues of will-power with Aristotle's enkratic agents, since such people cannot observe the golden mean without effort and struggle. It has been previously shown, however, that the virtues of will-power can be practised without inner conflict or self-intervention, and we have argued that the need for self-control, especially in not very demanding situations, may be indicative of a certain deficit of such virtue. Moreover, it seems misleading to picture self-control simply on a model of internal struggle or mental exertion. In the colourful words of Max Scheler (1950: 10): exercising self-control is not always 'schwer und schweissig' (hard and sweaty); on the contrary, the ease of grace with which many techniques of self-intervention are exercised may make it more appro-priate to speak in terms of limber elegance than of crude effort.[5]

I think that with regard to the actions of the bearer of the virtues of will-power, however, the doctrine of the mean is reasonably illuminating. Take, for example, the virtue of *resolve*, which among other things involves fidelity to a principle or commitment to a decision. Some people exhibit clear deficiency in these respects: time and again they are beset by doubts, reconsider their decisions too soon, adjust their views too often, are swayed too easily. Such agents suffer from a vice or defect which might be called *inconstancy*. On the other hand, there are people who seem excessively stubborn. Such people keep to their decisions at all costs and refuse to change their minds even where there are overwhelming reasons for doing so. Such persons are characterized by the vice of *obstinacy*. The bearer of the virtue of resolve, however, will not change his or her course too soon, or too often, or for the wrong reasons, nor will he or she stick to his or her objectives against better judgement come what may. His or her actions, in short, lie in a reasonable mean between inconstancy and obstinacy.

It also seems possible to offer a comparable analysis of other virtues of will-power. We may claim plausibly enough that the actions of those who possess the virtue of patience are in a mean between impatience and something like resignation or submissiveness, and similarly, that courageous actions avoid the excesses and defects of cowardice and foolhardiness.

If we assume the correctness of this particular application of the doctrine of the mean, possession of the virtues of will-power will entail not only control of conflicting inclinations, but also the influence of a certain type of preference. If preferring a certain action means being motivated by the belief that performing such an action is, all things considered, the best thing to do, bearers of virtues of will-power will – along with those (the virtuous) who are immune to vices of excess or deficiency and those (the akratic) who are not – prefer actions that are in the mean. Because exercising virtues of will-power consists in performing actions that are in the mean, the bearer of such virtues performs right actions: and in so far as that person believes that performing such actions is the best thing to do, his or her preferences are appropriate.

It is consequently a significant educational implication of the internal relationship of virtues of will-power to appropriate preferences, that if we propose to cultivate such virtues as persistence, fortitude and resoluteness, we cannot confine ourselves to training skills of self-intervention. We also need to ensure that the young person will prefer actions that are in the mean, and quite different – essentially intellectual – capacities are needed for the formation of such preferences. In so far as the formation of such preferences involves determining the mean – which is essentially a process of weighing the pros and cons of alternative courses of action – the young person requires certain deliberative capacities in the interests of judging maturely how to act in a given situation. It is only via certain capacities of practical deliberation (*phronesis*), that a young person may come to decide the appropriate course between Scylla ('too much') and Charybdis ('too little'), and therefore also to appreciate when it is right or appropriate to give rein to the exercise of self-intervention skills.

In the preceding section I began by suggesting that virtues of will-power, by contrast with virtues of benevolence, compassion, impartiality and fairness, are *non-moral* by nature. Is this claim consistent with the view that virtues of will-power never the less entail capacities of normative appraisal: that exercising such capacities also involves preference for the performance of right actions? And what else should we call someone with such preferences but a moral person?

It is clearly a mistake to assume that actions in a mean are automatically or necessarily morally right. According to R. M. Hare (1981: 192–4), traits like perseverance, temperance and courage are *instrumental* virtues, important in so far as they are vital to the effective realization of our plans, to carrying out our projects and to attaining our long-term objectives. But to the considerable extent that the deliberations presupposed to practising virtues of will-power are of a purely means–end kind, the sense in which the bearer of the virtues of will-power prefers right actions is merely functional or instrumental. It is a sense, at any rate, perfectly consistent with conduct which places the agent's interests above those of other people. Indeed, in so far as the virtues of will-power can be pressed into the service of all manner of ends – non-moral, amoral and even immoral – action in a mean which effectively realises the agent's ends is by no means necessarily morally right.

## Conclusion

The upshot of my analysis is that virtues of will-power involve both deliberative capacities and capacities for self-control. To that extent, parents who wish their children to develop into adults with virtues of will-power should teach them both how to determine the mean and how to control conflicting inclinations. But my analysis is not yet complete, for while these two different kinds of capacities are severally necessary for virtues of will-power, they are less clearly jointly sufficient. What is still missing?

To attribute a certain capacity to someone is ordinarily to indicate that the person can do something; but crediting him or her with a virtue normally implies that he or she is also *willing* to do certain things. In her celebrated essay on virtues and vices, Foot (1978: 4–8) rightly argues that virtues – as opposed to such capacities as memory and concentration – are internally related to desires, wants or attachments: 'a virtue is not . . . a mere capacity: it must actually engage the will' (p. 8). Consequently, virtues of will-power are composed not only of capacities to form appropriate preferences and control conflicting inclinations, they also presuppose a willingness to act in the appropriate fashion. Put otherwise, possessing virtues of will-power involves being motivated to exercise associated capacities under appropriate circumstances.

To be thus motivated is hardly conceivable in the absence of some standing commitment or attachment, although it is important to notice that the virtues of will-power logically imply no *specific* commitments or concerns. Such virtues differ, in this respect, from the run of moral virtues, for people who are just, tolerant or benevolent *are* committed to certain moral principles, attached to particular moral ideals or otherwise concerned with aspects of human welfare. Hence, if we want young people to develop into adults capable of pressing virtues of will-power into the service of moral concerns and commitments, we also need to teach the *moral* virtues, as part of that much broader educational undertaking known as 'moral education'.

## Notes

1 This corrective function of the virtues of will-power is not typical of the moral virtues. Foot (1978: 8–9) also defines the virtues of will-power in terms of a specific corrective function. She distinguishes between two ways in which virtues function as correctives. Virtues of will-power, like courage and temperance, are corrective because there is some 'temptation to be resisted', whereas traits like justice and charity, which can be regarded as typical moral virtues, are corrective because there is some 'deficiency of motivation to be made good' (p. 8). In agreement with Foot, Carr (1984/5; 1991: 204–5) also argues that the corrective function of the virtues of will-power is not characteristic of moral virtues. But contrary to Foot, he does not maintain that moral virtues are corrective in a different way. He labels such traits as charity, kindness and sympathy 'the other-regarding virtues of attachment', and – instead of regarding, as

Foot does, this group of moral virtues as corrective of human nature – he sees them as built on human nature, in particular on the pro-social tendencies that are typical of human beings as social creatures.

2 According to Von Wright (1963: 146–9), all virtues are forms of self-control. Carr (1984/5; 1991: 195–8) rightly rejects this view. He distinguishes between two classes of virtues, the virtues of self-control (such as courage, temperance and chastity) and the virtues of attachment (such as generosity, benevolence and humility). According to him, only practising virtues of the former category is connected with exercising self-control. Regarding the virtues of attachment, the need for self-control can be a sign that these virtues are not fully present (p. 200). In my view, however, Von Wright's account can be criticized even more radically. Even practising such virtues as temperance and courage does not always involve exercising self-control (cf. Roberts 1984a: 228 (note 2), 246) – and, again, the need for self-control can indicate that these virtues are underdeveloped.

3 In several experiments on deferred gratification in children, Walter Mischel and his colleagues have shown that such self-intervention techniques can be very effective. I have elsewhere (1988: 107–10) summarized their research results, with particular attention to so-called self-distraction and cognitive transformation techniques.

4 The capacities of self-control I have in mind are forms of skilled self-control. There are also, perhaps, more elementary or primitive forms of self-control which do not consist in using techniques of self-intervention. These forms are called 'basic self-control' and 'brute self-control' by Roberts (1984a: 244, 245) and Mele (1987: 26, 58) respectively.

5 Carr (1984/5; 1991: 205) also defends the view that such virtues as temperance and courage should be conceived as means between vices of defect and excess. Unlike the view I expound, however, he argues that practising such virtues is intrinsically connected to the exercise of self-control (see note 2). Consequently, Carr's temperate or courageous person looks very much like Aristotle's *enkrates*. Moreover, by interpreting (some) virtues of will-power as varieties of self-control, one is driven to the peculiar position of conceiving the corresponding vices as varieties of under-control and over-control respectively. Thus, vices corresponding to the virtue of temperance are explained by Carr as 'submitting too much or too little to sensual pleasure' (p. 205).

# References

Alston, W. P. (1977) 'Self-intervention and the structure of motivation', in T. Mischel (ed.) *The Self: Psychological and philosophical issues*, Oxford: Blackwell.

Aristotle (1925) *Nicomachean Ethics* (Ethica Nicomachea), trans. W. D. Ross, Oxford: Oxford University Press.

Brandt, R. B. (1979) *A Theory of the Good and the Right*, Oxford: Clarendon Press.

Carr, D. (1984/5) 'Two kinds of virtue', *Proceedings of the Aristotelian Society* 85, 47–61.

—— (1991) *Educating the Virtues: An essay on the philosophical psychology of moral development and education*, London: Routledge.

Foot, P. (1978) *Virtues and Vices and Other Essays in Moral Philosophy*, Berkeley/ Los Angeles: University of California Press.

Hare, R. M. (1981) *Moral Thinking: Its levels, method, and point*, Oxford: Clarendon Press.

Mele, A. R. (1987) *Irrationality: An essay on akrasia, self-deception, and self-control*, New York/Oxford: Oxford University Press.

Mischel, W. and Mischel, H. N. (1977) 'Self-control and the self', in T. Mischel (ed.) *The Self: Psychological and philosophical issues*, Oxford: Blackwell.

Peters, R. S. (1981) *Moral Development and Moral Education*, London: Allen and Unwin.

Roberts, R. C. (1984a) 'will-power and the virtues', *The Philosophical Review* 93, 2: 227–47.

—— (1984b) 'Solomon on the control of emotions', *Philosophy and Phenomenological Research* 44, 3: 395–412.

Scheler, M. (1950) *Zur Rehabilitierung der Tugend*, Zurich: Arche Verlag.

Sherman, N. (1989) *The Fabric of Character: Aristotle's theory of virtue*, Oxford: Clarendon Press.

Steutel, J. W. (1988) 'Learning the virtue of self-control', in B. Spiecker and R. Straughan (eds) *Philosophical Issues in Moral Education and Development*, Milton Keynes: Open University Press.

Urmson, J. O. (1973) 'Aristotle's doctrine of the mean', *American Philosophical Quarterly* 10, 3: 223–230.

—— (1988) *Aristotle's Ethics*, Oxford: Blackwell.

Von Wright, G. H. (1963) *The Varieties of Goodness*, London: Routledge and Kegan Paul.

# 10

# VIRTUE, *AKRASIA* AND MORAL WEAKNESS

*David Carr*

## Weakness, reason and will

Can a person who is convinced that a particular course of conduct is the best to pursue in some circumstances, nevertheless deliberately or *intentionally* adopt an admittedly worse course of action? Despite the fact that many have considered such conduct to be a familiar feature of human practical experience, the problem of so-called 'weakness of will' or 'clear-eyed *akrasia*' continues to figure among the most intractable of philosophical problems. More-over, though the issue is a problem for understanding practical life and human agency in general, it has its original source in the earliest of ethical or moral enquiries: where, it might also be said, the difficulty must arise in a fairly acute form. For if, as many philosophers have also argued, moral ideals and principles constitute the most sincerely or deeply held of human motives or commitments, it must be well nigh incomprehensible how human agents could fail to pursue what they affirm to be the highest of human goods.

It is important to be clear here that what is in question is a *deliberate* turn-ing aside from what one knows is right or feels one should do. Circumstances in which people fail to achieve what they consider to be for the best through inability, inefficiency, pain, fatigue or insurmountable obstacles are at once familiar, understandable and forgivable. What seems less comprehensible – as well as less forgivable – are circumstances in which someone knows what is better, is empowered so to do and yet apparently prefers what is admitted to be worse.

While it would be vain to hope that the present essay might have much to offer by way of a final solution to this problem, I nevertheless believe that a virtue-theoretical perspective on the nature of practical (primarily moral) knowledge may assist us to a rather clearer picture of the difficulties. I wish to explore this question with some reference to its educational implications.

To begin with, it seems wise to forestall some potential confusions inherent in received terminology. While, as already observed, the Greek term *akrasia* is frequently rendered 'weakness of will', it is also often said that the Greeks in fact had no conception of the will (e.g. Charlton 1988). In order to dispose of this apparent anomaly, we should first distinguish between different senses of 'will': or, perhaps better, different connotations of 'voluntary', or the sense in which an action might be said to be performed 'of one's own free will'. Under one interpretation, an action may be said to be 'voluntary' or 'willed' to the extent that it is not accidental or coerced and is performed by an agent for a particular reason or purpose. There can be little doubt that the ancients had a concept of agency as expressive of free will in this sense; this is more or less the account of voluntary action given by Aristotle himself. There is, however, a more substantial and controversial understanding of 'will' according to which voluntary actions are the causal products of 'acts of will', or of what have some-times been called 'volitions' or 'conations'.

This notion of the will – which is commonly held to be a Judaeo-Christian inheritance with no precise counterpart in pagan Greek thought – has not fared particularly well in modern philosophy. For many, indeed, the final death knoll of any idea of the will as a distinct psychic faculty has been sounded by the cri-tiques of Wittgenstein (1953) and Ryle (1949) – in whose wake such modern philosophers as Anscombe (1959) have proceeded to show, very much under the influence of classical Greek philosophical accounts of agency, that ideas of freedom and voluntariness are readily explicable in terms of rational action, without recourse to volitions, conations or 'acts of will'. Thus, in what follows, I shall assume that understanding the problem of so-called 'weakness of will' does not entail commitment to some distinct idea of the will and its acts, and shall proceed to treat the issue as primarily about the nature, status and role of practical knowledge, reasons and principles in human agency.

It is certainly in some such terms that the problem of akrasia or weakness of will first arises in western philosophy. As far as we can tell from early Plato, Socrates had argued that virtue is knowledge of the good, in which case no one who knows what the good is could possibly act contrary to that knowledge, and vicious action is not comprehensible other than as a product of ignorance. In short, no one errs knowingly and no one is coherently blameable for moral misconduct. Although it would seem that Plato was not entirely happy with some of the more counterintuitive aspects of this simple Socratic story, and tried somewhere between the middle and late dialogues to develop a rather more complex moral psychology, it may be doubted whether his ultimate position on the possibility of 'clear eyed *akrasia*' represents any radical depar-ture from Socrates. The point of the tripartite theory of the soul which Plato proposes in the *Republic*, so far as one can see, is that there is a bit more to virtuous conduct than propositional knowledge and that those who apparently act against such knowledge – perhaps in circumstances where we would say their judgement was swayed by passion – do so on account of a certain failure of nerve, initiative or 'spirit'. From this point of view, good moral education is more than just academic education (which can leave a person with 'less backbone than is decent') and also requires some training in resolve or endurance, which Plato apparently held to be the main function of physical education.

However, in so far as Plato's third part of the soul is construed primarily as a higher kind of desire – the seat of more assertive inclinations of human nature – it is not at all clear what, if anything, it has to contribute to resolving the specifically Socratic problem about moral weakness. As Plato himself concedes, there can be men of energy who are rough, uncivilized and dissolute, and it is no foregone conclusion that spirit will act in the service of reasonable virtue rather than devil-may-care vice. Thus, any inability to explain why reason sometimes fails to control the baser appetites must also affect the question of how, if it does, reason is able to influence spirit in its favour.

If only in this respect, the Platonic introduction of spirit and initiative into the problem of moral motivation may call to mind, not so much the Judaeo-Christian notion of the will, but that belief-desire theory of action which seems to have entered modern philosophy via Hume's skepticism about the causal efficacy of reason in human agency (Hume 1969 [1736]). Hume, of course, subscribed to a more explicit conception of knowledge as motivationally inert; since reason is in and of itself impotent to move men to action, something with more the motivational force of passion or desire is required for effective agency. Indeed, a hallmark of the modern account is a more or less complete assimilation of the difference between feeling-based desire and reason-based knowledge and belief, to a distinction between subjective but motivationally effective states of affect, and objective but motivationally indifferent cognition. But it is just this assimilation which necessitates the involvement of both desires and beliefs in any full explanation of human agency, since just as desires are needed to give point, purpose and impetus to agency, beliefs are needed to advise and inform it. Thus, the story goes, just as we cannot predict what an agent will do on the basis of his or her beliefs without some knowledge of what he wants, nor can we can predict on the basis of his desires without some information concerning his beliefs. (See McNaughton 1988 for some useful discussion of these issues.)

This could well be what gives rise to problems – ancient *as well as* modern – about moral motivation. For if we care to ask whether value judgements in general, or moral judgements in particular, are to be defined cognitively as beliefs or affectively as desires, either response seems to land us in trouble. Notoriously, Hume characterised moral judgements as subjective states of affect and in so doing effectively removed morality from the realm of rational concern. In responding to Hume, Kant [1785] tries to have the cake of moral objectivity and eat it subjectively by construing moral judgement in terms of a universalizing process of self-legislation. But any such compromise seems prey to the dilemma that in so far as one construes the deliverances of universalizable prescription as objective truths of reason, it cannot be clear how they motivate, and in so far as they are conceived as products of self-legislation, it must remain unclear in what respects they are really objective. Indeed, the post-Kantian moral theory which has gone furthest towards coming clean about this problem is the unashamedly non-cognitivist constructivism of modern prescriptivism (Hare 1952).

Thus, prescriptivists bite the bullet of Humean distinctions between fact and value, description and prescription, by recasting Kantian universal prescriptivity in the more subjectivist guise of consistent personal commitment. To the extent that judgements of moral value are generalised acts of commendation, prescriptivism preserves *internalism* – the requirement that sincerely held moral principles and commitments should issue in appropriate conduct – at the fairly heavy price of moral objectivity. Judgements of moral value are evaluative rather than factual, morally prescriptive rather than descriptive. It also effectively disposes of the problem of *akrasia*, since on one plausible view, it is difficult to regard what an agent *sincerely* (rather than ostensibly) believes as reflected in anything other than what he actually does.

In the light of the belief–desire account of agency, the principal alternative to a moral non-cognitivism which defines value judgements pro-attitudinally would be a kind of moral realism: broadly, the view that value judgements have some basis in considerations which are independent of our personal desires. The trouble is that any such realism seems attainable only at the cost of an implausible *externalism* which leaves it unclear what would motivate an agent to act on his moral judgements, especially if those moral judgements conflict with what a person otherwise desires in the way of pleasure or ambition. The belief–desire theory explains why, given a particular goal and beliefs about the way to achieve it, an agent acts the way he or she does; but on the assumption that moral judgements are cognitive rather than affective, it becomes hard to see what would compel action upon moral beliefs alone.

On this view, the problem known as *akrasia* or weakness of will again evaporates, not for the prescriptivist reason that there is an internal connection between non-cognitive value judgements and action, but because there is *no* necessary connection between value judgements cognitively construed and action. As Hume himself says, 'tis as little contrary to reason to prefer even my acknowledge'd lesser good to my greater, and have a more ardent affection for the former than the latter' (Hume 1969 [1736]: 463). In short, any such story takes it to be a fact that agents often do act against what they consider to be their greater good, by claiming implausibly that this consideration has no special motivational force for them.

Anachronism aside, Plato may also have held, in a not dissimilar fashion to modern belief–desire theorists, that since reason is not infrequently overmastered by passion, it cannot of itself be sufficient to move men to action and requires the assistance of an executive psychological power to ensure that value judgements issue in right action. Hence, Plato seems to introduce spirit or initiative into his account of moral agency, for much the same reason as desire is invoked by Hume: whereas reason indicates the correct path, desire gets things done. But since Plato as a moral realist held value judgements to be in some sense expressive or descriptive of an objective order of eternal moral verities, it is difficult to see – on any assumption that reason is not sufficient, without the help of desire, to motivate action – how some form of *externalism* might be avoided. The trouble is that whatever powers of spirit, energy or initiative are imported into the story to assist reason to action, it can only be a contingent matter whether they are able to do so, if they are defined in some opposition to reason. Briefly, if the spirit is itself a kind of knowledge of the good then it is clear how it inclines to right action, but one is then no further on with the question of how it can control the non-rational sources of motivation. On the other hand if the spirit is a kind of desire distinct from knowledge of the good, there seems no clear answer to the question why it should obey the dictates of right reason rather than the siren song of brazen pleasure.

What is striking, in the context of the educational implications of moral weakness, is that the unsuccessful Platonic attempt to preserve both moral realism and internalism is conspicuously reproduced – though this is a large claim on which I must here be brief – in most influential post-war theorising about the nature of moral education.

To begin with, it seems to have been taken as largely axiomatic by the liberal theories of education which have lately held centre-stage that any genuine account of *moral* education must involve *rational* initiation into a form of knowledge or understanding grounded in extra-personal considerations. It is also probably safe to say that most latter-day attempts to construct a liberal rational account of moral education have sought a broadly Kantian basis for moral knowledge and understanding, though not always coherently so. There cannot be much doubt, for example, that the moral developmental theory of Lawrence Kohlberg (1984) – perhaps the single greatest influence on post-war thinking about moral education – is mainly inspired by a kind of Kantian universalism. Kohlberg's account is in fact a highly eclectic and unstable mix of post-enlightenment elements of prescriptivism, contractualism, pragmatism and so on. It also pays homage to Plato, and it is striking that Kohlberg adopts what seems to be a very Platonic solution to a very Socratic problem about his theory. Indeed, Kohlberg seems to have been among the first to appreciate the apparent failure of his theory to account for circumstances in which agents appear to know exactly what they should do for the best, but fail to act accordingly. However, his proposal to solve this problem via the cultivation of a range of executive 'ego-strength' virtues of self-control, perseverance, patience and so forth, fails – in attempting to introduce an executive motivational power external to moral reason – for much the same reason as Plato's proposal in the *Republic* to deal with weakness through the training of spirit or initiative.

There can also be little doubt that most, if not all, other liberal theories which have attempted to ground moral education in an objective form of knowledge and understanding are prey to similar objections about a possible shortfall between judgement and action. From this point of view, it may seem surprising that the problem of weakness of will seldom seems to have been directly addressed by contemporary educational philosophers. A notable exception here, however, is Roger Straughan (1982) who has directly attempted to deal with the question in terms of a distinction between differ-erent sorts of reasons for action.

Basically, Straughan argues that the very idea of a reason for action is ambiguous between what he calls 'justificatory' and 'motivational' reasons. In his view, the problem of the akrasiac is that although he acknowledges a strong justification for acting other than he does – a reason such that acting contrary to it makes his present conduct appear weak – the reason is not presently *motivational* for him. But this explanation will not do, for reasons already considered. Either the motivational reason has equal status with the justifica-tion as a *real* reason – in which case it remains unclear why the agent fails to act upon that which he takes to have greater rational authority – or its motivational force derives from its character as a desire or impulse in cognitive disguise. In that case, Straughan's attempt to have it both ways in the form of some hybrid of reason and desire also fails, and his motivational reasons totter on the brink of a non-cognitivist theory of moral motivation.

For Richard Peters, one of the founding fathers of post-war analytical philosophy of education, Kohlberg's main problem lay in his failure to appreciate the importance for moral development of moral training. He not infrequently invoked the then not very fashionable authority of Aristotle to sup-port his view that 'the palace of reason has to be entered by the courtyard of habit' (Peters 1966: 304). But, despite his subtle and impressive interweaving of ideas from various philosophical sources, Peters' (1981) own 'externalist' use of training to plug the gap opened up between reason and action by moral weakness also clearly fails to deal with the problem of weakness, especially in the light of his own commitment to a fairly unreconstructed Kantian moral foundationalism. To this end, although I believe Peters comes closest to the root of the difficulty in recognising the importance for understanding the growth of moral knowledge of Aristotle's ideas about moral habituation, he seems not to have recognised the insuperable extent to which an Aristotelian view of practi-cal reason is at odds with any kind of moral deontology.

## Aristotle, virtue and moral reasons

Aristotle, of course, is a key theorist of moral weakness. First, his ethical writings are the source of a rich moral psychology incorporating a complex tax-onomy of types of moral failure and weakness. Second, this moral psychology is built around a highly original and distinctive conception of moral reason, called by a major modern philosopher (Anscombe 1959), 'one of Aristotle's best discoveries'. Third, he is also the author of a sustained discussion of the problem of weakness which is still regarded – along with Plato's account of Socrates' original formulation of the problem – as a *locus classicus* for discussions of this issue.

Briefly, in Book VII of the *Nicomachean Ethics* (NE), Aristotle identifies three basic types of moral excellence – heroic virtue, virtue and continence – and three kinds of vice – incontinence, licentiousness and bestiality – though the live distinction in his account of moral defect is that between incontinence and vice or licentiousness. The distinction between the virtuous and continent is basically between those who have mastered moral virtue to a degree where they no longer experience conflict between their best judgement and their natural inclinations, and those who – whilst still prey to conflict and temptation – are yet invariably successful in exercising self-control in the light of reason. The distinction between the incontinent and vicious, on the other hand, is between the morally weak – who, though they know at some level what is morally better, yet pursue the worse – and the wanton who care little for what is morally better or worse but simply pursue present pleasures. In addition, Aristotle suggests further significant distinctions between types of moral weakness. First, parallel to the distinction between the *enkrates* (continent person) and the *akrates* (incontinent person), he draws a distinction between the *karterikos* or tough person and the *malakos* or soft person. This latter distinction cuts across the first, since a person who is good at enduring hardship may be easy prey to pleasure, and someone who is self-controlled about pleasure may be poor at withstanding pain. Second, Aristotle also recognises a difference in the sphere of *akrasia* between intemperance (*astheneia*) and impetuosity (*propeteia*), regarding the latter as less culpable than the former on the grounds, among others, that outbursts of anger are more episodic and amenable to rational control than the sways of appetite.

Much, if not most, past discussion of Aristotle on *akrasia* seems to have had either the exegetical intent of explaining what Aristotle may actually have thought the problem or its solution to be (e.g. Ross 1964; for a useful review of such work see also Hardie 1971), or the critical purpose of using his discussion as a point of departure for the construction of an alternative positive view (Davidson 1988). There is, to be sure a good deal of uncertainty about Aristotle's conception of the problem, and much controversy whether he did in fact recognise the possibility of 'clear eyed *akrasia*'. At the start of Book VII of the *Nicomachean Ethics*, Aristotle seems inclined to disagree with Socrates' apparent denial of the possibility of incontinence, but all his own treatments of the problem seem to indicate that the morally weak agent has something rather less than complete knowledge of the good upon which he or she fails to act, and his discussion contains a grudging acceptance of the 'position that Socrates sought to establish' (*NE* 1147b15). Via a battery of distinctions of his own original logical and metaphysical devising, Aristotle seeks to show that at the crucial moment of moral action, an akratic agent fails to know *fully* or *clearly* what is required by right judgement, and is therefore led to pursue what he or she would otherwise regard as wrong. Either he or she possesses the necessary knowledge dispositionally but not ocurrently, or he or she acts in ignorance of this or that premise of practical argument, or he or she fails to connect the premises of a practical inference correctly and to follow it through to its proper practical conclusion. It would seem, however, that to whatever extent these various explanations of moral weakness in terms of failures of cognitive processing contribute to our understanding of moral error in general, they do not adequately account for the possibility of *akrasia* or weakness of will, understood as perverse action in the light of a clear view of some better alternative.

I shall not rehearse what has been previously said for or against Aristotle's account of incontinence in the extensive exegetical literature. Rather, I shall try to sketch a virtue-ethical perspective on the problem, which may go some way towards explaining the appearance of action against our better knowledge, even if it does not ultimately vindicate 'clear eyed *akrasia*' in any unqualified sense of this expression. Although this account is not – so far as I can tell – actually given by Aristotle, it relies for the most part on resources available in his wider account of the nature of *phronesis* or practical knowledge, and its role in the cultivation of virtue. (Moreover, Aristotle's remarks at the end of Book VII Chapter 4 of the *Nicomachean Ethics*, about the problem having something to do with failure of *perceptual* knowledge, may be suggestive of some such account.) I believe, in the light of this wider account, that akratic failure – or what generally passes for such – needs to be understood as a particular kind of non-intellectual failure of practical knowledge. On the face of it, however, any such suggestion must appear problematic, since Aristotle repeatedly insists that practical wisdom is quite *incompatible* with incontinence; after all, the practically wise person is the *virtuous* person, and the virtuous person is, by definition, above both incontinence and continence.

But the idea of *phronesis* – practical knowledge or wisdom – is ambiguous in Aristotle. In one rather narrow sense, practical knowledge appears to refer to little more than a particular mode of reasoning or inference. As such, Aristotle's first concern is to distinguish *phronesis*, as a form of practical means–end deliberation concerned with pursuit of the good, from theoretical reasoning concerned with the pursuit of *truth*. However, the means–end deliberation characteristic of *phronesis* is also a feature of what Aristotle calls productive reasoning (*techne*). And although differences between types of practical reason have sometimes been blurred by modern logicians more interested in the formal features of practical inference, Aristotle is concerned as much to separate practical wisdom from productive reasoning as he is to distinguish it from theoretical reasoning.

Basically, while Aristotle conceives *techne* as the mode of reasoning which underpins the efficient and effective exercise of *skills* for productive purposes, *phronesis* is deliberation concerned with the proper articulation and expression of the values and virtues which make us morally good. From this point of view, Aristotle is quite explicit that *phronesis* as a mode of deliberation requires the *virtues* as much as the virtues require *phronesis*, and that deployment of practical means–end reasoning apart from an appropriate value base is liable to issue in mere sophistry or 'cleverness'. In short, *phronesis* as a form of reasoning is essentially concerned with the production of virtues – constitutive of human excellence – via the clear recognition, expression and actualization of values conducive to human flourishing.

On this account, to possess practical wisdom in the sense which Aristotle claims to be incompatible with incontinence, requires more than a capacity to grasp patterns of practical deliberation: it also involves possessing inclinations consistent with virtue. But it is crucial to recognise that for Aristotle, acquiring virtuous *inclinations* and coming to make the right sorts of value judgements, or to engage in the correct processes of practical deliberation, are not two *separate* matters. On many of the post-Humean perspectives on value-judgement noted earlier in this chapter – particularly those wedded to the belief–desire theory of action – there is a clear separation of judgement and desire which precludes any explanation of rational action in terms of reasons or desires alone. It would appear, however, that any such split between the cognitive and the affective is foreign to Aristotle in particular, if not to pre-modern thought in general. Indeed, it seems likely that the post-Humean alignment of fact and value with reason and affect is just a particular expression of the Cartesian separation of mind from world – a schism which marks the fall of modern philosophy into a new dualism – against which John McDowell (1996) has inveighed in recent times. Having divested the world of any non-subjective value in the name of a new scientific objectivity, modern moral philosophy was bereft of resources to account for moral objectivity in any terms other than subjective preference or the various constructivisms of consistent commitment and interpersonal agreement. Since, for Aristotle, any such clear separation of knowledge from affect or motive, desire from perception and judgement, or value from reason can hardly be intelligible, his conception of moral rationality and of the relationship of knowledge to virtue indicates an understanding of moral weakness markedly different from modern accounts.

Aristotle's explicit adoption of a non-dualist philosophical anthropology separates him not just from many post-Cartesian philosophers, but also from Plato. For Aristotle, reason and other cognitive capacities function – unlike Platonic intellects or Cartesian minds – within a wider economy of human operations which cannot be characterised independently of social, practical and affective considerations and implications. Moral reason is not distinct from moral sense, and the raw material from which *phronesis* seeks to construct moral knowledge and virtue is experience of the everyday rough and tumble of interpersonal association. Nature has equipped us with a range of morally salient sensory and affective responses to the world – pleasures, pains, love, fear, anger and so on – which it is the task of parental and other nurture to bring in line with some defensible conception of individual and social flourishing. However, since practical moral knowledge is concerned more with helping us *become* good (*NE* II 2) via systematic cultivation of the moral virtues than with any theoretical definition of 'the good', early moral education needs to be focused less on the inculcation of a body of received moral opinion – though this is by no means an unimportant part of moral education and training – and more on the fostering of a range of sensibilities and sensitivities to the feelings and needs of others, the reinforcement of positive attitudes and attachments to others, and the basic control of potentially destructive selfish and anti-social tendencies.

It would be a peculiarly modern mistake to think of such cultivation of positive inclinations and affections as something less than, a mere precondition, of moral knowledge. On the contrary, it seems clear that such positive inclinations are for Aristotle part and parcel of what it means to have moral knowledge, and there cannot, in any full sense, be any such thing in their absence. (See on this, for example, various essays in Nussbaum 1990.)

Possession of moral knowledge in this sense is quite incompatible with incontinence, or even, for that matter, continence. In so far as possession of moral knowledge is neither more nor less than the fine tuning of one's sensibilities to the requirements of virtue in accordance with the deliverences of *phronesis* (understood as appreciation of appropriate 'means') it is inconceivable that anyone whose sensibilities have been so attuned could act contrary to their better judgement. In this sense, practical experience is a key component of practical knowledge or wisdom: hence Aristotle's well known analogy between acquiring virtues and mastering skills, which suggests that we learn to be honest or courageous much as a craftsman improves by practice. Moral knowledge is, in short, a matter of acquiring *dispositions* more than grasping propositions, and the role of *phronesis* is to inform or order our practical experience in the interests of effective moral agency. All the same, this analogy may be misleading if it is taken to mean that virtues are apt for acquisition, in the manner of at least some skills, as mechanical routines. Some recent commentators on Aristotle (e.g. Dunne 1993) are at pains to emphasize that the main respect in which *phronesis* requires to be distinguished from both *techne* and *episteme* is that the former is inextricably tied to the contingent particularities of practical experience, and quite unsusceptible of articulation and expression in any kind of general rules or principles. I think this point can also be liable to overstatement, but it does seem to be true that there is something irredeemably personal and particular about the the practical knowledge Aristotle attributes to the virtuous agent.

Of course, that a mode or form of knowledge is personal and particular does not make it *subjective*. On the contrary, in so far as practical wisdom is dependent upon the development of a range of situation-specific sensibilities precisely concerned to enhance powers of moral discrimination and agency, an agent may be demonstrably mistaken about what he or she takes to have moral

147

salience in some situation, and it may well be a determinable matter whether the agent has behaved well or badly in the light of his or her understanding. But insofar as effective practical wisdom must depend to a large extent upon fine attunement to a morally problematic situation, it also seems likely that agents who are directly privy to the peculiarities of such situations are going to be better placed than others for full appreciation of them.

It seems to follow from this that although we can certainly communicate the deliverances of practical wisdom in the familiar terms of ordinary moral usage, it does not follow from the fact that people are differently placed to profit from the lessons of experience that moral discourse reduces to a babel of private languages: there is a clear sense in which I cannot give others my moral knowledge in the way I might give them my scientific, mathematical or even musical knowledge.

This constitutes an enormous problem for the teaching of moral wisdom. It is a problem which is repeatedly recognised by Aristotle when he claims that one needs to have reached years of discretion in order to appreciate the lessons of practical wisdom, and that the young are hardly fit, precisely by virtue of their inexperience, for serious moral discussion; but it is also a problem for the teaching and learning of practical wisdom in general. This difficulty is, I believe, the key to understanding the appearance of *akrasia*.

In this light, let us return to consider whether an akratic driver who takes one drink too many, when he knows it is not merely legally but morally wrong, is someone whose powers of reasoning have broken down in the ways indicated by Aristotle in his own treatment of the problem: that is, his knowledge of the wrongness of the act is temporarily absent, or he is failing to pursue the premises of a practical argument through to its logical conclusion. Surely there is a perfectly intelligible sense in which this is *not* generally true of akratic agents: in which, indeed, we would not call them akratic if it was true. What is perplexing about akratic agents is that they can often rehearse arguments for not doing what they are about to do with considerable precision and sincerity. But the sense in which akratic agents can be said, in so rehearsing, to know what is better, depends crucially upon the earlier noted ambiguity concerning the status of *phronesis* as a form or mode of knowledge. In such cases, while phronetic reasons are appreciated as valid reasons for action, they are not entertained as Aristotelian *practical* reasons. On the wider Aristotelian view it is clear that the reasons which inform virtue and the moral life are not simply cognitive states, but states of a peculiarly character-instantiable kind. However, in so far as neither the incontinent nor the continent are in full possession of such reasons, they are prey to temptations that the virtuous person does not even experience. To some extent, Aristotle's point that the *akratic* agent has moral knowledge, just as the drunk is able to mutter Empedocles, comes near the heart of the problem. But the idea seems a little spoiled by the suggestion that at the time of action an *akratic* agent lacks any present awareness of communicable knowledge of right conduct.

For is it not true that even psychopaths and sociopaths who have committed the most heinous crimes can clearly and coldly tell us what is right or wrong, and that there is, therefore, a perfectly intelligible sense in which they can be said to have moral knowledge? The trouble is that those whose crimes we attribute to pathology rather than free moral agency are, as often as not, individuals whose interpersonal sensitivities have been stunted or disordered in early years to such an extent that they may be forever beyond the kind of experiential appreciation which makes moral reasons meaningful for the rest of us. On the Aristotelian view, any development of moral qualities has to be seen as the cultivation or perfection of certain natural sensibilities and inclinations, and if these have been fatally stifled or inhibited during early socialization, it may well leave an individual tragically beyond the pale of serious moral instruction. However, we do not regard the *akratic* agent as one who is pathologically damaged in this way, but, precisely as one who can be blamed because he or she could or should have known better. This, indeed, is the pivotal moral issue about the problem of *akrasia* as originally defined by Socrates; for as Socrates maintains, if a person does evil it can only be because he or she is ignorant of the good, and someone thus ignorant cannot be blamed. But if we have now defined the person of practical wisdom as someone who has acquired the kind of experiential insight into virtue which gives motivational bite to his moral reasoning, is it not also true that anyone who lacks the experiential insight cannot have the moral knowledge and cannot therefore be blamable?

Aristotle (*NE* Book III Chapter 5) shows perhaps about as well as could be shown that the Socratic inference does not go through; the *akratic* agent, unlike the psychopath, could have done otherwise, or have become the kind of person who could have done otherwise. Thus even if there is a sense in which drunken drivers or treacherous adulterers do not have the practical knowledge of the virtuous person – for if they had that they would not act viciously – the means to obtain practical knowledge through responsible acquisition of available relevant information and the exercise of choices consistent with such information are nevertheless available to them. Everything here hinges, once again, on the ambiguity already noted in the notion of practical knowledge. The drunken – or even continent – driver could not (by definition) know, in the sense of the practically wise person, that such action is morally irresponsible, but any plea of ignorance in a court of law can be no excuse if relevant information was readily available to manifestly sane agents. After all, the continent person who also lacks the true practical wisdom of the virtuous, and is subject to the same temptations as the *akratic* agent, can make the right choice and act contrary to his or her impetuous or self-indulgent impulses. Thus, morally relevant knowledge in this attenuated informational sense is not sufficient for practical wisdom, but it is necessary, and is surely crucial to the difference between continence and incontinence. If an agent of otherwise sound intellectual capacities claims he or she did not have it, he or she will be culpably wanton for not having sought it; and if he or she had it but did not exercise it, he or she would be irresponsibly *akratic*.

All the same, complete insurance against *akrasia* is only ultimately possible via cultivation of that practical knowledge of virtue which renders even continence redundant. For Aristotle, this entails nothing less than systematic experiential initiation – via the patterns of nurture and training discussed elsewhere in this volume – into a way of life exalting certain forms of conduct as noble and others as base. Only through the practical guidance of parents and other mentors in a particular context of moral evaluation, the cultivation of some affections, inclinations and sensibilities and the extinction of others, can a young person be put firmly on the road to a live appreciation of the long term lessons of practical wisdom: to a love of one's noblest inclinations because they are noble, and to unswerving rejection of one's baser instincts because they are base. Only through such a complete union of heart and mind can we recognize that moral reasons *are* moral reasons just to the extent that they resonate with what we should regard – if only our inclinations were rightly educated – as conducive to our practical perfection.

From this point of view, it is not hard to see how we can and do successfully assist young people to appreciate the intrinsic value of some dispositions over others, by affording them first hand exposure – through story, example and otherwise – to the positive personal and interpersonal benefits of fairness, sincerity, charity, friendliness and generosity over greed, hypocrisy, selfishness, distrust and meanness. What better way to teach a child the value of a charitable or generous spirit than via exposure to the ways in which mean and spiteful acts can blight the lives of authors as well as victims of such acts?

However, some of the knowledge of what not to do that we want young people to acquire is of a potentially life-threatening kind, and this is distinctly more problematic for the idea of a crucial experiential dimension to moral knowledge. Learning the benefits of benevolence via some experience of how personally demeaning it is to be spiteful is one thing, but learning by experience the devastating effects that sexual promiscuity or drug abuse can have on lives is quite another. Thus, a problem which has always exercised teachers of health and sex education – and is increasingly coming so to do in an age of greater personal freedom, greater sexual hazards, increased availability of drugs and some association of drugs and promiscuity with the glamour of popular culture – is how to communicate the wisdom of experience without exposing those we wish to protect to the very real hazards of such experience. In this context, supplying second-hand knowledge which ought to persuade someone to choose what is clearly the wiser path can be notoriously ineffective in the case of those who are bent on exercising the wings of their independence through adventure, experiment and risk.

I have no more space here to address a problem which is every parent's nightmare. It must suffice for now to say that I believe Aristotle to be the author of a moral psychology of unsurpassed insights into the complexities of moral motivation (including numerous valuable distinctions between kinds of moral failure) which philosophers are only beginning to explore with the kind of depth and seriousness of treatment they deserve: insights which could well bear fruit in relation to these and other difficulties.

## References

Anscombe, G. E. M. (1959) *Intention*, Oxford: Basil Blackwell.

Aristotle (1925) *Nicomachean Ethics* (Ethica Nicomachea), trans. W. D. Ross, Oxford: Oxford University Press.

Charlton, W. (1988) *Weakness of Will: A philosophical introduction*, Oxford: Basil Blackwell.

Davidson, D. (1988) 'How is weakness of will possible?', in D. Davidson, *Essays on Actions and Events*, Oxford: Clarendon Press.

Dunne, J. (1993) *Back to the Rough Ground: 'Phronesis' and 'techne' in modern philosophy and in Aristotle*, Notre Dame: University of Notre Dame Press.

Hardie, W. F. R. (1971) 'Aristotle on moral weakness', in G. W. Mortimore (ed.) *Weakness of Will*, London: Macmillan.

Hare, R. M. (1952) *The Language of Morals*, Oxford: Oxford University Press.

—— (1963) *Freedom and Reason*, Oxford: Oxford University Press.

Hume, D. [1736] (1969) *A Treatise of Human Nature*, Harmondsworth: Penguin Books.

Kant, I. [1785] (1948) *Groundwork of the Metaphysic of Morals*, trans. H. J. Paton under the title *The Moral Law*, London: Hutchinson.

Kohlberg, L. (1984) *Essays on Moral Development*, Volumes I–III, New York: Harper and Row.

McDowell, J. (1996) *Mind and World*, Cambridge, Mass.: Harvard University Press.

McNaughton, D. (1988) *Moral Vision*, Oxford: Blackwell.

Nussbaum, M. (1990) *Love's Knowledge*, Oxford: Oxford University Press.

Plato (1961) *Protagoras* and *Republic*, in E. Hamilton and H. Cairns (eds) *Plato: The collected dialogues*, Princeton: Princeton University Press.

Peters, R. S. (1966) *Ethics and Education*, London: George Allen & Unwin.

—— (1981) *Moral Education and Moral Development*, London: George Allen & Unwin.

Ross, D. (1964) *Aristotle*, London: Methuen.

Ryle, G. (1949) *The Concept of Mind*, Harmonsworth: Penguin Books.

Straughan, R (1982) *I Ought to but. . . A philosophical approach to the problem of weakness of will in education*, London: Windsor.

Wittgenstein, L. (1953) *Philosophical Investigations*, Oxford: Blackwell.

# Part 5

# RELATIVISM AND RIVAL TRADITIONS

# 11

# VIRTUE, TRUTH AND RELATIVISM

## John Haldane

## Moral philosophy and virtue

One of the main tasks of philosophy is to determine orders of priority. The precise object of this task may differ from one area to another. In logic the concern is to establish priorities among propositions, relevant to determining entailments between them. In metaphysics it is to show what is prior and what is dependent with respect to substance and attribute, particular and universal, event and process, and so on. The business of epistemology involves establishing priorities between observation, testimony and inference. In ethics, conceived for the present as moral theory (rather than meta-ethics, to which I shall return) a major concern is to establish the relative priority of intention, act and outcome.

In one sense, of course, it might seem as if there could be no doubt as to proper order. The outcome is what results from the act, and the act realizes the intention. Even this may not be so simple, however, since the issue can be raised as to whether that ordering is logical, causal or temporal. May the three elements or aspects not be co-present in a single episode? If so, can the ordering relation be a causal one? To pursue these questions would be an exercise in the metaphysics of action and that is not the point of present interest. For there is another kind of priority with which we may be concerned, namely that of *evaluative explanation*. Suppose I ask whether one outcome is morally preferable to another. Is the answer to be derived from an assessment of the moral worth of the actions that produce it, or is their value to be determined by a prior assessment of the value of the outcome? Proceeding in one direction we arrive at *deontology*; proceeding in another at *teleology*.

The debate between advocates of the evaluative priority of action and of outcome has dominated moral theory from the nineteenth century onwards; first in the form of a contest between Kantians and utilitarians, and later in a more generalised form in the debate between critics and advocates of consequentialism. As with all fundamental philosophical disputes it has proven difficult for members of either party to find arguments likely to convert their opponents. Even the method of deriving purported absurdities has been tried and found wanting. This failure is wittily illustrated in an entry in the *Philosophical Lexicon* defining the term 'outsmart' (after J. J. C. Smart, one of the most famous advocates of utilitarianism):

> **outsmart,** v. To embrace the conclusion of one's opponent's reductio ad absurdum argument. 'They thought they had me, but I outsmarted them. I agreed that it was sometimes just to hang an innocent man.'
>
> (Dennett 1982: 14)

Against this background of unresolved opposition the suggestion of a 'third way' is liable to be welcomed with some enthusiasm. This is one reason why in the last twenty or so years there has been much interest in virtue ethics. What the appeal to virtue suggests is that the primary focus of moral evaluation is neither action nor outcome, but *character*. The other aspects are not entirely set aside, but they are interpreted in the light of this distinctive feature. Consider, for example, the familiar case of sheltering an innocent and of then being asked by his would-be executioners whether he is on the premises. The consequentialist moves straight to a calculation of outcomes while the deontologist worries about what sorts of actions would be involved in doing one thing rather than another. To resolve this, the latter might appeal to some abstract device such as pairs of lists ranking types of actions positively and negatively. On that basis it might be held that while an act of lying is bad as such, an act of saving an innocent is good, and sufficiently so to outweigh any bad aspect. One thing to be said about this view is that it begins to look like consequentialism again. Another is that it seems to miss the point so far as serious evaluation is concerned. What we want to know is what should be done in the specific circumstances with all their human complexities, and the best guide to that would be the thoughts and deeds of a wise and good person. What weight to give outcomes, and how to rank types of action, are subordinate to the task of determining what virtue or goodness of character requires. As one influential writer (John McDowell) puts it:

> According to this different view (not one which sees the primary topic of ethics as the nature and justification of principles of behaviour) . . . the question 'how should one Live?', is necessarily approached via the notion of a virtuous person.
>
> (McDowell 1998: 50)

A second and related reason why virtue ethics has seemed appealing is that it avoids the isolation of moral thinking. Instead of partitioning off certain behaviour as 'moral', virtue theory takes a broader view, arguing that we should be concerned with nothing less than the goodness of our overall lives.

Rather than aim to be specialists in moral mathematics (as in consequential-ism), or experts in moral taxonomy (as in deontology), we should aim to acquire settled habits of feeling and choice, the exercise of which will give our whole existence meaning and value.

In shifting focus from outcomes and actions to people, virtue ethics promises a rich moral psychology and interesting links with philosophical anthropology. Depending on how central and extensive is the place of virtue in human life, one might even say that becoming virtuous is becoming a properly human person. The interest of this for education is clear. Since antiquity – and even today – it has been widely held that the general point of education is to enable the learner to develop into a rounded figure; to acquire abilities to make evaluative discriminations; to have and to control feelings important for life, and so on: in short, to become virtuous.

A third reason for the appeal to virtue in recent moral philosophy is that it may provide a different way of thinking about the objectivity of value and practical reasoning. Deontology and consequentialism are theories of evalua-tion and deliberation; accounts of the proper objects of assessment and of the appropriate form of justification. As such, they do not address the question of the metaphysical status of value and requirement. This point is sometimes overlooked owing to the fact that advocates of one or other view tend also to be committed to an accompanying meta-ethical position. Many utilitarians, for example, tend to be objectivists about the value of the end in terms of which right action is defined. It is not always so, however. Smart, for example, combines utilitarianism as a moral theory, with subjectivism as a meta-ethical one: we ought to maximize utility, but utility is not something good in itself, it is simply something we are disposed to favour.

If it is sometimes forgotten that moral theory needs supplementation by meta-ethics, it is impossible to overlook the difficulties in arriving at a satisfactory account of the status of value and requirement. In particular, objectivism has been challenged with the claim that what we now know of reality leaves no scope for the existence of non-natural values, let alone of 'free-floating' requirements and prohibitions. Wittgenstein is reported to have described how in his last meeting with Frege he asked the great mathematical logician whether he ever found difficulty in his theory that numbers are objects. Frege is said to have replied, 'Sometimes I *seem* to see a difficulty – but then again I *don't* see it' (Anscombe and Geach 1973: 131). Meta-ethical objectivism faces the task of showing how there could be such 'objects' as moral facts and values, and this has proven a real difficulty. At the same time, however, the reduction of value to preference and sentiment has seemed contrary to experience and liable to undermine commitment to right action.

One might wonder how an ethics of virtue could fare any better in these respects. Given the distinction between moral theory and meta-ethics, even if we adopt the virtue approach there remains the issue of objectivity. That observation is true so far as the mere idea of virtue is concerned, but once one broadens this out and links it with aspects of human nature it may be that the metaphysics of virtue is less problematic than that of consequentialism and of deontology. The most prominent advocates of virtue ethics have been neo-Aristotelians and it is no accident that they emphasize the importance of relating virtue to an account of human nature. Peter Geach, for example, argues that virtues such as prudence, temperance, justice and courage are as necessary as health and sanity in order to achieve and maintain a good life (Geach 1977: ch. 1). The goodness of such a life, for the Aristotelian, is not to be understood in terms of the presence in or around it of 'values' in the philosophically familiar sense of metaphysically distinct entities. Rather it consists in the integrated and balanced operation of various natural functions, including physiological, psychological and social ones. Goodness in human life is metaphysically neither more nor less mysterious than goodness in the life of plants.

If this is so then there is no special philosophical problem involved in the claim that virtue requires that one act in a certain way. More generally, it will be in order for those charged with the education of others to provide guidance in virtue, just as one might with regard to diet and exercise. Moral educators will still have problems to deal with in deciding *what* to teach but they need not carry the burden of many educators who believe that neither they nor anyone else can give an objective foundation for their instruction. Virtue theory appears to make moral education a real and rationally defensible possibility. No wonder philosophers of education have shown considerable interest in it (Carr 1991).

## MacIntyre and the challenge of relativism

Is the account of the previous section too good to be true? Setting aside claims of innocence and superiority made on behalf of consequentialism and deontology, there is an issue about the viability of the sort of naturalistic position just described, and ironically grounds for doubt about this arise from within the family of virtue ethicists.

Forty years ago Elizabeth Anscombe adopted the method of slash and burn so as to prepare the terrain for the reintroduction of virtue in her essay 'Modern Moral Philosophy' (Anscombe 1981 [1958]). Among the bold and very interesting theses she presented is the claim that the basic moral vocabulary of requirement and of prohibition, 'ought', 'ought not', 'must', 'must not' and so on, is one of the cultural remains of an earlier religious way of thinking, according to which morality consists of a series of divine commands. Since people in general no longer subscribe to such a view (indeed it is uncommon even among Christian moral theologians) Anscombe proposed that it be abandoned in favour of the language (and the philosophy) of human virtue and flourishing.

Twenty years later Alasdair MacIntyre took up both this historico-concep-tual analysis, and the option for virtue. In *After Virtue* (1981) he argued that ethical language has become an incoherent assemblage of disordered fragments left over from earlier moral systems. However, whereas Anscombe focused exclusively on the remains of divine law and proposed the readoption of a traditional Aristotelian approach, MacIntyre discerned the vocabulary of virtue ethics itself amidst the babble of competing moral claims; and argued that as things stand, modern secular liberal consciousness is no better placed to make sense of virtue talk than it is of the strongly prescriptive vocabulary of the Judaeo-Christian moral law. In both cases what we lack are the historical and cultural contexts that give meaning to these ways of evaluating and com-mending character and conduct.

A further point of important difference between Anscombe and MacIntyre is that while she seemed to believe that we could reconstruct the philosophical anthropology by which Aristotle was able to prescribe a natural end for human kind, realization of which constitutes well-being or flourishing (*eudaimonia*), MacIntyre regards this sort of quasi-philosophical anthropology as being committed to a form of ahistorical, acultural 'metaphysical biology', which philosophy itself, as well as the natural and social sciences, has shown to be no longer tenable.

Before discussing this difference with respect to the philosophical foundations of ethics, it is important to stress MacIntyre's agreement with the general character of Aristotelian moral psychology. For in keeping with this he argues that the value, and indeed the moral meaning, of actions flows from habits of action and avoidance whose standing as virtues derives from their orientation towards ends constitutive of good human lives. Like Anscombe and other neo-Aristotelians, therefore, MacIntyre hopes to restore coherence to morality by relating it to an account of life as teleologically ordered; but in part for the reasons mentioned, and in part because of conclusions drawn and retained from his earlier studies in Marxism and sociology, he views that order in terms of social practices rather than culturally invariant natural functions. In asking the question 'what ought I to do?' one is, in effect, asking a question about the kind of person one should be. The unit of moral assessment is not, strictly, individual actions but the form of life from which they issue and the agent's overall character. Furthermore, this moral character is formed and developed in a social context, out of participation – originally unchosen and not reflected upon – in practices whose meaning is given by their traditional goals. On this account moral maturation involves reflection upon the kind of life one's finds oneself living, and the construction of a personal narrative in terms of which actions, habits, episodes, trends, commitments, aversions and so on, can be judged as failings or achievements, as vices and virtues.

In summary, to understand the moral identity and value of individual actions one has to relate them to the agent's life, and through this to the traditional practices and social forms of his or her culture. The very obvious problem presented by modernity, therefore, is that there is no single unifying culture and hence no shared set of values and virtues by reference to which actions may be interpreted and judged. As MacIntyre observes:

> The rhetoric of shared values is of great ideological importance, but it disguises the truth about how action is guided and directed. For what we genuinely share in the way of moral maxims, precepts and principles is insufficiently determinate to guide action and what is sufficiently determinate to guide action is not shared.
>
> (MacIntyre 1990b: 349)

For example, and superficial appearances to the contrary, modern societies lack substantial agreement on such basic questions as whether or why lying is bad. (Anyone tempted to doubt this might contemplate the record of public deception by the President of the United States and the varying reactions of the American people to this undisputed fact.) In traditional societies, by contrast, actions are subject to sets of norms appropriate to various roles (though these norms are not always codified or codifiable); and these prescribe what is honourable and dishonourable, vicious and virtuous.

The considerable interest of MacIntyre's explorations of these issues is testified to by the attention his work has attracted (Horton and Mendus 1994; McMylor 1994). Yet his thoughts also raise a problematic question about the claim to objectivity of the virtue ethics approach. If the standards of moral assessment are not given by extra-moral and uncontested values, or by ahistorical principles of practical reason, but are immanent within the particular social traditions and practices in which agents are situated, then how is relativism to be avoided? If what is right is determined by virtues whose form and content is specific to a tradition, how can it even make sense to raise questions about the morality of conduct from an evaluative perspective outside that tradition? Since the diagnosis of modernity, and a *fortiori* of 'post-modernity', is that there is no single moral order, the threat of relativism is not merely speculative, it is real.

MacIntyre's concern with the question of competing moral traditions is reflected in the title of the book that followed *After Virtue*, namely, *Whose Justice? Which Rationality?* (MacIntyre 1988). In this, and in the sequel *Three Rival Versions of Moral Enquiry* (MacIntyre 1990a), he developed a dialectical account of how one tradition of reflection can establish its rational superiority over another. In broad outline he maintains that while norms of reason are immanent within, and particular to, traditions of enquiry, a tradition may run into philosophical difficulties and recognize this fact without having the resources to solve the problems. It might yet, however, be able to appreciate that another, rival tradition does possess the means to diagnose and to resolve these difficulties. Acknowledgement of these facts therefore amounts to recognition of the superiority of the rival. Additionally, MacIntyre maintains, in the fashion of Aristotle and of Aquinas (his relatively new-found hero), that the defining goal of enquiry is truth and that the only adequate conception of this is a realist one which regards it as an objective relation of conformity between mind and world (*adaequatio intellectus ad rem*). As he remarks, 'claims to truth, thus conceived, are claims to have transcended the limitations of any merely local standpoint' (MacIntyre 1994: 18–19). Thus, while styles and principles of enquiry may be tradition-specific, the ultimate goals of enquiry – truth for theory, goodness for action – are tradition-transcendent.

## The subjects and objects of thought and action

Virtue and the associated habit of right reason – for the Greeks *orthos logos* and for the Latins *recta ratio* – are cultivated in interpersonal contexts. Can that fact really be squared with claims to transcendent objectivity? MacIntyre believes himself to have provided the basis for a positive answer, but I think we are not yet entitled to say 'yes'. We need to develop further the philosophy of thought and action.

First, then, his proposed escape from immanentism. For this MacIntyre acknowledges a debt to Peter Geach and to what the latter, modestly, has attributed to another, calling it the 'Frege point' (Geach 1972). In brief it is this. Truth is conceptually linked with assertion in the respect that to assert 'p' is to hold that 'p' is true. I say 'conceptually' to indicate that one would not know what to make of someone who said, for example, 'it is raining, but it may not be raining'. Assertion is not to be confused with assertiveness. The former is a logical category, the second a psychological one. Assertiveness may be aimed at commanding the attention of others; of its nature assertion aims at truth. This latter fact emerges in connection with inference, which is the proper focus of the Frege/Geach point. The interpretation of compound sentences involving logical connectives (p *and* q, p *or* q, if p *then* q, etc.) depends upon an understanding of these as governed by a common standard, that is, truth. This is not to say, of course, that the various elementary and compound sentences are true, but only that the possibility of their entering into logical relations depends upon them being truth assessable, that is, being such as to have truth values. To illustrate this, one of the more common patterns of inference is *modus ponendo ponens* (the method by which affirming affirms): if p then q; p; therefore q. In order for the inference to be valid it must be the case that there is no equivocation in meaning, which is to say that the constituent propositions (p and q) must function in the same manner in each of their occurrences. If inferential validity is to be preserved it cannot be the case that what 'p' *means* in the conditional 'if p then q', and then by itself is something different. Resolving for consistency we must conclude that in the two occurrences 'p' has the same meaning and is truth-apt. MacIntyre's thesis, then, is that assertions involve claims to truth: to assert is to present as true.

Accordingly, while there may be competing understandings of the virtuous life, those who assert them must be committed to the idea that there is a fact who, if anyone, is correct: 'So too justifiability has to be already understood in terms of truth and not vice versa' (MacIntyre 1994: 17).

Whether or not this deserves to be accepted as conclusive, it is not likely to be adopted without question by anyone familiar with recent literature on truth and objectivity. For there is a line (more strictly, 'lines') of reasoning associated in the first instance with David Wiggins (Wiggins 1980) and then with Crispin Wright (Wright 1992, 1995), according to which it may be possible to distinguish different varieties of truth. At one extreme there are minimalist understandings of 'truth' sufficient to apply to each premise in an inference, as illustrated above, but which carry no philosophical baggage. At the other extreme there is truth so full-blooded as to entail metaphysical claims about the nature of reality: 'a property of intrinsic metaphysical *gravitas*', as Wright puts it (Wright 1995: 213). If this thesis of a variable truth predicate is correct, then the relativist has a route to follow. He or she can allow that someone who, from *within* a tradition, expresses a claim to the effect that acting out this or that virtue is good, is certainly making an assertion and hence is holding it to be true. Yet he or she can also insist that, without further 'substantiation', there is no reason to regard the kind of truth in question as anything more than an artefact or governing principle of discourse and hence not something that ought to command universal assent as conforming to objective fact.

How MacIntyre himself might reply to this is an interesting question, but the more pressing issue is how anyone interested in the objectivity of virtue should respond. One 'technical' rejoinder involves a return to the Frege/Geach point and to the thought that only truth-assessable sentences can feature in inferences. It might seem that Wright's position is untroubled by this since he can maintain that inference is secured by the universal applicability of a minimalist truth predicate. However, matters may not be so simple. Consider the following inference:

1    Salt and vinegar ice cream is disgusting.
2    This is salt and vinegar ice cream.
3    Therefore, this is disgusting.

If we suppose that the truth predicate applicable to 'Salt and vinegar ice cream is disgusting' is immanent and/or sensibility-cum-community relative, whereas the truth predicate appropriate to 'This is salt and vinegar ice cream' is transcendent or enjoys realist status, then surely we will not be able to derive (3) from (1) and (2), since there is no common notion of truth to be preserved across the inference. Contrariwise if we think the inference is valid then this implies that truth is univocal, and hence that what is meant by asserting a proposition is the same in each case. Further argument will then press the case for the truth of (1) being understood as implying no less objective a fact than that of (2).

It is fairly clear, however, what Wright's response will be to this replay of the Frege/Geach point. For he may insist that there is only one truth predicate (that which is preserved in valid inferences); and add that what is at issue in questions of objectivity is what else may obtain when that predicate is applicable, the obtaining of the second and subsequent things being a matter not of the meaning of truth, but of the particular subject matter under consideration.[1] So we are returned to the question, what does truth amount to in the sphere of claims about the good life? A further borrowing from contemporary philosophy of language will be of help, but before coming to that a historical reflection may prove beneficial.

Echoing Augustine's anti-sceptical reflection 'if I err I am' (*si fallor sum*), Descartes famously reasoned 'I think therefore I am' (*cogito ergo sum*). In response to Descartes, Lichtenberg observed that what was licensed by Cartesian reflection on phenomenal consciousness is not '*I think*' but 'there is thinking' or 'thinking is going on' (Lichtenberg 1990). This is usually seen as a corrective endorsement of a non-centred view of thought similar perhaps to Hume's subjectless cluster of impressions and ideas. Without entering into exegetical disputes, however, I take it that Lichtenberg's comment may be treated as a *reductio ad absurdum*, showing that the form of Descartes' doubt about his own existence is incoherent, and that the peculiarly Cartesian attempt to deal with it leads to nonsense. Thought is mental activity; activity requires an agent; thinking is done by thinkers.

On this account the 'I', which in Kant's formula accompanies all my perceptions, is not a mere transcendental condition of experience but a substantial reality, a metaphysical precondition of acting. In a letter of 1786 Lichtenberg wrote 'we only know of matter and soul because of the forces through which they manifest themselves and with which they are identical'. His concern was to show that the ideas of a fully substantial but immaterial soul, and of a fully substantial but inert material body, are erroneous abstractions. In the course of another dialectical engagement (with Averroism and Augustinianism), Aquinas observed that it is one and the same thing or substantial unity that breathes, moves and thinks. As he puts it: a *man* walks, sees and thinks by means, or in virtue, of 'one and the same soul'.(Aquinas 1969: Ia, q.75, a.4). The common conclusion of these reflections is that the subject of deliberation, and hence of judgement, is an incarnate agent, a *rational animal*.

A second important idea associated with Aquinas is that all actions are aimed at the good. Just occasionally this is (mis)interpreted as saying that all is for the best. Aquinas, however, was not expressing moral optimism: he was making a point about the internal constitution of agency. Action is intentionally characterized behaviour, and as intentional it is aimed towards something conceived of as worthy of effort, and thus as good so far as the interests of the agent are concerned. Those interests may be misidentified or in some way disordered, but the fact remains that if we are to see individuals as acting at all, then we must interpret what they do in terms that show that it is directed to an intelligible goal.

So far, this may seem to do little to establish a foundation for ethics. All we have is that the subjects of action are rational animals and that they operate under the direction of what they conceive to be goods. Surely this can hardly establish the objectivity of value, let alone gives any determinate content to values? Let us see.

About thirty years ago Donald Davidson began to make good the old idea, to be found in Frege and in Wittgenstein, that we know the meaning of an utterance when we know the conditions associated with its truth (Davidson 1984). In the vocabulary of Aquinas's scholastic followers, 'signification is ordered to truth'. Davidson's idea was to try to construct a theory of meaning for a given language (a fragment of English as it happens) by articulating, and in a technical sense 'proving', a truth theory for it. We need be concerned only with the fact that on this account you know the meaning of a sentence when you know, or can identify, the relevant truth specification for it. I know the meaning of the German sentence 'Schnee ist weiss' if I know that 'Schnee ist weiss' is true if and only if snow is white. Accordingly, I know the meaning of all sentences of German if I know the corresponding truth specification for *each* of them. It took Davidson's followers in Britain and in the United States to see that if this approach is to work then much more needs to be done deploying the meaning-truth equivalence in the context of a broader theory of action interpretation. In the circumstance first characterised by Quine (1960) (Davidson's teacher) as one of 'radical translation' we are to imagine that we find ourselves parachuted into the midst of an alien (but human) group. How are we to determine the meaning of their words and deeds?

If we follow Aquinas's lead then we will know that something is an *action* if it is ordered to the good, as that is conceived by the agent. If we follow Davidson we will know that something is an *utterance* (at any rate an assertory indicative) if it is equivalent to the specification of its own truth condition (as that is envisaged by the speaker). Very well, but how does this help in the circumstances of radical ignorance proposed by the thought experiment? If we know what someone is saying or doing, we can identify the truth or value at which they are directing themselves. However the equivalence also permits us to work in the opposite direction.[2] If we know what truths or values are salient in the circumstances, given what we can determine from looking around and studying the lives of the beings themselves, then we can begin to trace lines leading back from these objective and publicly observable facts to the significance of the subjects' activities. Put briefly, the very possibility of interpreting human behaviour depends upon the possibility of 'retrojecting' from the true and the good as we conceive them, to the beliefs and motivations of others. This is, of course, a transcendental deduction of common epistemic and moral values.

It might now be objected that this argument does not establish the *actuality* of truth and goodness but only the presupposition of the ideas of them. To this there are two lines of replies, the first of which comes in two versions. Version one is a familiar Kantian idea, re-expressed in a linguistic key by Habermas; namely, that no more is required, and no more is available to be had, than transcendentally deduced inter-subjectivity. Version two is inspired by pragmatism and is a case of what Hilary Putnam has termed an 'indispensability argument' (Putnam 1994). The latter may be characterised as follows (this is not Putnam's formulation): if x is indispensable to y and y is basic and pervasive within our thought or practice, then x cannot be criticised from any rationally superior vantage point.

The second line of reply draws upon pre-modern philosophy, in particular that of antiquity and the middle ages, and is more ambitious in its aim of establishing objectivity. Consider again the task of interpretation. I want to know what someone is doing or what they are saying. Mindful of the fact that much action and utterance is marginal to a subject's guiding concerns, it remains the case that for anything that has the life of a rational animal there is much serious business to be done and there are many truths to be discovered and reported. Interpretation by projection from truth to meaning and from value to intention requires that one identify unambiguously-salient features of the present circumstances with which the subject is evidently involved. That is to say it involves observation and evaluation of what present themselves as *facts* and cannot even be conceived as anything other than *facts*. Of course, on occasion one may be mistaken, but what is being relied upon is one's own very best estimate of reality and its impact upon the existence of another animal. At this level, short of total skepticism of a sort that threatens any notion of an objective world, there is no proper sense to be made of the idea that for all one really knows there is in actuality no such thing as true judgement and correct evaluation. This line of reply should remind us of the kind of naturalism in ethics introduced earlier, which relates questions of virtue to the common facts of human nature. On this account, questions of value and conduct are to be referred back, at the fundamental level, to philosophical anthropology.

## Conclusion

As we saw earlier, MacIntyre's inclination has been to reject appeals to nature conceived as something metaphysical antecedent to contingencies of time and circumstance, and to look instead to social history as a foundation for value. This proposed alternative would seem curiously *ad hoc* were it not that MacIntyre has continued to see history in quasi-philosophical terms, even though he has long ago abandoned the Marxism he once preached. The idea, then, is that culturally-situated narrative history can serve in place of a philosophical anthropology in what remains a broadly Aristotelian account of the foundations of virtue.

MacIntyre's rejection of a deeper grounding in universal nature is based on his claim that Aristotle's teleology presupposes a metaphysical biology which we 'must reject' (MacIntyre 1981: 152). It is not clear to me why he thinks this. If the suggestion is that some of the things Aristotle believed about biology, concerning human reproduction for example are false, that is hardly likely to provide grounds for rejecting a role for biology as such. On the other hand if the idea is that what is wrong is the appeal to functions and purposes, as against causal mechanisms, then I contest the reductionism implicit in this, and express surprise that it should be subscribed to MacIntyre. We come closer to his reason, I think, when he writes of 'deep conflicts' in our cultural history over what human well-being (and hence human nature) consists in. But again there is an ambiguity: the presence of disagreement does not imply the absence of objective fact, so unless he is saying that there are no facts of human nature, we remain in a position that allows for the possibility of appealing to them.

If MacIntyre's rejection of universal human anthropology has not been shown to be warranted, he is surely right to emphasize the importance of second nature: what time, place and community add to what God or evolution have established. Our movement towards self-realization is in no small part as beings nurtured and formed by the communities of our birth, adoption, education or career. What this suggests, though, is not that Aristotelian anthropology is redundant, but only that it must needs be more historical than Aristotle himself might have supposed. And as MacIntyre himself has come to emphasise, there need be no opposition between *historicism* understood as the claim that reason has a variety of starting points, and *realism* conceived as the view that truth, which is the goal of enquiry, is something transcendent of local perspectives, yet attainable through situated dialectics.[3]

Drawing the various threads together, I want to suggest that the epistemology and metaphysics of virtue are less problematic than has been suggested by some twentieth-century critics. Of course, the discernment of deep facts has never been an easy business, but claims to moral knowledge are not disqualified on the grounds that there is contest or indifference. We simply have to take stock of what is going on and then ask: does this advance human interest? That is, is this an intelligible goal of intentional activity? And if so, does its intelligibility satisfy the conditions supplied by our considered opinion of what is good? The method of retrojective interpretation involves continuous probing of public terrain until we find secure common ground upon which to build an account of the meaning and point of the behaviour of others and ourselves. The more radical the cultural differences, the harder we need to press to reach through them to the basic, but extensive, facts of the lives of rational animals.

Any attempt to take seriously the idea that the content and methods of moral education should answer to norms beyond those of prudence and instrumental efficiency is going to encounter intellectual and human difficulties.

The former flow from the philosophical issues discussed here. The latter include the fact that any serious thought about how we ought to live must be accompanied by a preparedness to find that one's own activities and those of colleagues, friends, fellow community members, and so on may be indefensible. Virtue is not easily cultivated or maintained, but it is all the more necessary for precisely that reason.

## Notes

1 See Wright 1995: 215: 'I should emphasise, lest there be any misunderstanding, that the pluralism I am canvassing would not involve the idea that 'true' is ambiguous'. Prior to that he writes, 'Depending on the type of statement with which we are concerned, the constitution of truth may sometimes reside in factors congenial to an intuitive realism, sometimes not'.

2 Here I am applying an insight of David Wiggins (Wiggins 1980b; also Wiggins 1987). The original inspiration is Davidson himself: see 'Radical Interpretation' (Davidson 1984).

3 I discuss the character and coherence of MacIntyre's account of the structure of rational enquiry in Haldane 1994.

## References

Anscombe, G. E. M. (1981) [1958] 'Modern moral philosophy', in G. E. M. Anscombe, *Ethics, Religion and Politics*, Oxford: Blackwell (originally published in (1958) *Philosophy* 33).

Anscombe, G. E. M. and Geach, P. T. (1973) *Three Philosophers*, Oxford: Blackwell.

Aquinas (1969) *Summa Theological vol.23: Virtue*, trans W. D. Hughes, London: Blackfriars/Eyre and Spotiswoode.

Carr, D. (1991) *Educating the Virtues: An essay on the philosophical psychology of moral development and education*, London: Routledge.

Davidson, D. (1984) *Inquiries into Truth and Interpretation*, Oxford: Clarendon Press (Section 1).

Dennett, D. (ed.) (1982) *The Philosophical Lexicon*, Newark, Del.: American Philosophical Association.

Geach, P. (1972) 'Assertion', in P. Geach, *Logic Matters*, Oxford: Blackwell.

—— (1977) *The Virtues*, Cambridge: Cambridge University Press.

Habermas, J. (1989) *Moral Consciousness and Communicative Action*, Cambridge Mass.: MIT Press.

Haldane, J. (1994) 'MacIntyre's Thomist revival: What next?', in J. Horton and S. Mendus (eds) *After MacIntyre: Critical perspectives on the work of Alisdair MacIntyre*, Cambridge: Polity Press.

Horton, P. and Mendus, S. (eds) (1994) *After MacIntyre: Critical perspectives on the work of Alasdair MacIntyre*, Cambridge: Polity Press.

Lichtenberg, G. (1990) in R. J. Hollingdale trans. *Aphorisms*, London: Penguin.

McDowell, J. (1998) [1979] 'Virtue and reason', in J. McDowell, *Mind, Value and Reality, Cambridge*, Mass.: Harvard University Press (originally published in (1979) *The Monist* 62).

MacIntyre, A. (1981) *After Virtue*, London: Duckworth.

—— (1988) *Whose Justice? Which Rationality?* London: Duckworth.

—— (1990a) *Three Rival Versions of Moral Enquiry: Encyclopedia, genealogy and tradition*, London: Duckworth.

—— (1990b) 'The privatisation of good', *Review of Politics* 42.

—— (1994) 'Moral relativism, truth and moral justification', in L. Gormally (ed.) *Moral Truth and Moral Tradition: Essays in honour of P. Geach and E. Anscombe*, Dublin: Four Courts Press.

McMylor, P. (1994) *Alasdair MacIntyre: Critic of modernity*, London: Routledge.

Putnam, H. (1994) 'Pragmatism and moral objectivity', in J. Conant (ed.) *Words and Life*, Cambridge, MA: Harvard University Press.

Quine, W. V. (1960) *Word and Object*, Cambridge Mass.: MIT Press.

Wiggins, D. (1980a) 'What would be a substantial theory of truth?', in Z. van Straaten (ed.) *Philosophical Subjects*, Oxford: Oxford University Press.

—— (1980b) 'Truth and interpretation', in Leinfellner et al. (eds) *Language, Philosophy and Logic*, Vienna: Hölder-Pichler-Tempsky.

—— (1987) 'Truth, and truth as predicated of moral judgements', in D. Wiggins, *Needs, Values, Truth*, Oxford: Blackwell.

Wright, C. (1992) *Truth and Objectivity*, Cambridge, Mass. Harvard University Press.

—— (1995) 'Truth in ethics', *Ratio* 8.

# 12

# JUSTICE, CARE AND OTHER VIRTUES

## A critique of Kohlberg's theory of moral development

*Paul Crittenden*

## Sources and influences

Lawrence Kohlberg considered that the ethical and educational ideas in his theory of moral development could be seen as a modern statement of the Socratic view of these matters. In forging this alliance he was particularly critical of what he called Aristotle's 'bag of virtues' view with its insistence on the role of habit, or 'learning by doing', in the development of moral virtue. More immediately, the account of stages of moral development which Kohlberg began to devise in the early 1960s (Kohlberg 1981: 29–48) took its inspiration from Piaget's general theory of cognitive development and, more specifically his account of moral thinking among children (Piaget 1932). Kohlberg also followed Piaget in espousing an essentially Kantian conception of morality in terms of universal ethical principles of justice rationally grasped by the autonomous individual. The idea that Kantian ethics could subsume Platonist, or more specifically Socratic, ethics was a later inspiration. Among other sources, Kohlberg was much influenced by John Dewey's theory (Dewey 1908) of the educational growth of the child through invariant, ordered sequential stages into adulthood; but he was not convinced by Dewey's ethical naturalism and challenged his support for an Aristotelian-type view of habit formation.

Kohlberg's attitude to Aristotelian ethics was shaped importantly by his familiarity with well-known studies in psychology concerned with moral education and the virtues. The classic example of such work was the study by Hartshorne and May (1928–1930) in which school-aged children were tested for virtues such as honesty and self-control in situations offering opportunities for telling lies, cheating and stealing. The study indicated that positive correlation between virtue or character education, and actual practice of the virtues, was quite low; and the authors were drawn to conclude that, while we can identify honest and dishonest acts, we are not entitled to speak of honest or dishonest people. Later studies, notably by Havinghurst and Taba (1949) on the basis of an enlarged list of virtues, appeared to tell a similar story.

In Kohlberg's eyes, moral education in the virtues, and the view of morality it embodied, was thus discredited. He would describe it as the 'bag of virtues' view or the 'Boy Scout' approach ('be honest, loyal, brave . . . '). That the 'Boy Scout' approach never the less continued to dominate American moral education could be attributed in part to the influence of Dewey; but its most direct affinities, Kohlberg considered, were with the views of Aristotle (Kohlberg 1981: 31). In a word, a certain conception of Aristotelian ethics and its traces in American educational practice constituted the problem for which the young Kohlberg sought a solution.

Kohlberg's response was to bring forward an account of moral development based on the identification of graded forms of moral reasoning specifically in relation to questions of justice. Given the idea that reasoning in the moral sphere could be correlated with more general patterns of cognitive development, the proposal carried the prospect of an account of moral development which could be tested empirically and which would be universal. In these scientific and open terms, the new approach would provide the basis for an acceptable and effective programme of moral education, especially in the enlightened liberal state where questions of justice could be taken to be paramount. At the same time, the focus on moral reasoning could draw support from the towering figures of Kant and Socrates as marking out, in their ethical thinking, the highest level or end-point of moral development for human beings generally. In this company, furthermore, it could be shown that an Aristotelian-type approach, based on the attempt to inculcate moral virtues, belongs to a lower, more immature stage of moral awareness. With all this far-reaching promise, the Kohlbergian research program in moral psychology emerged rapidly into prominence in the 1960s and was established as the dominant theory in the field by the early 1970s.

## The six stages of moral development

Kohlberg's central thesis is that there are six stages of moral development, marked by distinct and developing ways of thinking about questions of right and wrong. The stages are grouped in pairs in three levels of social awareness, preconventional, conventional and postconventional, as follows:

### Level A. Preconventional Level
*Stage 1. The Stage of Punishment and Obedience*
Right is literal obedience to rules and authority, avoiding punishment, and not doing physical harm . . .

   The reasons for doing right are avoidance of punishment and the superior power of authorities.

*Stage 2. The Stage of Individual Instrumental Purpose and Exchange*
Right is serving one's own or other's needs and making fair deals in terms of concrete exchange . . .

The reason for doing right is to serve one's own needs or interests in a world where one must recognise that other people have their interests, too.

### Level B. Conventional Level
*Stage 3. The Stage of Mutual Interpersonal Expectations, Relationships and Conformity*
The right is playing a good (nice) role, being concerned about the other people and their feelings, keeping loyalty and trust with partners, and being motivated to follow rules and expectations . . .

Reasons for doing right are needing to be good in one's own eyes and those of others, caring for others . . . (Golden Rule).
*Stage 4. The Stage of Social System and Conscience Maintenance*
The right is doing one's duty in society, upholding the social order, and maintaining the welfare of society or the group . . .

The reasons for doing right are to keep the institution going as a whole, self-respect or conscience as meeting one's defined obligations . . .

### Level C. Postconventional and Principled Level
*Stage 5. The Stage of Prior Rights and Social Contract or Utility*
The right is upholding the basic rights, values and legal contracts of a society, even when they conflict with the concrete rules and laws of the group . . .

Reasons for doing right are, in general, feeling obligated to obey the law because one has made a social contract to make and abide by laws for the good of all and to protect their own rights and the rights of others  One is concerned that laws and duties be based on rational calculation or overall utility . . .
*Stage 6. The Stage of Universal Ethical Principles*
This stage assumes guidance by universal ethical principles that all humanity should follow . . . Principles are universal principles of justice: the equality of human rights and respect for the dignity of human beings as individuals . . .

The reason for doing right is that, as a rational person, one has seen the validity of principles and has become committed to them.
(Kohlberg 1981: 409–12)

The identification of stages was made in conjunction with cross-sectional and, in time, longitudinal studies of the ways in which children and adolescents – all male subjects – responded to a series of hypothetical dilemmas involving conflicts of rights.[1] While the specification of the stages (and the scoring system) underwent modifications over the years, the substance of Kohlberg's major claims remained unchanged.

The stages are presented as distinct, qualitatively different ways of thinking about the same problems. Each stage is a 'structured whole' which marks out a consistent pattern of thinking, which is held distinguishable from the actual content of responses. The stages are hierarchical integrations, forming an invariant sequence from less to more integrated structures of increasing differentiation, generality and adequacy. The invariant sequence, which holds universally, is not affected substantially by epoch or culture, or by class or gender difference. Movement through the stages occurs on the model of an interaction between the individual and external structures, especially the social environment. Finally, the six stages form a complete set, although to cope with anomalous data Kohlberg later introduced sub-stages at the conventional level and a transitional Stage $4^{1}/_{2}$ between the conventional and postconventional levels, and he speculated about a 'seventh stage' of higher morality incorporating, but going beyond, justice.

The empirical studies, involving a complex scoring system, carried the promise of showing how subjects, from early childhood through to maturity, are distributed across the six stages. The resultant pattern would be explained in turn by the general data relating to cognitive development, associated importantly with age, level of experience, and the social environment (for example, the degree of opportunity for open discussion of moral issues and for role-playing). In general, children up to around ten were found to be at Stage 1 or 2; adolescents were normally assigned to Stage 3 or 4; from the beginning, Stages 5 and 6 were taken to define an adult level of attainment.

How did Kohlberg arrive at his account of levels and stages of moral development? One commentator has supposed that the stage descriptions were derived from (empirical) data (Puka 1982). This is completely implausible, certainly for Stages 5 and 6. Kohlberg himself made clear that his psychological theory 'grew out of . . . Kant's formal theory in moral philosophy and Piaget's formal theory in psychology' (Kohlberg 1981: 192) and that, from the start, the psychological inquiry was guided by (Kantian) epistemological and ethical principles (ibid: 85). Specifically, Kohlberg drew on Kantian ideas on lines which were being developed contemporaneously by John Rawls (Rawls 1963; 1971). The psychological theory, grounded on the philosophical claim that the stages become progressively more adequate in moral terms, supposed that individuals would advance as far as their understanding would take them. But, as Kohlberg acknowledged, the philosophical claim would be put in question if the facts of moral advance did not fit with its psychological implications (Kohlberg 1981: 194). Piaget held that, in structural contexts, the pyramid of knowledge does not so much rest on foundations as hang by its vertex, the ideal point towards which it moves (Piaget 1968: 341). The idea of universal ethical principles focused on justice played this critical role in driving Kohlberg's research program.

## Kohlberg's Kantian ethics

The fundamental ethical assumption is that 'the core of morality and moral development is deontological, that it is a matter of rights and duties as prescriptions' (Levine, Kohlberg and Hewer 1985: 95). Morality can be defined, according to this view, in terms of the formal character of moral judgements independently of content; thus the primary marks of moral judgement are impersonality, impartiality, universalisability and preemptiveness; and such properties are to be looked for in the reasoning on which moral judgement properly rests. More specifically, the core of mature deontological morality is indicated fundamentally in principles of justice. The assumption of the primacy of justice is linked with Kohlberg's conviction that morality is primarily concerned with the resolution of conflicts between competing claims of individuals or groups:

> *Moral* judgments or principles have the central function of resolving interpersonal or social conflicts; that is, conflicts of claims or rights. Such judgments also define duties relative to these rights. Thus moral judgments and principles imply a notion of equilibrium, balancing, or reversibility of claims.
>
> (Levine, Kohlberg and Hewer 1985: 98)

Following Rawls, Kohlberg was satisfied that if one imagines a society ordered by a social contract among equals (as in Stage 5), one could derive principles of justice or equal rights (Stage 6 morality) as the only foundation to which rational individuals would consent in the hypothetical original position from which the contract is determined. Thus, in achieving moral maturity, the individual – of whatever time and place – is seen as recapitulating the two main theories of modern ethical liberalism, utilitarian and Kantian ethics respectively. In addition, the emphasis on justice and moral reasoning, as Kohlberg came to argue, could also seek support from the more ancient source of Socratic ethics.

## Socrates, virtue, and the primacy of justice

Kohlberg's summary of the Socratic view involves three principal claims: one, that virtue is one, not many, and that it has the same ideal universal form, the name of which is justice; two, that virtue is knowledge of the good (the good being justice); and three, that one who knows the good chooses it (Kohlberg 1981: 30). In taking up loosely recognizable Socratic theses, Kohlberg secures his case for the primacy of justice by assuming what was to be established. While Socrates argued that virtue is knowledge of the good, he did not hold that virtue and the good, of which it is knowledge, bears the name justice.

On the evidence of Plato's early dialogues, Socrates recognised a number of virtues, chiefly courage, temperance, justice and wisdom. Thinking of virtue on the lines of a craft and essentially as a form of knowledge (which ensures virtuous action), Socrates was led to conclude that the virtues are all one, that is, knowledge of good and evil. But for Socrates, what is true of justice in this respect is no less true of courage or temperance, for example, even if justice is sometimes accorded a general or inclusive sense (as Aristotle also recognised). Nor does the idea of virtue as knowledge of the good dispense with the need for the virtues named by courage, self-control, justice and so on. More generally, the claims that virtue is constituted essentially by knowledge and that there is just one virtue, knowledge of the good, are not easily defensible (as Plato's later dialogues indicate). But even if the Socratic claims could be defended, they do not lend support to the Kohlbergian assumption that all moral issues are fundamentally matters of justice, or to his remarkable claim that justice is mainly about settling conflicts and that '*most social situations are not moral, because there is no conflict between the role-taking expectations of one person and another*' (Kohlberg 1971a: 192: emphasis added).

In response to mounting criticism, Kohlberg eventually explained that, given the core importance of justice, he chose reasoning in this domain as 'the cognitive factor most amenable to structural developmental stage analysis' (Levine, Kohlberg and Hewer 1985: 92); and he went on to suggest that his theory might be seen, even retrospectively, as a rational reconstruction of the ontogenesis of justice reasoning. In response to Carol Gilligan's work in particular, consideration was given to ways of thinking about justice in relation to 'issues of care and response in real life dilemmas as well as . . . a concern about the issue of how such dilemmas are resolved in practice' (Levine, Kohlberg and Hewer 1985: 96). But while he was led to concede that justice is not the whole of morality, the acknowledgement was made without any revision of the way in which the focus on principles of justice at Stage 6 shapes the specification of each of the stages from beginning to end.

Kohlberg's invocation of Socrates was linked, as noted earlier, with the rejection of what he called Aristotle's 'bag of virtues' view. The summary objection to Aristotle is that, having marked off moral from intellectual virtues, he supposes that moral virtue is acquired, not by teaching, but by habit (Kohlberg 1981: 31). This objection, made without qualification, treats the Aristotelian emphasis on 'learning by doing' as a form of mindless habituation effected by indoctrination. Two brief comments are appropriate. First, Kohlberg overlooks the considerable role which Aristotle attributes to intellectual aspects of moral development. This is apparent in his discussion of choice in virtuous action, for example, and in his account of practical wisdom, especially the insistence that the acquisition of moral virtue involves practice in assessing situations, getting a sense of what is appropriate in concrete circumstances in the light of general considerations, and developing an overall understanding of how one should live. Second, Aristotle is on strong ground in supposing that openness to moral argument, as one grows up, rests importantly on having had a good affective formation in one's early childhood, especially in relationships of love and trust with parents and others. The Kohlbergian focus on moral reasoning fails to take account of, or simply assumes, the broader context of human relationships in which such argument can have an effective place.

More generally, Kohlberg takes the view that virtues are relative to particular conventional cultural standards; that this approach is restricted, therefore, to the conventional level of moral development, Stage 3 or 4; that what counts as a virtue is highly variable; that any attempt to settle on a set of virtues will be largely arbitrary (hence the dismissive phrase 'bag of virtues'); and that the teaching of virtue in this context will be a form of indoctrination. There is also the argument, drawn from psychological research, that education in the virtues does not work. The overall conclusion to which Kohlberg is drawn is that there are no such things as virtues or vices at all. There are no stable personality traits, or dispositions, of the relevant kind, but rather, 'virtues and vices are labels by which people award praise and blame to others' (Kohlberg 1981: 34).

The concerns which Kohlberg expresses are not unimportant, as the history of ethics bears witness; on the other hand, the conclusion is drawn too easily and is, in any case, inconsistent with his basic thesis that there is one genuine virtue, namely justice. Kohlberg's defence is that justice is indeed a character trait, but not in the usual sense; not in the manner of honesty or self-control, for example, because it involves universal principles. Having regard for associations between virtues, the question is whether one could say of Socrates that he was a just man, but beg to leave open the question whether he was wise in practical concerns, and an honest, truthful, temperate, or courageous person.

## Testing the theory at the higher stages

The cognitive-developmental theory looks to ethical and epistemological principles as fundamental to its justification. What is distinctive of the account as a whole, in Kohlberg's own terms, lies in the co-ordination of the right philosophical and psychological theories and the facts of development (Kohlberg 1981: 85). Each body of theory raises its own set of questions. In general, there is the question whether Kantian ethical theory does provide an adequate account of moral maturity; again, there is the the question whether Piagetian cognitive-developmental stages are generally valid and, if so, whether the proposed moral stages meet the criteria. Then there is the question of the facts of moral advance, at least to the extent that facts of this kind can be identified through the assessment of responses to hypothetical dilemmas relating to conflicts about claims and rights.

In the first years of the research programme, with the focus on children and adolescent and their development into early adulthood, the post-conventional level was bound to have been no more than a projection or postulate. In the early 1970s Kohlberg confidently proclaimed, on the basis of some limited cross-cultural studies, that the same basic ways of moral valuing are found in every culture and develop in the same order, providing evidence of the general recognition of a universal set of moral principles of the Stage 6 kind (Kohlberg 1981: 23-7). In the event, the expectation of empirical confirmation of progression to the higher stages was not fulfilled. What the studies eventually indicated was that very few people, even within the educated circles of Western culture, could consistently be assigned to the post-conventional or principled level. It appeared that, even in the most favourable conditions, no more than 2 to 4 per cent of subjects met the Stage 6 profile; and this figure plummeted further under the revised scoring system.

In an updated formulation of the theory in 1983, Kohlberg and associates proposed that Stage 6 be withdrawn from the sequence of stages and that it be designated rather as a 'theoretical construct in the realm of philosophical speculation', to be used as an interpretative principle in relation to the other stages (Levine, Kohlberg and Hewer 1985: 97). There was also an acknowledgement in this source that the philosophical assumptions which guided the programme were controversial; but it was supposed that their continued use could be justified on the grounds that they had led to empirical findings (presumably in relation to earlier stages). This appeal to empirical fruitfulness appears deeply problematic. The ethical and meta-ethical assumptions shape findings at the earlier levels, most directly by setting a narrow focus for moral development; on the other hand, what is narrated about moral outlooks at the preconventional or conventional levels is compatible with quite different meta-ethical assumptions.

With the removal of Stage 6 from the sequence, Kohlberg nevertheless continued to report into the mid-1980s that studies confirmed his thesis of a culturally universal invariant sequence, now specified as extending over Stages 1 to 5 (Kohlberg, Levine and Hewer 1983: 112–13). In fact, the evidence for the existence of Stage 5 as a consistent pattern of reasoning in any culture was also shown to be quite low (Vine 1985). No doubt, the idea that moral judgements are to be linked with an assessment of general benefit is not uncommon. But the terms of Stage 5, with a focus on basic rights and legal contracts, build in the perspective of 'a rational individual aware of values and rights prior to social attachments and contracts', and suppose that one is motivated to do what is right (even in regard to family and friends) out of a feeling of obligation arising from the idea of having made a social contract. A framework of this kind has a particular place in modern Western political theory, where it has also long been subject to serious criticism. Almost certainly, Kohlberg was influenced in the choice of Stage 5 by Rawls' imaginative re-invention of a social contract theory in the 1960s. But the idea that we have here the universal form of moral reasoning, which will in turn lead to Stage 6 principles, strains credulity.

Given the theoretical provenance of the idea of social contract in liberal thought and the lack of empirical evidence for this form of reasoning in moral psychology, it seems reasonable to suppose that Stage 5, like Stage 6, can also be designated as a theoretical construct in the realm of philosophical specula-tion. At this point, Kohlberg's argument that moral education should be based on the developmental stages is seriously weakened, for there is no longer any definite point towards which the development proceeds. The higher stages in their specific forms are at best possible ideals, to be considered along with other ideas of moral maturity. More directly, the theory of development cannot proceed as if nothing were changed at the lower levels, since the earlier stages have themselves been shaped and ordered in terms of the postulated point of development and the associated conception of moral maturity.

## Questions about Stages 1–4

The most obvious downward influence of the higher stage mentality lies in the narrow conception of moral development across the theory as a whole. The supposition is that moral development is indicated uniformly at the different levels by the way in which subjects respond to hypothetical dilemmas about conflicting rights and claims. Apart from the significant presumptions involved in assessing moral outlooks on this basis, the approach means that significant areas of children's behaviour fall outside the privileged perspective: for example, how they express and respond to affection, learn about trust, kind-ness and friendship, show concern and generosity, share things, put up with illness, and so on. Such considerations are already relevant to the first stages of development. Clearly, one can take account of them only by attending to a wider range of moral situations than are encompassed by conflicts about claims or defined by punishment, obedience and the making of deals.

Again, the higher level mentality bears on the order in which stages are ranked in terms of moral adequacy. Thus, Stage 4 is counted as morally more adequate than Stage 3 since it is taken to involve a more general level of think-ing, as manifested in a person's adopting a general societal standpoint in contrast to the 'personal concordance morality' of Stage 3. Allowing that a higher stage is treated as subsuming a lower stage, this ranking never the less begs the question in supposing that moral reasoning is better fundamentally for being more general. The possibility is that, with generality, various specific factors which are important in moral judgement are overlooked. This is espe-cially so as generality in Stage 4 is made to rest on a limited conception of the social order in terms of laws and duties; and the different form of generality involved in the dispositions characteristic of the caring person allocated to Stage 3 are overlooked.

Reasoning at a more general level would be less morally adequate if, for example, it were less sensitive to particular situations and circumstances, less flexible in recognizing and responding to difference, and more inclined to rely on general rules or the invocation of an impersonal principle. Precisely these issues are relevant if one compares Kohlberg's account of adequacy in moral reasoning with an Aristotelian-type account of practical wisdom. Specifically, the question of particularity and generality was to come to the fore in Gilligan's critique of Kohlberg's stages (Gilligan 1982) in the context of an ethic of care. The adoption of a narrow focus, in this case the privileging of generality in the public sphere, may be reflected in stereotypical thinking. There is perhaps an indication of this in an early study in which there is reference to Stage 3 as 'a functional morality for housewives and mothers', but not for professionals and businessmen (Kohlberg and Kramer 1969).

The problems which affect the ranking of Stages 3 and 4 raise the question whether the two stages can be clearly distinguished in the way the theory supposes; and doubt is then cast on the claims embodied in the theory as a whole (especially the postulate of holistic structures arranged in an invariant sequence). In this case, one could hypothesize that Stage 4 was introduced into the theory specifically as marking a step to the higher stages. The collapse of a clear division between Stages 3 and 4 is further indicated by the fact that, under the test data, most adults fit into a mixed pattern of the two. In short, the whole conception of the conventional level of moral development would need to be re-thought around an enlarged and more adequate conception of moral maturity.

## The social perspective

The need to go beyond the conventional level of ethics, as Kohlberg saw it, arises from the inherent limitations of its thinking. The suppositions are, one, that moral thinking at this level fails to provide a guide to the treatment of people outside the social order which defines its perspective; and two, it fails to provide a rational basis for social change in terms of new laws or norms. Kohlberg is thus led to postulate the need for a post-conventional level of ethical thinking which, in the curious logic of the situation, must be derived from a source outside the social order. He thus turns to an essentially individualistic and ahistorical framework in which the individual is thought of as arriving at guiding principles in advance of entering into social relations – 'the prior-to-society perspective – that of a rational individual aware of values and rights prior to social attachments and contracts' (Kohlberg 1981: 412); and the claim is made that, at this level, the individual 'clearly has a perspective necessary for rationally creating laws *ex nihilo*' (Kohlberg 1971a: 200).

Allowing that the real world falls far short of the ideal, the limitations of working from within a social perspective are not necessarily as problematic as Kohlberg supposes. The question is whether, for human beings, there is a genuine alternative even if self-sufficiency is thought of as an important dimension of moral maturity. In any case, there is no inherent reason why social conventions may not include definite guidance for the fair and proper treatment of outsiders, or embody appropriate provisions, formal or informal, for social change. It is true that socio-moral conventions may be maintained in a largely uncritical way, simply 'to keep the social order going' as the description of Stage 4 subjects puts it. But equally, the social perspective offers scope for thinking critically about moral goodness and for seeking to develop the guiding principles, the attitudes of mind and dispositions of character which would make its achievement possible. There are various long-established moral traditions which work fundamentally within a framework of this kind. It follows that the demand for a perspective from which laws might rationally be created *ex nihilo* or from which fair social arrangements could be derived is not well-founded.

The leap outside the social order also affects the idea of universal ethical principles which Kohlberg envisages as characteristic of Stage 6. What is presented is a notion of justice conceived as a universal principle rationally grasped by the autonomous individual, 'a rule of choosing that we want all people to adopt always in all situations' (Kohlberg 1981: 39). Kohlberg is concerned to insist that the ethical principle of justice, upholding the equality of human rights and respect for the dignity of human beings as individuals, is not to be treated as if it were a set of rules. This is reasonable. But the question is whether the universal principle can be given substantive moral expression in the conditions of human life. The difficulty is one of moving from a formal principle – such as the categorical imperative – to substantive moral views of any kind without proceeding in a question-begging way. Thus, Kant was able to arrive at his substantive moral position, concerning the virtues for example, only by drawing on an enlarged conception of rationality as the need arose. In taking the high ground of a moral point of view from which social arrangements derive, the Kohlbergian Stage 6 subject is cut off in effect from the world of social and moral relations.

This consequence is at odds with the general emphasis which Kohlberg places on social interaction and with the overall importance which the theory attaches to fair and equitable social arrangements. But even at its best, the approach is built on a limited conception of social and moral relationships, focused on issues of conflict resolution typically between individuals. This is a world of impersonal principles and fundamental rights and duties, in which caring about the people one loves might appear problematic or to lie outside the moral domain altogether. It might also be a world which reflects a predominantly male point of view. These criticisms of Kohlberg's theory were given particular prominence in Carol Gilligan's book *In a Different Voice* (1982) in the name of an ethic of care.

## Care and other virtues

It is not possible in a short discussion to do justice to Gilligan's original argument, much less to her later work or the extensive debate which has surrounded her ideas in the past fifteen years.[2] Even so, a schematic account of the main themes of the different voice is an essential element in considering the last period of Kohlberg's research programme.

The primary focus of Gilligan's critique is Kohlberg's conception of justice at the post-conventional level and its role in generating a specific line of development in which the stages mark the individual's quest for identity and autonomy through separation from others. The argument is that what is offered in these terms as universally true relates only to a psychology and an understanding of morality which is characteristically male. From this premise, Gilligan's fundamental response is that the Kohlberg story needs to be complemented by a different account, a conception of morality in which the primary focus is on a reflective care for others. This different ideal generates its own line of development in which a simplified set of stages marks the individual's quest for a sense of integrity and self-worth through caring attachment to others (the 'post-conventional' level in the alternative line). Gilligan holds that the different voice she describes 'is characterized not by gender but theme' (Gilligan 1982: 2); but the story of care is told entirely through women's voices in a framework in which it appears as a complement to Kohlberg's story of justice identified as a male way of thinking.

In espousing a twin-paths account of development (while looking towards their integration), Gilligan effectively endorses the Kohlberg stages as valid for males. Her contribution at this point is to place the cognitive-developmental emphasis within a psychoanalytic theory in which male identity is typically effected through separation and independence, while female identity is developed through attachment and intimacy. Given this basis, the primary contrast between the different ethical ideals can be stated succinctly. The central insight of the ethic of care is that self and other are interdependent, while the ethic of justice relates to a fragmented world of self-contained individuals. Care is associated with relational networks and webs, justice with hierarchical order and authority. Care is concerned with mending relationships in situations of conflict, justice with determining rights and duties. In these terms, the ethical superiority of care over justice appears obvious.

Given this argument, Gilligan's endorsement of Kohlberg in relation to male moral development remains puzzling. For the problems which affect his conception of justice as an ethical ideal draw in the stages as a whole and show that the account does not provide an adequate measure of moral development for anyone. In other words, the thesis that the two ethics are complementary is questionable. It might still be feasible to say that care and justice stand for two different modes of ethical thought, one more typical of women, the other of men. But this does not provide support for the conclusion that Kohlberg's theory accounts for male moral development. There is the original flaw in the ethical conception which structures the stages; additionally, there is evidence that hardly anyone, male or female, can be allocated to Stages 5 or 6 or consistently even to Stage 4. (This is consistent with recognizing that the account nonetheless involves a gender bias.)

The complementarity thesis is also linked with an artificial separation between the leading ideas of care and justice and the dubious assumption that an adequate ethics could be expressed in terms of a single value. Care for others, for family and friends for example, needs to include a concern for justice in their regard and more generally for justice in the community at large, if only because injustice threatens the concerns of care. Justice therefore is integral to an ethic of care. Part of the problem is that Gilligan did not work out in any detail the presuppositions and implications of an ethic of care in relation to other values. In an approach which rightly emphasizes the moral significance of particular associations (the love of family and friends, for example), there is the danger of failing to recognize the importance of generality in attending to the particular. In addition to justice, care and the related ideas of nurturance and responsibility towards others embrace such things as practical wisdom, goodwill, sensitivity to others' needs, compassion and friendship as values of general importance in human life; and care could hardly be exercized over any length of time without the need for courage.

Again, there are certain forms of behaviour and ways of life which are incompatible, in a clear and indefeasible sense, with care, for example, behaviour exhibiting ill will, hatred, cruelty, self-indulgence. Equally, there are general forms of behaviour and ways of life which are characteristic of care, such as expressions of goodwill, love, kindness, sensitivity, courage, self-control. Care is typically related to particular connections; but it properly calls for a background of general values and commitments. What is needed, then, in relation to mature moral awareness is an approach, developed through experience, which attends with care to the concrete and the particular under the guidance of general considerations. (A primary account on these lines is to be found, of course, in Aristotle's discussion of practical wisdom in the *Nicomachean Ethics*, Book VI).

An ethic of care enlarged on these general lines could be a plausible candidate for the integrated ethics which Gilligan envisages, but leaves unexamined in this source. In any case, it would constitute a common ideal of moral maturity (though its realization could be manifested in many different ways among different people). I have argued elsewhere that the different moral voice which Gilligan found in women reaches back across the modern era of liberalism and the Enlightenment to revive important themes in Greek ethical thought, especially in Greek tragedy and in Aristotle (Crittenden 1990: 94-8). An emphasis on community and the importance of developing good affective relationships in early childhood, in contrast to the individualist and overly intellectualist framework which Kohlberg's theory enshrines, would be prime examples. Of course, Greek thinking was subject to serious bias in regard to women and other groups, not least in Aristotle's ethics and politics. Nevertheless, an approach which emphasizes care, justice and other virtues within the idea of community holds out the best promise for a satisfactory conception of moral maturity (and for thinking about moral development and education); and the current provenance of these ideas might now make a considerable difference.

## Notes

In writing this paper I have drawn on a fuller discussion of the topics in Crittenden (1990) c. 3; to note one other secondary source among many, there is a good discussion of the issues in Flanagan (1991).

1 For an account of the dilemmas, see Kohlberg and Turiel 1971.
2 Among sources see Blum (1988); Brown and Gilligan (1992); Gilligan, Lyons and Hanmer (1990); Hekman (1995); Kittay and Meyers (1987); Larrabee (1993).

## References

Blum, L. (1988) 'Gilligan and Kohlberg: Implications for moral theory', *Ethics* 98, 3: 472–91.

Boyd, D. (1980) 'The Rawls Connection', in B. Munsey (ed.) *Moral Development, Moral Education, and Kohlberg*, Birmingham, Alabama: Religious Education Press.

Brown, L. M. and Gilligan, C. (1992) *Meeting at the Crossroads: Women's psychology and girls' development*, Cambridge, Mass.: Harvard University Press.

Burnyeat, M. F. (1980) 'Aristotle on learning to be good', in A. O. Rorty (ed.) *Essays on Aristotle's Ethics*, Berkeley: California University Press.

Colby, A. and Kohlberg, L. (1984) *The Measurement of Moral Judgment* (2 vols.), New York: Cambridge University Press.

Crittenden, P. J. (1990) *Learning To Be Moral*, Atlantic Highlands, N.J.: Humanities Press.

Dewey, J. (1908) *Ethics*, in J. O. Boydston (ed.) *The Middle Works, 1899–1924* (vol. 5), Carbondale and Edwardsville: Southern Illinois University Press.

Flanagan, O. (1991) *Varieties of Moral Personality*, Cambridge, Mass.: Harvard University Press.

Gilligan, C. (1982) *In a Different Voice*, Cambridge, Mass.: Harvard University Press.

Gilligan, C., Lyons. N. and Hanmer, T. (eds) *Making Connections*, Cambridge, Mass.: Harvard University Press.

Hartshorne, H. and May, M. A. (1928–1930) *Studies in the Nature of Character* (3 vols.), New York: Macmillan.

Havinghurst, R. J. and Taba, H. (1949) *Adolescent Character and Personality*, New York: Wiley.

Hekman, S. J. (1995) *Moral Voices, Moral Selves*, Cambridge and Oxford: Polity Press.

Kittay, E. and Meyers, D. (1987) (eds) *Women and Moral Theory*, Totowa, N.J.: Rowman and Littlefield.

Kohlberg, L. (1969) 'Stage and sequence: The cognitive-developmental approach to socialization', in D. A. Goslin (ed.) *Handbook of Socialization: Theory and research*, Chicago: Rand McNally.

—— (1971a) 'From is to ought: How to commit the naturalistic fallacy and get away with it in the study of moral development', in T. Mischel (ed.) *Cognitive Development and Epistemology*, New York: Academic Press.

—— (1971b) 'Stages of moral development as a basis for moral education', in C. M.

Beck, B. Crittenden and E. V. Sullivan (eds) *Moral Education: Interdisciplinary approaches*, Toronto: Toronto University Press.

—— (1981) *Essays on Moral Development* (vol. I), San Francisco: Harper and Row.

—— (1985) 'A current statement on some theoretical issues', in S. Modgil and C. Modgil (eds) *Lawrence Kohlberg: Consensus and controversy*, Lewes: Falmer Press.

Kohlberg, L. and Gilligan, C. (1974) 'The adolescent as philosopher: The discovery of the self in the post-conventional world', in P. H. Mussen, J. J. Conger and J. Kagan (eds) *Basic and Contemporary Issues in Developmental Psychology*, New York: Harper and Row.

Kohlberg, L. and Kramer, R. (1969) 'Continuities and discontinuities in children and adult moral development', *Human Development* 12: 93–120.

Kohlberg, L. and Turiel, E. (1971) *Moralization research: The cognitive developmental approach*, New York: Holt, Rinehart & Winston.

Kohlberg, L., Levine, C. and Hewer, A. (1983) *Moral Stages: The current formulation of Kohlberg's theory and a response to critics*, Basel: S. Karger.

Larrabee, M. J. (1993) (ed.) *An Ethic of Care*, London: Routledge.

Levine, C., Kohlberg, L. and Hewer, A. (1985) 'The current formulation of Kohlberg's theory and a response to critics', *Human Development* 28: 94–100.

Piaget, J. (1932) *The Moral Judgment of the Child*, trans. M. Gabain, New York: The Free Press.

—— (1968) *Structuralism*, trans. C. Maschler, London: Routledge and Kegan Paul.

Puka, B. (1982) 'An interdisciplinary treatment of Kohlberg', *Ethics* 92: 468–90.

Rawls, J. (1963) 'The sense of justice', *Philosophical Review* 72, 3: 281–305.

—— (1971), *A Theory of Justice*, London: Oxford University Press.

Sorabji, R. (1980) 'Aristotle on the role of intellect in virtue', in A. O. Rorty (ed.) *Essays on Aristotle's Ethics*, Berkeley: California University Press.

Vine, I. (1985) 'Moral maturity in socio-cultural perspective: Are Kohlberg's stages universal?', in S. Modgil and C. Modgil (eds) *Lawrence Kohlberg: Consensus and controversy*, Lewes: Falmer Press.

# 13

# LIBERAL VIRTUE AND MORAL ENFEEBLEMENT

## Eamonn Callan

### I

Liberal politics is repugnant to virtue. That is a common charge nowadays. A familiar rejoinder is that liberal politics requires a distinctive family of virtues, including tolerance, moderation, and open-mindedness. By itself, the rejoinder cannot be decisive because no one denies that liberal politics depends on virtue-like dispositions of some sort. The real worry is that these are mere simulacra of virtue, disguising an essentially amoral or immoral conception of persons and society. I claim that liberal virtue is the genuine article. But the grounds for saying that it is depend on conceiving liberal morality and its educational requirements as closer to traditional conceptions than many think they are.

### II

Liberalism is widely understood as a set of political practices that it becomes reasonable to adopt once we cannot base co-operation on a common understanding of moral goodness. When social relations occur against the background of a comprehensively shared moral understanding, the reasons you and I have to be morally good secure political concord once they have enough motivational force. A close if not seamless fit holds between the first-person-singular moral perspective (e.g. I ought to do or not do A) and the first-person-plural political perspective (e.g. as members of this polity, we ought to prescribe or proscribe A). But when we no longer understand moral goodness in concordant ways, our divergent moral reasons threaten to pull us towards social discord. Liberal politics contains the threat by insisting on respect for the freedom to live according to conflicting moral beliefs.

The trouble is that the discipline of mutual respect seems to require us to reject whatever reasons we have to live in full fidelity to the convictions that shape our lives outside politics. The person who believes abortion is an abhorrent violation of the sanctity of human life but says it should be politically tolerated will seem to many more feebly, perhaps even less honestly, committed to acknowledging the evil of abortion than the person who maintains that his or her grounds for abhorrence are sufficient for public prohibition always and everywhere. The reasons we have for endorsing liberal politics appear to be reasons we can make our own only at the cost of an enfeebled acceptance of the ethical values we claim as our own.

The ideal of liberal moderation raises the problem of enfeeblement in an especially striking way. Although moderation figures in just about everyone's catalogue of virtue, its paradigmatic role is as an inhibition against excess and deficiency in the indulgence of appetite. The peculiarity of the liberal version is that it seems to operate as a constraint on moral judgement itself, and to be motivated, in part at least, by a form of moral skepticism. I argue that the relevant skepticism is not incompatible with virtue; it is rather a necessary element within any public morality that honours reasonable disagreement among people who aspire to live in mutual respect. But I also claim that we have to tell a broadly Aristotelian story about how the virtues internal to liberal morality, such as moderation, are to be elicited in human life. Liberals cannot assume that once the correct procedures of moral reasoning have been learned, virtue will somehow take care of itself or become unimportant. Moreover, they need an account of moral education that not only acknowledges the importance of processes of habituation and the moulding of emotional susceptibilities, but that can reconcile the good of the self and the rightful claims of others.

## III

Stephen Macedo's remarks on liberal moderation give us a good beginning:

> The principled moderation I am defending is a liberal virtue justified by the respect owed to our shared reasonableness and the difficulty of occupying a common moral standpoint, of exercising our common capacity for reasonableness in the same way . . . The best solution [in political controversy] may sometimes be to give something to each side. Moderation in the face of very strong competing cases offers a way of honoring not simply the best case but also the case that is very strong.
>
> (Macedo 1990: 72)

This is puzzling. The best case must be the one that supports the most morally defensible policy. Therefore, any concession to those who make a strong but inferior case must have morally undesirable consequences which would have been avoided had the best policy been implemented without compromise.

Macedo cites the abortion controversy as one in which moderation is needed. But if the best case favours a less restrictive policy than the strong but inferior case, 'giving something' to opponents of the best case must involve some

185

restrictive concessions. This means some women will not obtain an abortion, or have greater difficulty in obtaining one than they would have had if the best case alone had determined policy. Conversely, if the best case supports more restriction than the strongest rival argument, any loosening of restriction will lead to some morally unjustified abortions which would not have otherwise occurred.

So moderation, on Macedo's account, cannot be construed as sheer magnanimity toward those whose arguments are strong but ultimately unsuccessful in reasoned political debate. His moderation carries at least a grave risk of injustice toward those who are disadvantaged when we retreat from the policies that the best arguments support. The freer the rein we give to moderation in the face of moral disagreement in politics, the farther it will carry us away from what is right and good. If we want public deliberation to function in ways that are morally best, why not adopt a winner-takes-all rule in political argument? And if we retreat from that rule in the name of moderation, are we not merely hiding our moral weakness behind a bogus language of virtue?

Part of the argument against a winner-takes-all rule can be made through the following analogy. Suppose you are on a committee adjudicating an essay competition in philosophy. You decide before the committee meets that one essay is the best, but you believe another comes in a close second. When the committee does meet, a colleague argues intelligently that the essay you put in second place should really be first. You remain unconvinced, and the discussion is inconclusive. A third member of the committee is inclined to share your judgement. But she suggests that the first prize be shared because of the uncertainly that always besets very close comparative judgements about philosophical merit and the inconclusiveness of this particular dispute.

The suggestion of the third member of the committee might be taken to reflect the virtue of moderation. Why? The point surely is that there is much room for reasonable doubt about whose essay really deserves to win, and to deny this bespeaks an intransigence which is itself a lapse from reasonableness. But then the example suggests that Macedo's characterization of moderation is not quite right. Moderation is not aptly depicted as a way of honouring the case that is very strong along with the best case. If it were, its status as a virtue would be baffling because of the moral costs we incur when we move away from a winner-takes-all rule in circumstances where we really know which case 'wins' and which is only very strong. A better conception of moderation – call it 'the skeptical conception' – might see it as a way of honouring the doubts that reasonable people experience when they acknowledge the failure of reason clearly to reveal the difference between the very strong and the best case. At least this will do as an initial, rough characterization. I refine the skeptical conception a bit further in the next section.

One thing that should be emphasized straightaway is that my use of 'skeptical' here does not invoke any blanket skepticism about the right and the good. It points rather to the discriminating variety evinced when we adjust the content of our beliefs, and the degree of assurance with which we hold them, to reasonable doubts that others raise against them in a given social context. A winner-takes-all rule for political argument would be compelling if we could always identify the truly deserving 'winners' with a high degree of warranted assurance. But we very commonly cannot, and therefore moderation becomes an expression, rather than a denial, of our reasonableness.

Liberal moderation has an ever-expanding role in our civic lives, the more we find ourselves favouring political policies that seek to accommodate the diversity of reasonable views our fellow citizens advocate, rather than what each of us alone takes to be the one best view. On the skeptical conception, this requires an increasing internalization of reasonable doubts that arise about the moral judgements we are inclined to make prior to collective deliberation. The growth of moderation is thus tied to the growth of a certain kind of moral skepticism, and in this it works against putative virtues at odds with such skepticism.

Suppose I am a conservative Christian who believes that a foetus is as much a child of God as any adult, and therefore as much a person. Then I come to have strong doubts about that belief, and as a consequence, come to support a more moderate policy on the regulation of abortion than the absolute prohibition I had originally espoused. Notice that the pressure of doubt that brings about this moral change is also a powerful cultural force toward moral homogeneity. This is precisely where worries about the enfeebling effects of liberal politics become acute. Christian charity may well be compossible with a developed liberal moderation, but it will be a tamed charity, one whose differences from the kindness of the infidel are scarcely detectable because both have been moulded by the skeptical pressures of moderation to take on the same public countenance.

Part of the liberal response to this is obvious. Wherever ways of life exist that are in conflict with the requirements of some supposed virtue, the diffusion of the latter will take some toll on the former. This counts as ethical enfeeblement in a sense we could rationally deplore, only if the ways of life that are undermined in the process embody moral truth, and the dispositions whose cultivation threatens them embody error. So it is an open question whether the fading cultural presence of some established mores or ideals that liberal morality induces is good or bad. But this is a question that some philosophical critics of liberalism evade rather than answer.

Alasdair MacIntyre sometimes maintains that the liberal state is no more than a mechanism for adjudicating the claims of narrow self-interest (e.g. MacIntyre 1988: 335–8). The dispositions on which its survival depends must then be hostile to any genuinely moral construal of social relations. They might include a propensity to compromise in the face of political disagreement. But on MacIntyre's account, the propensity could be no more than the habitual cunning of those who have learned to bargain when they cannot have all they want (MacIntyre 1988: 336). His argument obscures the way in which liberal moderation is animated by reasonable doubt about the truth of one's prereflective moral judgements, doubt to which someone who cares about the moral truth must be open in deliberation with others when their arguments show that one might not, after all, have a monopoly on knowledge how human beings should live. Learning to be open to such doubt is integral to learning to care about the moral truth, and whatever enfeebling effects this may have on some ways of life is no matter for serious regret.

This point helps to dispatch much that is worrying about the problem of enfeeblement as I originally described it. That description depicted us as bringing our moral convictions to public deliberation fully formed, and then, when others cannot or will not agree, seeming to betray them for the sake of maintaining co-operation. The description dovetails nicely with one influential model of liberal politics, as a social contract among self-interested individuals for whom conditions of scarcity and mutual vulnerability make orderly co-operation necessary. But if narrow self-interest reigns in politics, the dispositions that secure its sovereignty could not be real virtues, and their inculcation would have to be demoralizing. The argument traced so far is enough to show why this is wrong. The convictions we bring to public deliberation are properly open to modification according to the moral reasons others marshall against us, and even if at the end of the day a gap remains between our considered judgement and theirs, we may be sufficiently doubtful that our own view is right, that splitting the difference between us will come to seem the best course. Moderation is the virtue we need for these circumstances.

A deeper worry cannot be dispelled so easily. Liberal moderation on the conception I have endorsed harbours skeptical tendencies. But what is to prevent the acids of skepticism from penetrating the core of the moral life? The skepticism intrinsic to moderation inclines us to compromise when immoderate zealots would insist on the unassailable correctness of one view. Why does moderation not counsel a similar flexibility when we confront predatory egoists or those who would argue for patently illiberal or anti-democratic practices? The exemplar of liberal moderation will commonly strike a skeptical posture within the liberal moral life. But he or she cannot so easily adopt that attitude about the liberal moral life without undercutting his or her own moral agency.

To cope with this, we need to see the skeptical element within liberal virtue not as a free floating hospitality to rational doubt, but as an attitude that flows from, and is closely circumscribed by, the subtantive commitments of liberal morality.

## IV

I want to identify some necessary aspects of what we could all recognize as a liberal politico-moral sensibility.[1] The point is to bring into relief commitments that *cannot* be compromised if we are to recognise the propensity to compromise in the face of reasoned public disagreement as integral to liberal virtue.

The phrase 'liberal sensibility' is more than a shorthand way of talking about a particular package of beliefs. The commitments that comprise the sensibility form an ensemble of mutually supporting perceptual, affective, and motivational dispositions. These dispositions are internally related to certain bedrock moral beliefs but are irreducible to them. The commitment to tolerance that operates within a liberal sensibility, for example, is more than a bare conviction that tolerance is a good thing. It is also, for example, a disposition to 'see' occasions for the proper exercise of tolerance that others might miss, a propensity to outrage in the face of egregious intolerance, and an inclination to act tolerantly even against the grain of countervailing desires. Furthermore, to possess the sensibility is to see its adequate expression in dealing with others as part of one's own good, and not merely an obligatory deference to their rightful claims. To show tolerance when one is tempted to do otherwise is not only to respect another's rights, it is to protect one's dignity against the stain of intolerance, and so on. This is an aspect of a liberal sensibility whose educational importance will emerge in Section VI.

For those who think that liberal virtue is authentic, a liberal sensibility is needed if our lives are to keep faith with the true moral platitudes at its core. For those who insist that liberal virtue is bogus, the same sensibility is supposedly cut adrift from any genuine moral beliefs or is tied to false moral beliefs. Yet here are three plainly moral beliefs that a liberal sensibility will comprise, and I doubt that many of liberalism's self-styled critics would really want to say that they are false.

First, those with whom we seek to co-operate politically are our equals. Each has a worth which properly commands the respect of all, regardless of the affinities or enmities that link or divide human lives in any particular society. Second, even though the design of political institutions that embody respect for equal citizens is a matter of ongoing disagreement, our differences arise within boundaries that have evolved over time, and whose acceptance has now become one criterion of a liberal sensibility. More precisely, political institutions must include some scheme of rights to protect the weak and vulnerable among us and provide security to all. Third, the idea of rights is connected to the other grand abstraction of the liberal tradition, the idea that citizens are not merely equal but free. No comprehensive vision of the good life, as specified, say, within a religious creed, should be politically enforced. Citizens have a right to pursue their own, divergent conceptions of the good within wide limits set by the rightful authority of the state.

The platitudinous ground of liberal politics is important for my purposes because liberal moderation cannot operate apart from it. Suppose someone advances a proposal that flatly contradicts something at the consensual core of liberal politics. The proposal is for the reinstatement of pre-modern forms of torture for criminals, or the massive exploitation of certain groups because of their inferior intelligence or despised ethnicity. Our sensibility does not respond with the openness to iconolastic proposals that might be fitting in other circumstances; the fitting response is outrage, and it is no lapse of moderation to find the thoughts behind such proposals repulsive in a way that makes them virtually unthinkable.

This reveals some need for qualification to my original characterization of the skeptical conception of moderation. My initial suggestion was that moderation is a way of honouring the doubts we experience when the shared exercise of moral reason cannot bring us to a single conclusion in collective deliberation. This leaves out the necessary context to deliberation, a context I have made explicit through the notion of a liberal sensibility. Fundamental to the sensibility is not a general openness to rational doubt, but a respect for others as free and equal partners in the venture of political co-operation. By virtue of differences in experience, culture or the like that abound in any free society, others will be disposed to reason in public deliberation in ways that yield conclusions in conflict with ours (Rawls 1993: 54–8). If we are to respect them and they are to reciprocate, we must each be open to the doubts about our partisan claims that the arguments of the other will rightly provoke, and moderation is demanded of all as we seek to find policies adjusted to the enduring fact of reasonable disagreement. Never the less, some claims in public discourse deny the fundamental presuppositions of mutual respect. A refusal even to entertain them is no failure of liberal moderation; it is rather an affirmation of the practice without which liberal moderation loses its point.

So liberal moderation seems to combine two elements: a steadfast adherence to a common practice of mutual respect, whose basic shape is fixed by the liberal platitudes, and a willingness to accommodate reasonable disagreements among those who share the practice. To call this the 'skeptical conception' of moderation gives salience to the second element within the virtue, but that can only be understood within the overarching context of the first. I want to ask now how the two elements might be related.

The question has to be understood against the background of the wider question of how liberal public morality is to be justified. That background is important because it is the source of some influential objections to the authenticity of liberal virtue. A common claim among critics of liberalism is that as far as it might claim to be a moral conception at all, it is yoked to an untenable Kantian model of moral justification. First, the model cannot furnish arguments for any substantive moral conclusions, and therefore, the content of a liberal sensibility must be an arbitrary and unstable melange of conviction and doubt. Second, the Kantian model is rationalistic in a sense that slights the importance of virtue in our lives, by suggesting that once we adhere to correct procedures of moral reason, virtue will somehow take care of itself or be unnecessary.[2]

## V

One target of Kant's moral criticism is the appeal to the wisdom of tradition against the deliverances of moral theory: 'Such illusory wisdom imagines it can see further and more clearly with its mole-like gaze fixed on experience than with the eyes which were bestowed by a being designed to stand upright and scan the heavens' (Kant 1970 [1793]: 63). The object of that jibe is almost certainly

Burke's *Reflections on the Revolution in France*. We see far and clearly as moral beings only by prescinding from our diverse ends, including attachment to hallowed institutions, and asking what is required of us as rational agents in a world we share with other such agents. That at least is what Kant would have us believe.

Recall that our problem is to understand the distinctive combination of moral assurance and susceptibility to doubt that a liberal sensibility embodies in the exercise of moderation. The exponent of the Kantian project might say that from a rational perspective which discounts the contingencies of our ends, we can see both compelling grounds for the liberal platitudes, and the need for moderation in common deliberation that proceeds within their limits. But even some liberals worry that so ethereal a level of abstraction cannot have that much justificatory power. Perhaps it only appears to have that power when we are insensitive to the effects of our own, culturally conditioned liberal sensibility on attempts to uncover the moral substance of 'pure' practical reason.

Other ways of conceiving the task of justifying liberalism are available than the one that drives the Kantian project. The moral reason we learn, exercise, and teach in the historical context of liberal politics might better be construed as 'the immanent rationality of a tradition in which habitual action and reflective thought are related dialectically' (Stout 1988: 143–4). At any given moment in the history of that tradition, some moral beliefs will reasonably be held as matters of virtual certainty. But that is because of what the tradition has shown can be said in their favour, including what conversation (and conflict) with the bearers of rival traditions has disclosed. Furthermore, what can be said in their favour is more than some thin abstraction about the nature of practical reason or the like; it depends rather on their central role within a web of beliefs and practices that is the fruit of many generations' experience and that defines a way of life we cherish as inheritors of the tradition.

Certainty is not underwritten here by a reason torn away from what Kant ridicules as a 'mole-like gaze fixed on experience'. What sustains a robust commitment to human equality within liberal politics, for example, is perhaps a recognition of the self-serving reasons that have buttressed arguments for natural social hierarchy throughout history, and an emotionally engaged awareness of cruelties and abuses, both petty and terrible, sponsored by moral codes that deny basic human equality. The 'mole-like gaze fixed on experience' of those whose gaze included the sufferings of the Third Estate under the *ancien régime* might have furnished another, and better reply to Burke than the appeal to pure practical reason. Similarly, the justification of our openness to rational doubt, and willingness to compromise within the limits of the liberal platitudes, may depend critically on our historical experience of oppression rationalized in the name of a comprehensive conception of the good and the right.

But suppose for the moment that the Kantian project could succeed in justifying the liberal platitudes. (My sketchy remarks about the liabilities of the project and the promise of a tradition-centred alternative hardly suffice to show that it could not succeed.) It would still remain obscure how we might interpret the relationship between the dictates of pure practical reason and the situated standpoint of moral agents who evince a liberal sensibility within the flow of ordinary moral life. Consider one possible interpretation that beggars belief, although it has not been without influence. One might think that once the abstract argument for the liberal platitudes is understood and accepted, then either intellectual assent guarantees that one will see, feel, and be motivated as a liberal sensibility requires, or else assent makes it morally irrelevant whether one has the sensibility or not. Something like this idea seems to have been at work in Lawrence Kohlberg's theory of moral development. By examining the structure of moral reasoning that people exhibit when reflecting on schematic moral dilemmas, Kohlberg thought we could trace a developmental sequence in moral judgement, with Kantian-style reasoning ascendent at the terminus of the sequence (e.g. Kohlberg 1981). But there is a conceptual chasm between the skill in a particular species of reasoning which fixated Kohlberg and the possession of a liberal sensibility. There is also more at stake here than the conceptual possibility that one might achieve the object of Kohlberg's fixation and fall short of liberal virtue. Morally weak, unperceptive or evil people who are skilled at abstract moral reasoning are not unfamiliar beings.

Kant for one was acutely aware of the chasm between pure practical reason and the human embeddedness of moral agency. He knew that moral theory owes us an account of how moral considerations are to exert their authority in the lives of creatures whose patterns of perception, feeling and desire may support or thwart that authority. The 'anthropology of morals' that is the necessary companion to a 'metaphysic of morals' has been until recently a neglected corner of Kantian scholarship (Sherman 1997: 121–86). But to understand liberal morality in its distinctively human context is necessarily to return to questions about moral education and its relation to processes of habituation and the shaping of affect, as well as the growth of ratiocination. These were fundamental questions of ancient virtue ethics, and Kant understood their importance even if some of his contemporary devotees do not.

This is not to say that liberal morality can be construed entirely on the ancient model, with the liberal platitudes filling out a moral conception structurally identical to the classical prototype. A real structural difference does separate the morals of modernity from classical antecedents. But here too, once we ask how this is to be accommodated in the cultivation of morality, the difference is muted.

## VI

A truism in ancient ethics is that virtue links rational choice to human flourishing: choosing virtuously is choosing our own good. Our pre-reflective understanding of the good is likely to be distorted. Therefore, choosing virtuously and choosing our own good often appear to diverge. However, philosophy discloses a deep convergence between the good of the individual and the interests of others. A prime example of a concept that secures this convergence is Aristotle's notion of *philia*, which subsumes friendships, familial intimacy, and civic ties of solidarity (*Nicomachean Ethics* Book VIII-IX). If a good human life must include *philia*, then the moral claims of those whose lives intersect with mine through *philia* are not properly contrasted with reasons of self-interest. Thus to act ungratefully to my parents is not to choose my own good over my parents' welfare; it is to act against the more enlightened understanding of human excellence I would have if I appreciated the place of filial piety in a good life.

Yet this line of thought fits uncomfortably with the liberal platitudes. These affirm a worth that inheres in all human lives, regardless of affective ties that meld our own good with that of particular others. The rights which derive from that worth impose obligations of aid and forbearance which have no necessary connection to our good. And as long as people use their rights to pursue many different and conflicting ends, our longing for a polity that would be our own conception of the good writ large must be defeated. At the core of the liberal moral life is the inviolable worth of distinct human lives, lives of strangers as well as friends, the wicked as well as the saintly. The worth of each commands a respect we are obliged to give, irrespective of the promptings of even the wisest interpretation of self-interest. So liberal morality rests on a fractured conception of ethical value in which moral and prudential reasons have no necessary harmony. But there is less to this contrast with classical models than meets the eye, because liberal moral education has to find ways in which the formation of identity eases, even if it cannot eradicate, the split between self-regard and other-regard in practical reason.

Consider Christine Korsgaard's almost melodramatic description of the gap between the ancient understanding of virtue and the modern, liberal ethic of obligation: 'When we seek excellence, the force that value exerts upon us is attractive; when we are obligated, it is compulsive' (Korsgaard 1996: 4). What I have already said about self-interest and liberal virtue might appear to give some credence to this. But notice how bizarre it would be to *present* moral obligation in this light within the process of moral education.

Suppose a child has been involved in a fight in which racist insults were exchanged. Conversation with a parent or teacher reveals that his involvement was prompted by the desire to win the esteem of his peers. Now only a loss of the most elementary common sense could motivate the parent or teacher to present the episode to the child as conflict between the good of belonging to which self-interest draws us, and rules of right conduct we must cleave to in a spirit of unrelenting self-sacrifice. Then the child is left to ask why moral reasons are worth heeding at all. Why submit to the 'compulsive power' of obligation when it cannot attract us, and the good that does attract pulls us in a different direction? Any sensitive adult will be at least implicitly aware of that question, and will help the child to see that a belonging worth having cannot come at the cost of racism. To belong at that price is to degrade oneself.

This educational task has to do with an aspect of the liberal sensibility noted in Section IV. To possess that sensibility is to think that meeting our moral obligations is intrinsic to a life worth living, and so to flout obligation is to diminish oneself and not merely to do wrong to others. Unless one comes to regard morality in this way, it must remain an essentially threatening force outside the self. Then moral virtue must be an unintelligible aspiration, given that weaving moral propensities into the fabric of identity is necessary to virtue. If justice, for example, can be coherently conceived as a norm that repels even as it compels, and this in fact is how I habitually experience the demands of justice, the norm must be external to the constitution of my identity, which is to say that it has not been internalized as virtue requires.

Now we confront the most interesting formulation of the problem of ethical enfeeblement. The liberal platitudes delineate a moral life in which no necessary convergence holds between reasons of self-interest and the rightful claims of others. Yet induction into the liberal moral life requires some reconciliation of these competing reasons. Thus we tell our children that a belonging that comes at the cost of injustice is no good. But the point might not be to teach them something true about their good; it might be to manipulate our children's beliefs and desires so that they will conceive their good according to our morality. Then if the liberal platitudes are really understood, the gap between the right and the good will also be understood. Therefore, the inculcation of liberal virtue will seem at the end of the day a kind of hoax. That would surely be a morally enfeebling rather than an edifying insight.

I cannot here present a full response to this, but a few remarks will indicate what I take to be the beginning of one. First, to see moral obligation as having a deliberative weight fundamentally distinct from the allure of our own good obviously does not mean we have to think of each as pervasively opposed to the other. The severity and frequency of conflict between self-interest and moral obligation is biographically contingent in so far as the content of self-interest is fixed in part by the ends with which individuals come to identify (Badhwar 1993). If moral considerations enter into these ends, self-interest and altruism are to a degree psychologically integrated. That is the purpose of trying to teach children that a sense of belonging stained by racism is no good. This takes me to my final point.

In trying to teach children that their good cannot be found in something terribly wrong, we are engaged in a kind of ethical discourse which Charles Taylor calls 'strong evaluation' (Taylor 1989: 75–90). This is a discourse in which we discriminate possible objects of choice as good or bad, admirable or shameful, in ways that are irreducible to facts about the satisfaction of desire. Our ordinary concept of the good is wedded to strong evaluation, and resists reductive analysis (Kraut 1994). The idea of a liberal sensibility and its educational transmission helps to clarify why liberals cannot do without strong evaluation. To be sure, a form of skepticism sometimes associated with liberalism denies this, claiming that our knowledge of the good lacks cognitive content, even if objective principles of right and wrong are available to us. My final formulation of the problem of ethical enfeeblement shows why this is at best implausible.

If talk of what is good in Taylor's sense is just so much deceptive chatter about what we desire or want others to desire, then we might pretend otherwise when we teach children that a belonging bought at the price of racism is no good. Alternatively, we might not pretend at all, and merely condition them not to want to belong at that price. In either event, we might seem to have an education for liberal virtue that entails a thorough skepticism about the good. But in the first case, we could not be sanguine about the durability of a liberal sensibility once its dependence on the sheer manipulation of desire is recognised; in the second, we could not rationally hope for its development to begin with, because liberal virtue would not be presented as a genuine good at all, but only as something the child has reason to desire because of the rewards and penalties we apply. A defensible liberalism requires a plausible account of the education for virtue that sustains liberal practices across generations; and given the difficulties of an account that reduces what is good to what is desired, a defensible liberalism would seem to depend on an understanding of the morality in which questions about the good, and not merely about the right, have objective standing.

Although much that I have said here softens the contrast between ancient moral conceptions and liberalism, the distinctiveness of liberal morality remains. In teaching that the good of belonging is undermined by racism, the lesson cannot be credibly taught in the circumstances of our world as part of a larger, consoling story in which the good to which we are drawn and the claims of morality are in ultimate harmony. At least that is true for those of us whose liberal sensibility is not nested within a religious creed. Liberal morality begins in disagreement about the right and the good, and the liberal sensibility is alive to the significance of that disagreement. To cultivate that morality is to learn to live with an openness to the diversity of choice-worthy lives, and a sense of the fragility and imperfection of all our attempts to reconcile that diversity with the imperatives of mutual respect. But what is fragile and imperfect may be precious for all that.

## Notes

Thanks to Steve Macedo for helpful comments on an earlier draft.

1 I borrow the phrase 'liberal sensibility' from John Haldane (1996), which is not to say that he would commend the use I have made of it here.

2 Michael Sandel has developed this particular anti-liberal line. See Sandel 1982; 1996.

## References

Aristotle (1980) *Nichomachean Ethics (Ethica Nicomachea)*, trans. W. D. Ross, Oxford: Oxford University Press.

Badhwar, N. K. (1993) 'Altruism Versus Self-Interest: Sometimes a false dichotomy', *Social Philosophy and Policy*, 10, 1: 90–117.

Haldane, J. (1996) 'The individual, the state, and the common good', *Social Philosophy and Policy*, 13, 1: 59–79.

Kant, I. [1793] (1970) 'On the common saying, "This may be true in theory, but it does not apply in practice," in H.Reiss (ed.) *Kant's Political Writings,* Cambridge: Cambridge University Press.

Kohlberg, L. (1981) *The Philosophy of Moral Development*, San Francisco: Harper and Row.

Korsgaard, C. M. (1996) *The Sources of Normativity*, Cambridge: Cambridge University Press.

Kraut, R. (1994) 'Desire and the Human Good', *Proceedings of the American Philosophical Association*, 68: 39–54.

Macedo, S. (1990) *Liberal Virtues*, Oxford: Clarendon.

MacIntyre, A. (1988). *Whose Justice? Which Rationality?*, South Bend, Ill.: Notre Dame University Press.

Rawls, J. (1993) *Political Liberalism*, New York: Columbia University Press.

Sandel, M. (1982) Liberalism and the Limits of Justice, Cambridge: Cambridge University Press.

—— (1996) *Democracy's Discontent*, Cambridge, Mass.: Harvard University Press.

Sherman, N. (1997) *Making a Necessity of Virtue: Aristotle and Kant on Virtue,* Cambridge: Cambridge University Press.

Stout, J. (1988) *Ethics After Babel*, New York: Beacon Press.

Taylor, C. (1989) *Sources of the Self*, Cambridge, Mass.: Harvard University Press.

Part 6

# EDUCATING THE VIRTUES: MEANS AND METHODS

# 14

# VIRTUES, CHARACTER, AND MORAL DISPOSITIONS

*Joel J. Kupperman*

## Introduction

Much of ethical philosophy in the last two hundred or so years has centred on an impersonal decision procedure. Kant's categorical imperative can be regarded under that heading, although strictly speaking the categorical imperative is not intended to yield decisions *ex nihilo* but rather is intended as a test of maxims and the decisions that embody them. Given the preliminary work of formulating the maxims that underlie possible courses of action, the categorical imperative can be used as a way of deciding which are morally acceptable and which (because all of the alternatives are unacceptable) count as morally required. The decision procedure is presented as entirely impersonal, in that everyone can use it in much the same way. The utilitarianism of Bentham and of John Stuart Mill similarly is presented as an impersonal source of judgements of how it is best to behave.

One recent writer, Jerome Schneewind, has taken virtue ethics to task for what he sees (in contrast) as its relative uselessness in yielding ethical decisions (Schneewind 1997). This however rests on a simplistic view both of the function of ethical theories and of the precision of the decision procedures that seem to flow from them. The working of the categorical imperative requires judgement in relating the particular case to principle, and sometimes also the art of casuistry (Kant 1991b [1797]). Was Kant's personal maxim 'I will be celibate' (which could not be willed to be a universal law), or was it 'I will be celibate if I have a vocation for this (or have not met the right person)'? Does capital punishment pass the test of the categorical imperative? Kant firmly thought it did, but some Kantians would disagree (see Kant 1991a [1797]: 142–5).

Utilitarian decision procedures also are far less precise than they may look. How do we go about estimating the likely consequences, into the far future, of an action, or for that matter assessing their values? There will be a natural tendency, which Mill endorses, to assume that the sort of thing that generally worked well or badly in the past is likely to work similarly in the present case (Mill 1979 [1861]: 23–4). But if the decision procedure requires judgements of this sort, then here again how the case is viewed, classified, and compared will have a great deal to do with the judgement that will be arrived at.

It might be tempting to think of Kant and the utilitarians as offering something like computer morality software. If so, it is crucial how the data are fed into the computer, so that the software program can be applied. An old saying of computer people is 'Garbage in, garbage out'. The sensitivity and judgement of the person making the moral judgement turns out to be crucial after all. So are the habits, inhibitions, and general frame of mind of the moral agent. This is partly because so many moral decisions must be made very quickly, before there is time to reckon what likely consequences will be or even to formulate a maxim. Also it needs to be said that no sane person (and certainly not Kant or the classical utilitarians) assumed that moral choice was a constant feature of everyday life. To think otherwise would be to deprive life of normal human spontaneity. We need, then, something like a psychic mechanism to let us know that something morally significant may be at stake, and to trigger moral reflection. This is closely related to how sensitive, alert, and conscientious we are. So are the inhibitions that prevent a decent person from even considering some options for which specious reasons might be offered. Finally, even though Kant and the utilitarians (in an act of ruthless abstraction designed to promote the show of precision) tend to present moral choices as if they generally can be disconnected from the previous and future choices of the agent, this works well mainly for choices of a fairly simple and clear-cut kind. In the real world one thing leads to another: choices made now can look very different because of what went on before, and what we do now can have implications that constrain our future choices.

Sensitivity, judgement, inhibitions, moral habits, and characteristic patterns of response all fit under the heading of character. Part of what I have been suggesting is that even someone who possesses very good moral software will also need a good character. Further, if we want to understand what ethics is about, we need to turn some of our attention away from minute to minute specific decisions and look instead at what gives value and moral reliability to an entire life. We need, that is, to understand character and the virtues that go to making up a good character.

## Character

The focus on the entire life is one of the features of Aristotle's ethics, especially his account of *eudaimonia* (often translated as 'happiness' and sometimes as 'well-being'), the sum of what is worth seeking. Does Aristotle offer a decision procedure? He provides a sophisticated account of how one can best decide difficult cases, in his discussion of the 'mean' (*Nichomachean Ethics* (NE) 1106a–1109b). Beginners sometimes presume that Aristotle's emphasis on finding the mean can be read simply as praise of moderation. But Aristotle's main point is that the mean between two extremes (e.g. rashness and cowardice) requires judgement of individual cases and also flexibility. Advancing into danger for the sake of possible gains may make good sense in some cases and be simply rash in others. We need the ability (and the patience) to tell the two sorts of cases apart. From this point of view the coward and the rash person look very consistent: each always behaves in the same kind of way. But the courageous person does not simply follow a rule or adhere to an algorithm, but instead reasonably adapts conduct to circumstances.

In this discussion Aristotle is most emphatically not laying down a decision procedure, but rather coaching us on the necessity of fashioning our own. Does he recognize readymade decision procedures? Yes: there are some times (not so difficult cases) when we need merely to follow a rule. Adultery, theft, and murder are examples he gives (*NE* 1007a). There is no mean, so that it is not as if we need to commit adultery only with the right woman at the right time and in the right way. Instead, he says, the answer is simply 'no'. But Aristotle is hardly suggesting this as one of his contributions to ethical knowledge; his assumption appears to be that his readers already know this. (Similarly Kant makes it clear that he assumes that his readers already are familiar with the core requirements of morality, although his exposition of the categorical imperative appears to be designed to discourage people's tendencies to find exceptions. The classical utilitarians also presumed familiarity with core requirements of morality, so that any novelty in what their decision procedure might appear to yield was mainly in the sphere of social policy.)

It seems reasonable to regard the ability to find the mean in difficult cases, which Aristotle explores, as an aspect of character. But then we have to include such qualities as intelligence, moral imagination, and sensitivity within character, bearing in mind that all of these are not well formed at birth but need to be trained and developed. We also will need to limit the assumption that sane adults in general know right from wrong to the domain of decisions that are not difficult (e.g. cases in which what is right or wrong straight-forwardly follows from a familiar rule). Aristotle's view clearly was that in difficult cases many generally decent people do not know right from wrong. Confucius, the sixth century BC virtue theorist, is making a similar point when he says, 'The honest villager spoils true virtue' (Confucius 1989, XVII, No. 13: 213).

If character includes the intelligence and sensitivity to make difficult moral decisions, what does it not include? It is time to explore what character is, and also its relation to the virtues.

This is a complicated story, but two simple points should be made at the start. One is that character needs to be thought of, not merely as an array of dispositions and abilities, but also as what a person is like. Thus education of character should be regarded not merely as the implanting of something like software for problems of life; it involves shaping the development of what (at the start) are not in the fullest sense persons into ones of certain sorts. The poet

John Keats, in a long letter to his brother and sister in law in Kentucky, speaks of this world as a 'vale of soulmaking' (Keats 1954, letter 123: 266). In much this sense, character education can be said to make (or to shape) souls. Similarly, the commentators David Hall and Roger Ames speak of Confucius' ethics as an ethics of 'personmaking' (Hall and Ames 1987). Some of the implications of this will be explored shortly.

Secondly, the modern concept of character emphasizes aspects of what a person is that are closely related to good (or bad) ethical choice. This is not the whole story. Vicissitudes that are said to strengthen character often strengthen mainly the ability to persevere and to rebound from failure, and neither of these abilities is specifically ethical. A strong character requires these and also the marked tendency to maintain steadily an independent point of view even under pressure. A wicked person could have a strong character in this sense. Clearly then character cannot be regarded as straightforwardly and simply an ethical concept. Never the less, when we are describing someone's character, those features that are crucial to being morally reliable will be very prominent. It is natural to ask whether someone has a good character, as opposed to having a bad one (which may require a perverse strength) or no character. Tastes in food and clothing are not part of someone's character; honesty and compassion (or their absence) are.

In previous work (Kupperman 1991: 17) I arrived at a working definition of character as a person's normal pattern of thought and action, especially with respect to concerns and commitments in matters affecting the happiness of others or of that person, and most especially in relation to moral choices. This definition is best used if we reject some simplifying assumptions which can be especially appealing because simple views are so comfortable. First, 'normal pattern of thought and action' should not be read as always referring to what a person always or usually does or thinks. 'Normal pattern' is to be taken as shorthand for what is normal (or at least not distinctly abnormal) for a person in various circumstances, especially including highly unusual circumstances that we might regard as moral test cases. Thus someone's character may include the fact that he or she is capable of great cruelty, even if this refers to occasional (and not entirely predictable) cruel acts. A quality can be part of someone's normal pattern of thought and action, in the intended sense, without there being any specific occasion on which quality is likely to be expressed.

Secondly, we need not assume that either favourable or unfavourable judgements of someone's character in some area of life will extend uniformly to the entire character. Someone who has a good character with regard to matters of money may have a bad character with regard to the opposite sex, and for that matter someone who is honest in financial transactions with friends and neighbours may be dishonest in corporate finance. The classic *Columbia University Studies in the Nature of Character* concluded that correlations of virtuous behaviour in various kinds of situation are not high (see Hartshorne, May and Shuttleworth 1930).

202

Virtues are important in the assessment of character, even if (as the Columbia University researchers claimed) virtue is sometimes more spotty than we would like to think. People sometimes tend to perform very well in a specific area of life, across a range of contexts. Plainly a good character will include a number of virtues, such as honesty, fortitude, considerateness, and willingness to go to some trouble to help those in need. Are all of these moral virtues? The answer depends on how narrow or broad the sphere of morality is taken to be. Is being inconsiderate a species of immorality? Fortitude, which includes the ability to endure hardships unflinchingly, may manifest itself mainly in concerns not normally thought of as either fulfilling or violating moral requirements, such as success in starting up a business or in athletics.

There is also the question of whether character can be thought of as straight-forwardly the sum of various virtues, or various vices, or of a mixed bag of virtues and vices. There are great advantages in focusing on specific virtues and vices. It enables us to be fairly specific about qualities that someone has or lacks, and what would be required to display these. In some ways it is like genre criticism of the arts, in which we can sharpen our focus by asking not 'Is it a good poem?' but 'Is it a good sonnet?', or 'Is it a good epic poem?', and so on. However, just as some poems may not fit their genres neatly, so that their exellence is not best approached through genre criticism, it may be that some excellences or defects of character cross the boundaries that would separate traditional virtues or traditional vices. Further, it is arguable (especially if one assumes that no one is perfect) that anyone's virtues and defects will be intimately connected, and that the connections will be best appreciated in a range of behaviour. The seventeenth century moralist the Duc de la Rochefoucauld, both deeply religious and deeply cynical, developed this line of thought in his *Maxims* (see La Rochefoucauld 1959 [1665], maxim 182: 57; also Confucius IV, no. 7: 103). If there is any truth to this, then we can get a more balanced and complex view of someone through use of the concept of character than through examination of a series of (discrete) virtues and vices.

Having said this, one has to admit that it is (for the reasons just given) much easier to talk with some brevity about particular virtues and vices than about character. If we are trying to say why someone seems to us to be a good person, or deeply flawed, it usually will be easiest to specify the goodness in terms of particular virtues or the flaws in terms of particular vices. This is not only because the concepts of the virtues and vices partition the field of thought and behaviour, but also because the available words for particular vices and virtues have established traditions of employment which lend themselves to quick and clear communication. This is especially important when we begin the moral education of young children. Our goal, arguably, is to help in the development of good character, rather than merely this virtue and that virtue. But we are well advised to begin the process of getting across what is important by speak-ing of what it is to be honest, compassionate and so on, and what it is to lack these qualities.

JOEL J. KUPPERMAN

# Can virtue be taught, and if so how?

The question whether virtue can be taught resounds throughout the dialogues of Plato, which leave the door open to a skeptical answer. Here are two reasons why one might be skeptical. First, if one thinks of virtue in terms of having mastered the right moral software (as a few admirers of Kant or of utilitarianism sometimes seem to think), then what can we say of someone who knows the morally acceptable answers but has no clear motivation to behave accordingly? Plainly virtue requires more than just an ability to give the right answers. A similar comment applies to the view of those traditionalists who think that we have taught virtue if we have dinned into students an assortment of familiar moral rules.

Second, Plato believes (I think rightly) that even ability to provide acceptable answers plus some motivation is not enough to qualify as virtue: true virtue requires a high degree of moral reliability, even in situations that are disorienting or in which there are unusual temptations. The notorious experiments of Stanley Milgram could be taken to suggest that, world-wide, perhaps at most a third of the population could qualify as virtuous by this high standard (Milgram 1974). Plato very probably has in mind a far smaller percentage, judging by the account of a neardeath experience (in which someone sees the souls of the dead choosing new lives) reported in the last book of the *Republic* (614b–621b). What is needed, Socrates says, is philosophy as well as habit. In place of the common assumption that people by and large are either good or bad, Plato's remarks suggest a vision in which true goodness (and presumably also true badness) are fairly rare, and the great majority of people are in an in-between category of neither true virtue nor true wickedness.

Despite these compelling grounds for skepticism, let me suggest a case for the teachability of virtue: a teachability much less direct and reliable than the teachability of mathematics and geography (so that virtue cannot be taught in the way in which they are taught), and also in many cases leading to what would count as virtue by a lower standard than Plato would accept. If the reader will diminish her or his expectations, we can see what might be possible.

The two great philosophers who have had the most to say about the teaching of virtue are Aristotle and Confucius. Aristotle makes a useful distinction between what is appropriate in the early stages of ethical education and what is needed in the advanced stages. The foundation, in childhood and presumably in early adolescence, requires good habits (*NE* 1103a). The student who does not tend to follow passions and is ready to reflect on her or his life, and to think seriously about good and bad, right and wrong, already is a certain kind of person (*NE* 1095a). Aristotle I think clearly agrees with Plato that real goodness (at a high standard) requires philosophy as well as habit; yet the philosophical instruction, he insists, will be useless or inappropriate if the foundation has not been laid properly.

A crucial element in the formation of habits is pleasure and pain. They are crucial both to what counts as a good result, and to the process of reaching the result. The goal is not merely a person who always does the right thing: if there is no particular pleasure in it, and the idea of violation of norms is not especially painful, then such a person can be corrupted readily or in changed circumstances can slip into a different pattern of behaviour. This is far from moral reliability. Accordingly, Aristotle observes, 'We ought to be brought up in a particular way from our very youth, as Plato says, so as to delight in and to be pained by the things we ought' (*NE* 1104b11–13). The delight and pain represent to some degree a conditioned response. Our more mature delight and pain, that is, are the result of childhood experience (brought about by parents and others) of pleasure and pain, which in a rather Pavlovian manner establishes predispositions to feel pleasure and pain at certain things or thoughts. (The childhood pain, it should be pointed out, need not be physical; under certain circumstances silent reproach can be very painful.) All of this is central to early childhood education. 'In educating the young we steer them by the rudders of pleasure and pain' (*NE* 1172a21–22). Childhood patterning reinforced by pleasure and pain is crucial, in Aristotle's view, to the formation of good habits.

This does not mean that it is all that matters. Any philosopher, including Aristotle, is likely not to mention what seems too obvious for words, or to be generally already understood by the intended audience. It is probable that articulation of general norms governing such matters as murder and theft fell in that category for Aristotle. Dinning in moral rules is not a sufficient condition for the inculcation of virtue, but it may be close to being a necessary condition. Familiarity with moral rules provides quick guidance when there is not much time for a moral decision, and inhibits the tendency to look for rationalizations that would justify appealing transgressions. Aristotle's readers could be assumed to have known this.

There is also the important factor of whether parents and community leaders provide (or fail to provide) models of good life. Whether or not this would have been part of a fuller Aristotelian account of early moral education, it clearly was at the heart of Confucius' view. The role of parents was assumed (in the context of extensive regard for the importance of family life); the role of community leaders, especially of rulers, is made more explicit. This sometimes emerges in an unexpected way. To a ruler who asks how he can deal with an upsurge of thievery, Confucius replies that if the ruler were not greedy then people would not steal even if paid to do so (Confucius XII, no. 18: 167).

Aristotle is I think right that habit is at the heart of early education of character, and that significant development later is unlikely if a good foundation of habits had not been laid. People sometimes have the sense of reinventing themselves in late adolescence or early adulthood. But, as Erik Erikson has observed, 'The community often underestimates to what extent a long intricate childhood history has restricted a youth's further choice of identity change' (Erikson 1968: 160).

Habits however, including habits of connecting painful thoughts with certain kinds of transgressions, can never be entirely protective. Strong temptations can overcome them. Also the habits will have power chiefly when someone is faced with familiar options in familiar kinds of circumstance. Their power will be limited when the choice is among alternatives that may not be readily classifiable (so that someone may not identify what he or she is about to do as a transgression), or when the agent is disoriented by unusual circumstances. Familiar modern examples are choices made during wartime, or after social upheavals, or by people who have moved into occupations whose rules are not clear.

The formation of good habits therefore is only a first stage. As Aristotle puts it:

> The soul of the student must first have been cultivated by means of habits . . . like earth which is to nourish the seed . . . The character then must somehow be there already with a kinship to excellence.
>
> (*NE* 1179b23–27, 30–32)

The phrase 'kinship to excellence' is meant, I think, to do justice to the phenomenon of the very good child, who has not fully become a very good person, but who is clearly on her or his way and already has qualities that resemble those of a very good person.

But if Aristotle is right (and I think he is), there needs to be an advanced stage, at least if we have in mind a high standard of reliable goodness. It may be that people's personalities usually are largely determined by the time they pass from childhood to adolescence, and that their characters are not. We may know, that is, that so-and-so at the age of fourteen or fifteen is very likely always to be outgoing, fond of physical activity, and casually friendly to all sorts of people without knowing whether he or she is very likely to be a good person. If Nazis come to power, or if the circumstances of life become disorienting, the likeable adolescent might come to act in ways that we would find disturbing.

Neither Aristotle nor Plato has a great deal that is explicit to say about advanced education of character. Confucius does. This is very largely a function of the fact that students formed part of Confucius's extended household, and that what we have of Confucius consists of the account that these students compiled.

What is clearest for Plato and Aristotle is that philosophy is important to advanced moral education. This has many facets. Arguably the most significant for Plato was the awareness of value, of The Good. A philosopher ought to know that the things, such as money, power, reputation, and sensual pleasures, that tempt people into misbehaviour have limited value. Inner psychological harmony is far more important, and this requires virtue. A similar insistence runs through the *Analects* of Confucius. It is why average people are so concerned with luck (to which such things as money, power, reputation, and sensual pleasures are very much subject), and why someone with good values can be unconcerned about luck and therefore can remain calm (see Confucius VII, no. 36: 131).

Arguably this is implicit in Aristotle's view as well. The discussion of ultimate value, *eudaimonia*, in the *Nicomachean Ethics* attends carefully to the degrees to which various values are under our control. The highest, in this view, are most under our control; and in our lives we should keep this in mind. But Aristotle's discussion of the mean makes clear that advanced training in goodness requires also judgement and experience, a sophisticated awareness of how the world actually works that goes well beyond any available rules. The very good person is guided by empirical knowledge and not swept away by passions.

Confucius also repeatedly emphasizes empirical knowledge of the world as a guide to goodness, but his account brings to the fore factors of very different sorts. These include familiarity with ritual (which could be understood broadly as patterned social interactions, which include – to take a familiar example – such things as thanking someone for a present). What is important in ritual goes beyond compliance with established standards. Thus, in behaviour towards parents, Confucius remarks, demeanour matters a great deal (II, no. 8: 89). There also are repeated references to the importance for advanced ethical development of familiarity with the classics (seen as sources of ethical insight) and with the right kinds of music. These are an important part of the process of character refinement which one of Confucius's students, quoting a classic poem, character-izes as chiselling, filing (I, no. 15: 87). Music, Confucius observes, is more than bells and drums (XVII, no. 11: 212). Whether and how this might work (it should be said) remains speculative, although some recent writers have in effect accepted elements of Confucius's ethical psychology (see Richards 1924).

Confucius's most famous follower, Mencius (fourth century BC), develops a further suggestion. At the heart of Mencius' ethics (very like that of David Hume two thousand years later) is the claim that human nature includes an innate benevolence which, however, may well be overwhelmed on various occasions by selfish impulses. Mencius holds that an essential step toward true goodness is to be aware of this benevolence and to be able to channel it appro-priately. A famous passage describes a king who spared a sacrificial ox because, he later tells Mencius, he had looked in the eyes of the terrified animal and felt pity. Mencius congratulates him on this benevolence, but asks how it is that 'the means laid down for the people are sufficient neither for the care of parents nor for the support of wife and children. In good years life is always hard, while in bad years there is no escaping death' (Mencius 1970, I, part A, no. 7: 54-59). Plainly the king needs to extend the benevolence to the people he does not see that he applies to the ox he does see.

This falls under the heading of moral imagination. Arguably much of the harm in the world is done by people who lack a sense of the less obvious consequences of their actions or of how some of the victims experience them.

Simply being able to enter into the point of view of people different from oneself can make a major difference in one's humanity toward them. Advanced education of character needs to strengthen the moral imagination. Imaginative works of fiction, properly taught, can aid in this process. So can straightforward exercises in working out the consequences of actions that might seemingly be limited in their impact, and in trying to grasp the likely experiences of those affected by them.

Two other elements need to be mentioned, the importance of which to advanced education of character all of the philosophers cited would have regarded as too obvious for words. One is a sense of self as unified through time. The other is the role that experience of overcoming challenges has in strengthening character.

Quite possibly the unity of the self through time would have seemed obvious to the average person even a hundred years ago. Because of the acceleration of technological change, and also the influence of television, we live in an age of short attention spans and near horizons. In a complex, mobile society an individual will play many roles, not always closely related. This has promoted the fragmented self of post-modernism, and may have increased the numbers of students who cannot think at all far ahead to people that they recognize as theirselves.

This undermines virtues for which, as writers like Jane Austen (Austen 1970 [1814]) have pointed out, constancy is required. Sincerity is a good example. A first thought might be that sincerity consists in a person's words at any given moment being in accord with her or his thoughts and feelings. However, what if someone's attitudes change drastically from day to day, so that yesterday's words (while entirely in accord with the person's attitudes at that time) do not fit attitudes today? Sincerity is impossible unless there is some stability of thoughts, feelings, and attitudes through time. It would be unreasonable to suggest that people never change, but if they are to have significant virtues they cannot change frequently and quickly.

Any kind of good character also requires the ability to take (and maintain) responsibility for actions, and for that matter to feel gratitude for what was done more than a short while ago. Conversely short horizons, often combined with wishful thinking, can lead to ruinous actions. It may be useful to students to be able to think in some detail what their lives will be like five or ten years after, say, teen pregnancy.

The importance of experiences of overcoming challenges, especially those that require sustained effort over a considerable period of time, cannot be overestimated. In many American schools in the 1970s and 1980s (an era in which the smiley face logo came into prominence), teachers out of a misplaced kindness tried to make success easy and immediate for their students, and failure highly unlikely. This is a recipe for developing weakness of character. To point this out is not to advocate the opposite extreme, a policy which makes failure both likely and painful. There may reasonably be temporary failures on the way to success, and arguably it is beneficial to have the experience of dealing with failure; but ideally students should be offered the likelihood of ultimate success of some sort, without a sense that it is to be easy and immediate or that it is absolutely guaranteed.

Because of this, educational activities that at first glance seem unrelated to moral education can contribute greatly to the development of a strong character. This includes any academic enterprise that requires sustained effort and selfdiscipline, and even athletic activities in which native skills are no more important than sustained effort and selfdiscipline.

None of this is guaranteed to work, even for a very intelligent student. Part of the point here is that individual psychological development can have many twists and turns, and can be influenced by events in sometimes unexpected ways. Social psychology has been much more successful in predicting group behaviour, or how individuals are likely to behave, than in providing entirely assured predictions of how a given individual will act. In this respect, the inculcation of virtue always has an element of uncertainty.

# References

Aristotle (1984) *Nicomachean Ethics* (Ethica Nicomachea), in J. Barnes (ed.) *The Complete Works of Aristotle*, vol. 2, Princeton: Princeton University Press.

Austen J. [1814] (1970) *Mansfield Park*, London: Oxford University Press.

Confucius (1989) *The Analects*, trans. A. Waley, New York: Vintage Books.

Erikson, E. (1968) *Identity, Youth and Crisis*, New York: Norton.

Hall, D. L. and Ames, R. T. (1987) *Thinking Through Confucius*, Albany: State University of New York Press.

Hartshorne, H., May, M. A., and Shuttleworth, F. K. (1930) *Studies in the Organization of Character*, vol. 3 of the *Columbia University Studies in the Nature of Character*, New York: Macmillan.

Kant, I. [1785] (1991a) *Metaphysical First Principles of the Doctrine of Right*, in *Metaphysics of Morals*, trans. M. Gregor, Cambridge: Cambridge University Press.

Kant, I. [1785] (1991b) *Metaphysical First Principles of the Doctrine of Virtue*, in *Metaphysics of Morals*, trans. M. Gregor, Cambridge: Cambridge University Press.

Keats, J. (1954) *The Letters of John Keats*, Oxford: World's Classics.

Kupperman, J. (1991) *Character*, New York: Oxford University Press.

La Rochefoucauld, F. [1665] (1959) *Maxims*, trans. L. Tancock, Baltimore: Penguin.

Mencius (1970) *Mencius*, trans. D. C. Lau, London: Penguin.

Milgram, S. (1974) *Obedience To Authority*, London: Tavistock.

Mill, J. S. [1861] (1979) *Utilitarianism*, Indianapolis: Hackett.

Plato (1961) *Republic*, in E. Hamilton and H. Cairns (eds) *The Collected Dialogues*, Princeton: Princeton University Press.

Richards, I. A. (1924) *Principles of Literary Criticism*, London: Routledge.

Schneewind, J. B. (1997) 'The Misfortunes of Virtue', in R. Crisp and M. Slote (eds) *Virtue Ethics*, Oxford: Oxford University Press.

# 15

# HABITUATION AND TRAINING IN EARLY MORAL UPBRINGING

*Ben Spiecker*

## Introduction and formulation of the problem

When does moral education begin? Different answers to this question are discernible in the research literature of this field. Philosophers and researchers who take the development of moral reasoning to be the heart of moral education will often characterize the child's early years as a period during which moral reasoning – and therefore moral education – is not yet possible. At this non-moral stage young children can only be socialized, indoctrinated or trained. From the cognitive-developmental perspective, indeed, training children in desirable conduct is sometimes dismissed as the inculcation of a 'bag of virtues' (Kohlberg 1981: 31); only when a young child is capable of understanding moral reasons and justifications can moral education as a rational form of influence begin. On the other hand, for behaviour-analytic researchers – who take moral development to consist primarily in the acquisition of moral behaviour – moral education starts somewhat earlier; from early childhood on, behaviour is rewarded or discouraged in accordance with adult preferences. Moreover, the young child matches his or her moral behaviour to that of persons to whom he or she is attached, and acquires moral behaviour under the influence and guidance of familiar role-models characterizable as 'caring', 'helpful', 'honest' and so on. Moral behaviour may also be more indirectly shaped by the moral rules explicitly recommended, prescribed or practised by adults themselves (Peláez and Gewirtz 1995). All the same, on this approach early moral education consists in training, habituation, and conditioning, and is in consequence largely non-rational in nature.

These different approaches, which are clearly at some odds with each other, spring from different conceptions of moral education – which we may here call the rationalistic and the empiricist. It is arguable that neither conception does full justice to moral education generally, and – as I hope to demonstrate – to early moral upbringing in particular. For example, it seems that these views pay little or no attention to the affective dimensions of upbringing and development (Spiecker 1988; Oakley 1992). Indeed, one may be hard put to account for such dimensions on conceptions of moral education exclusively focused on either cognitive states or overt behaviour.

However, it is intuitively reasonable to suggest that the *first* concern of parents or caretakers is not that their children reach the highest (post-conventional) stage of moral reasoning, or that they conform to conventionally correct moral behaviour, but rather that they grow into friendly, caring, just and trust-worthy persons who are especially capable of friendship and loving inter-personal relationships. Briefly, one may plausibly claim that parents are mostly concerned with the promotion of *virtues*, conceived at least partly in terms of affectively based attitudes and attachments. Hence, I want to ask in what follows whether allegedly non-rational early moral training and habituation can be regarded as initially contributory to moral development – more precisely, to the formation of moral qualities conceived as virtues – and, if so, what early moral training and habituation have precisely to contribute to moral education so construed.

To answer this question we shall need to clarify the meaning of the central terms that are used. Following this, we shall also need – all the better to understand early moral habituation – to distinguish two types of habit. With regard to this distinction, some recent readings of Aristotle's ideas in the *Nichomachean Ethics* – as well as the so-called 'paradox of moral educat-ion' – will be examined. Some space will also be devoted to a consideration of the extent to which empirical research data regarding the mother-infant relationship does or does not contradict the theoretical analyses of this sect-ion. This will be in the interests of respecting Flanagan's Principle of *Minimal Psychological Realism* which says: 'Make sure when constructing a moral theory or projecting a moral ideal that the character, decision processing, and behaviour prescribed are possible for creatures like us' (Flanagan 1991: 32).

## The contexts of training and habituation

Training, so Melden (1971) warns us, can mean various things. Some training is designed to impart skills – for example, tennis skills or the skills of politics – and some is designed to impart habits or patterns of behaviour or thought, ranging all the way from eating habits to habits of the mind (Melden 1971: 119). Since I am interested mainly for the moment in educational uses of the terms 'training' and 'habit', I shall not here deal with those forms of habituation acquired in accordance with the laws of association. However, the term 'educational' – and consequently the expression 'educational context' – can be a source of troublesome ambiguities. For, while 'education' can sometimes mean upbringing in general, it can at others more narrowly mean 'schooling' and sometimes, even more narrowly, a specific kind of schooling (perhaps 'liberal education'). A systematic treatise on the philosophy of education, according to Passmore (1980: 22), would need to distinguish between education1 (upbringing), education2 (schooling), and education3 (the production of educated individuals). Taking this point to heart in the light of present concerns, I will distinguish two presently relevant contexts of training and habituation: namely, the contexts of family upbringing (in particular that of early childhood) and of schooling.[1]

In analytical philosophy of education, concepts of training and habituation are invariably treated in relation to schooling. Along with concepts of indoctrination and conditioning – and by contrast with those of teaching and instruction – it is rare for such notions to be associated with the promotion of rationality or intelligence. Hence, in much (particularly liberal) theorizing about schooling, notions of training and habituation are liable to some negative evaluation. On the usual view (see, for example, Scheffler 1965) teaching as the promotion of learning is subject to the limitations imposed by the framework of rational discussion. This circumstance, however, requires the competent teacher to train students in (among other things) those rational habits of mind which – together with a complex of dispositions, attitudes, and traits of character – are characteristic of the critical spirit. Examples of such habits of mind are the habits of reason seeking, of rational evaluation and of subjecting received reasons to critical scrutiny (Siegel 1997: 35).

However, in the context of early childhood upbringing – by 'early childhood' I refer especially to the first three years – the promotion of rationality is often not the parents' main concern. At this stage, caretakers are mostly concerned to initiate infants and toddlers into daily social practices – to help them to grow into little persons with well-defined character qualities, traits and dispositions – and their operations are motivated by the desire to promote the well-being of their offspring with particular regard to the acquisition of right conduct and feelings. Moreover, it is within the inter-personal parent-child context that feelings of love and care, loyalty, connectedness, attachment, security, and unselfishness assume a central place; it is these parental qualities – sometimes called *child-centered virtues* (Okin 1996) – which help the infant get a foothold in the moral and social world.

On the face of it, then, it would appear that training and habituation are variously evaluated in the different contexts of education – schooling and early childhood upbringing – I have distinguished. In the context of schooling it is often held that training counts as part of the teaching process only in so far as it assists the development of rational discussion: in particular, if it fosters rational habits of mind. Training which does not answer this task may be considered of little relevance to the educational enterprise. In relation to theorizing about early upbringing, on the other hand, training and habituation are valued to the extent they assist the infant to become a participant in our daily practices, although such initiation into social practices will also often be taken to include parental promotion of intelligent behaviour. Still, training and habituation (as processes) seem to be evaluated in both contexts by their outcomes or products: by reference, that is, to the dispositions they entrain.

## Types of habits

The *Oxford English Dictionary* defines 'habit' as 'a settled disposition to act in a certain way'. Speaking of good or bad habits in relation to the different contexts just identified can make sense only given a knowledge of the kinds of habit involved. Since I have from the outset connected habits with the idea of training, I shall not consider here cases of habituation which are not consequent upon training: for example, such 'blind' habits as nail-biting or putting on one's right shoe first. I have already indicated that in thinking about the aims of schooling, any talk of good habits is liable to refer primarily to rational habits of mind. I now propose to distinguish two types of habit relevant to understanding early (moral) training and habituation.

In a classic modern discussion of the differences between intelligent capacities and habits, Ryle (1963) distinguished between single- and multi-track dispositions. Multi-track dispositions are traits which are liable to variable expression in the light of a context-sensitive observance of rules. Referring to Jane Austin's sensitive description of the specific form of pride of her heroine in *Pride and Prejudice*, Ryle observes that this disposition cannot adequately be characterised in terms of any one standard form or pattern of action or reaction. On the other hand, Ryle considers reflexes and all habits to be single-track dispositions; to be an habitual smoker, for example, is just to be prone to light the cigar under such and such conditions. Ryle also draws our attention to another distinction between intelligent capacities and habits: the former are built up by training, the latter by drill: 'Drill dispenses with intelligence, training develops it' (1963: 43).

Scheffler notes, however, that Ryle incorrectly includes under 'habit' not only propensities – such as the smoking habit – but also facilities, that is, relatively routinizable competencies of a calculative or computational sort. According to Scheffler, facilities are – like critical skills – acquired through training: 'They are acquired . . . through a variety of procedures involving repeated trials and including, or at least capable of being facilitated by, the process of showing how, by description, explanation, or example' (1965: 101–2; see also Peters 1974: 318). Scheffler emphasizes that such facilities should be included within the sphere of knowing how to, despite the fact that they share certain common properties with more habitual propensities, particularly the possibility of becoming automatic. In line with both Ryle's distinction between types of dispositions and Scheffler's distinction between critical skills and habits, I propose to distinguish two categories of habit of particular importance to early childhood upbringing and moral training: single-track and multi-track habits.[2] A single-track habit is a propensity to behave in a set way under specific conditions, while multi-track habits are capacities for appropriate rule observance in variable circumstances. Unlike multi-track habits, single-track dispositions and habits have largely uniform expressions (Ryle 1963: 43).

In early childhood upbringing, single-track habits can be called *closed* habits or routines; once acquired, they are apt for relatively unreflective exercise. Much early childhood training, conditioning, and drill is aimed at acquiring such habits, for it is in this way that the infant is (for example) adjusted to day and night rhythm, trained to take solid food, pot trained and kerb drilled. Once acquired, such single-track habits or routines cease to be evaluated as 'good' habits; training in these single-track habits – think, for example, of being toilet-trained – is directed at a behaviour-shaping more or less equivalent to conditioning or drill.

By and large, parents try to instill such habits by positive reinforcement – above all avoiding any association of them with negative feelings – not least, as already noted, because early training is also aimed at assisting the infant to gain a foothold in the moral and social world. It is through sharing our feeding and sleeping habits and by becoming continent that the infant comes to participate in ordinary human practices or routines. (Hence, subsequent geriatric or other incontinence is invariably experienced as a loss of human dignity.) All the same, the logical distinction between the two types of habits does not preclude practical continuity. Initially, a young child may be drilled or trained to wash his or her hands before sitting down at the dinner table; however this single-track habit may become multi-track with further under-standing of the reasons for such hygiene, then he or she may sometimes come to recognize exceptions to such reasons. In such circumstances, the closed habit is – metaphorically speaking – broken open. But generally, the acquisi-tion of single-track habits assists the young child to participate in our routines of daily life and can to that extent be regarded as preconditional upon moral development and upbringing.

In early upbringing, however, training of multi-track habit also plays a crucial role. These habits are expression of dawning (and still incomplete) moral qualities or traits of character – of right conduct and appropriate affec-tion – which may also be called *moral habits of mind* (or of heart). A young child is trained by parents not to hurt other persons or pets, to comfort, stroke or caress others who are in distress, to return toys, to refrain from aggression, to respond appropriately to discipline and to have proper feelings of pity, care, and regret. In such cases parental training aims to produce what Oakeshott (1962) calls 'the (moral) habits of affection and behaviour'. The rules or values mostly observed in such habits are the basic rules and common values (of non-injury, respect for property, promise keeping and so on) of social membership (Peters 1974; Bok 1996). Indeed, young children are by and large trained to perceive interpersonal relations very much in terms of these rules or values.

In the course of such training parents will often explain or justify such rules or values *as if* the young child could already understand their point and purpose: hence, early moral habituation often aspires to a sort of teaching. Young children are trained to perceive, to be sensitive to, the weal and woe of others, and to react as reason would require. The habit of paying attention to the suffering of others would not, according to Peters, be itself a virtue, but it might help children to be moved by compassion on specific occasions (1974: 327). Such habits, however, may be regarded as multi-track dispositions: different emotional and behavioural responses may be underpinned by one and the same basic rule. It would seem to be through these socially implicated moral habits that young children are brought to share our moral and social world.

If this analysis is sound, then it is reasonable to suggest that moral upbringing and development begin with moral habit training: that acquiring multi-track dispositions of this kind constitutes a first crucial stage of moral development.[3]

## Habituation in early childhood

Distinguishing between these two types of early childhood habit may help forestall certain misunderstandings about early upbringing. As Sherman observes (1989: 158), it is largely the mechanical theory of habituation – whereby all habits are conceived as single-track dispositions – which serves to obscure transition from childhood to moral maturity. Indeed, what has been termed 'the paradox of moral education' would appear to be be based upon some such confusion about development. Thus, in the course of observing that children can and must enter the palace of reason through the courtyard of habit and tradition, Peters says, 'The problem of moral education is that of how the necessary habits of behaviour can be acquired in a way which does not stultify the development of a rational code at a later stage' (Peters 1974: 272; see also Kazepides 1979). A first general response to this 'paradox' might be to point out that imparting moral habits does not necessarily preclude the possibility of their submission to critical reflection.[4] But any such response clearly fails to show how we are to make sense of a moral education which starts with moral habituation and ends in critical moral understanding. Any serious examination of this issue is likely to begin with Aristotle's celebrated discussion of relationships between character, training and reason in the *Nichomachean Ethics* (*NE*).[5]

In Book II of *NE* Aristotle clearly states that the development of such virtues as justice and courage crucially depends upon the regular performance of acts of justice and courage:

> To sum up, then, in a single account: A state (of character) arises from [the repetition of] similar activities. Hence we must display the right activities, since differences in these imply corresponding differences in the states. It is not unimportant, then, to acquire one sort of habit or another, right from our youth; rather, it is very important, indeed all-important.
>
> (*NE* 1103b21–25)

Thus, adults have to see to it that young children are trained in good habits, which must also entail attention to the quality of their own conduct, especially to their practices of child rearing. Intellectual virtue or virtues of theoretical reflection develop mostly under the influence of direct instruction; virtues of character have their sources in habituation (*NE* 1103a15–17).

However, taking Aristotle's remarks on the training of character at their face value, character states have formerly been held to be the exclusive product of practical rehearsal: conceived, more often than not, in terms of non-rational training or blind drilling (Sherman 1989: 157). Contrary to this traditional interpretation, some philosophers have argued that moral habituation should not be conceived in *NE* as a mindless process (Sorabji 1980: 216; Crittenden 1990). In order to become good-tempered, for example, a child need not be trained to avoid anger in *every* situation. The trick is rather to learn to eschew anger on the right occasions, as well as, of course, to feel it on the right ones. Habituation, Sorabji emphasises, involves appraising the situation to see what is called for; it is grounded in a kind of intuitive perception.

The crucial question would now seem to be whether these acquired multi-track moral habits are necessary for further moral development or whether such habits themselves amount to moral goodness. On Sorabji's view, the habits acquired in early childhood are not complete virtues, but *habit-virtues*, that is, virtues not yet enriched by practical wisdom or reasoning. Since complete virtue requires practical wisdom, the virtues presupposed to practical wisdom are virtues in only an attenuated sense (1980: 212). It certainly seems that for Aristotle himself mere habituation is not sufficient: 'Arguments and teaching surely do not influence everyone, but the soul of the student needs to have been prepared by habits for enjoying and hating finely, like ground that is to nourish seed' (*NE* 1179b24–26).[6]

Multi-track habits presuppose a grasp of social rules and criteria, and since comprehension of such rules changes over time, habits are liable to develop along with them. In the spirit of Aristotle, Sherman defends an explicitly developmental conception of habits and habituation as liable to change with advanced understanding (1989: 159–160).[7] The trouble is, of course, that while affective and perceptual capacities can be trained and cultivated at an early age – and in early upbringing the cultivation of these capacities goes largely hand in hand – complete virtue is a complex of affective, perceptual and deliberative capacities, and rational capacities develop rather later. All the same, coming to feel emotions like anger, pity, regret or shame is inextricably linked to learning to discern features of circumstances which warrant such emotional responses (Sherman 1989: 167–8; 1997). It is via attention to such particulars that young children are brought to discern what is affectively salient in a given situation.

To this extent at least, early childhood training in habit-virtues and parental tutoring have a distinct cognitive dimension. Indeed, Sherman conceives habituation as an essentially critical practice (though, given the context of upbringing, I would prefer to use the term 'intelligent practice'). In consequence, it is arguable that talk of becoming just by doing just actions, temperate by doing temperate actions, is shorthand for something rather more developmentally complex (Sherman 1989: 178). By the rehearsal of multi-track habits children are gradually brought by caretakers to a more sensitive appreciation of their responses to circumstances, which is rational or intellectual as well as affective.

Thus, following recent readings of Aristotle, we may conclude that moral training and habituation in early childhood have a distinct cognitive dimension: the acquisition of multi-track habits or habit-virtues is not just preparatory to the development of moral reflection and deliberation but crucially constitutive of it. Clearly, however, a certain context of upbringing – a context of close parental nurture – is presupposed to this account of early moral training and habituation. Moreover, it would seem that the early one-to-one relationship of mother to child is of particular significance in this connection. We may now therefore ask to what extent empirical research into this relationship might shed light on the phenomenon of early moral training and habituation.

## The first relationship

Many theories of moral education and development appear to enshrine unexamined assumptions regarding the 'true' nature of newborn or infants. In discussing the paradox of moral education, however, McClellan (1976) claims that a psychological theory is not – whatever philosophers and psychologists may have thought – a scientific summary of brute facts. It should rather be regarded as a practical or moral theory about how we *ought* to raise children: 'The dominant machismo-infected theories of our culture, from the Books of Proverbs through S. Freud and L. Kohlberg, all regard children as barbarians outside the gates'. But 'children, from a disconcertingly early age on, are obviously persons and obviously inside the gates' (1976: 158–9). McClellan's point may therefore prompt us to ask afresh about the purposes of habituation. Are the young habituated to assist them inside the gates of humanity, or does such habituation only make sense in so far as caretakers conceive them as developing persons already?

Instead of speculating about possible answers, we will draw upon some allegedly empirical data of child development, especially the findings of early years research. If, according to Crittenden, 'the elaboration of an account of morality rests on a degree of concrete experience and a grasp of what is involved in the process of entering into social relations, learning about morality, and coming to be involved in moral practices' (1990: 104), what could infant research have to teach us about the first close relationships within which training and habituation occur? After all, as Burnyeat points out (1980: 70), Aristotle's developmental picture may well be far too simple, by comparison with what modern scientific research has to offer.

Mother-child research does appear to indicate that even the earliest of interactions are two-way affairs, in which there is mutual interpersonal adjustment. More precisely, infants cannot be conceived as asocial creatures; they are, on the contrary, socially pre-adapted, that is, they are well equipped or genetically programmed to deal with the most important attributes in their immediate environment: people. The sensory apparatus of newborn infants appears to have inbuilt selective attention mechanisms embodying, for example, a preference for faces and moving objects (Kaye 1982: 121). Maternal behaviour patterns seem especially attuned, unsurprisingly, to infant needs. Consider, for example, the mother's natural propensity for baby-talk, her exaggerated mimics and the way she often looks the infant straight in the eyes for more than thirty seconds while adults normally only make sustained eye contact for ten seconds on very special occasions (Stern: 1977). These early interactions may be considered pseudo-dialogues, initiated and sustained by the mother (or other caretaker) as he or she 'replies to' infant reactions, and in so doing, acts *as if* such reactions already have communicative meaning. ('You are bored, angry, hungry, enjoying yourself, aren't you?') The caretaker will constantly stimulate dialogue-like situations or co-operative actions, calling upon a number of dyadic techniques to do so. The game of peek-a-boo is a good example of this.

In the initial encounters with the young child the caretaker acts both for him- or herself and for the child and has therefore been colourfully characterized as a 'double agent' (Shotter and Gregory 1978). It would seem that evolution has produced infants who can fool their caretakers into treating them as more intelligent than they really are: 'it is precisely because parents play out this fiction that it eventually comes to be true' (Kaye 1982: 53). Caretakers take it as their special task to find out the wishes, interests and needs of their infants. Crying, for example, is almost always conceived as if it reflects a sense of agency.

Such mother–child (and caretaker–child) relations, then, make the very first of infant social encounters quite special and significant. In these interactions the caretaker regularly acts *as if* the young child's behaviour is intentional and *as if* his or her utterances have meaning. In this respect, the caretaker's conduct has a strongly contra-factual character: that is, his or her behaviour towards the child invariably presupposes a grasp on its part of rules and principles which have yet to be acquired (Spiecker 1984; 1990). To that extent, caretaker-child relationships are characterized by the caretaker's imaginative anticipation of dialogical possibilities: of the possibilities of rationality and intentionality.[8] Indeed, Atkinson points out that mothers interpret infant gestures and noises in terms of Grice-like maxims of 'sincerity' ('He's really faking when he makes that sound') and 'consistency' ('Won't you make up your mind what you want?'); in short, 'The mother is treating the child as if he behaved according to adult conceptions such as intention, purpose, sincerity, deceit and so on' (1982: 73). In the course of nurture the caretaker acts on behalf of the child by giving voice to his or her supposed needs, feelings, emotions and interests; from the outset, human capacities and personal qualities are projected on to the newborn.

Returning to the issue raised by McClellan, we may draw two cautious conclusions. First, the infant is by nature pro-socially adapted in a way which predisposes it to moral habituation and training; hence, the newborn are 'inside the gates' of humanity virtually by nature. Second, by virtue of the caretaker's initial contra-factual anticipation of early human responses, the infant is from the outset treated as a would-be person; in view of this, the newborn are well 'inside the gates', and this is amply exhibited in the internal dynamic of early moral habituation.

Does this research-based understanding of initial caretaker-child relationships shed any light on the contribution of early training and habituation to moral development? Although the largely one-sided nature of the contra-factual anticipation gradually diminishes, the caretaker continues to act on both his or her own and the child's behalf beyond the stage of relative childish independence. In helping children to acquire both the closed habits and the virtue-habits, caretakers will give voice to already developed reasons, emotions and intentions. For example, in preventing a child from accidently putting out the eyes of a pet, a parent might say, 'Now you don't want to do that, you will hurt our Felix'. Because of the mutually-encompassing character of this relationship, the training of habits of affectivity and conduct is often connected with reasons, affections, and emotions the child could (or should) have had. Thus, the young child is often 'instructed' or 'invited' to have feelings of relief, joy, and compassion, and parental projection of justifying reasons looks forward to the conversion of such responses into (future) multi-track habits.[9] In sum, early moral training and habituation take place within a framework of parental support generally characterized by contra-factual anticipation of rationality, affectivity and intentionality.

We may therefore conclude that the Aristotelian view of moral training and habituation is not generally incompatible with modern psychological research on early development. This would appear to confirm Okin's observation: 'How early does the moral development of children begin? Modern researchers – confirming Aristotle's observations or hunches – tend to think that it begins very early indeed' (1996: 221).

## The rehabilitation of early moral training and upbringing

We seem to have gone quite far towards answering our opening question, 'When does moral education begin?' From what has been said so far it would seem that moral upbringing starts as soon as children are trained, admonished, cajoled and instructed to treat human and other sentient beings as agents with interests and desires of their own, to which they should not be humanly indifferent (Melden 1971: 133). In early upbringing responsible caretakers draw children's attention to these interests and to the weal and woe of other species; they supervise the child's perception and project moral appraisals and traits on to the child. In the course of such shaping parents will naturally employ so-called *thick* ethical concepts: concepts, that is, which are both evaluative and descriptive. In conveying to the child that some action may hurt a pet, parents will simultaneously describe it as painful and evaluate it as 'naughty' or 'bad': as something that ought not therefore to be done (Williams 1985: 129; O'Leary 1993). It is by such training that children acquire appropriate habits of affect and conduct, the basis of good conduct by which injury to others as well as self-harm may be prevented. In this connection – responding to Kohlberg's criticism of the so-called 'bag of virtues approach' – Scheffler (1991: 79) has observed that he is less concerned with the moral stage of his fellow citizens than that he is able to walk the streets free of bodily assault; that after being stabbed, he would not be much consoled by the information that his attacker is moving in his own good time up the ladder of moral development.

Indeed, it may be hoped that by acknowledging the crucial place of moral dispositions or virtue-habits – including the important part played by feelings – in moral development and education, we may avoid a too rationalistic conception of morality and a one-sidedly intellectualist approach of moral education. We also need to pay considerable attention to the primary context of early moral training: namely, the first affective relationships between caretaker and child.

## Notes

1 The latter context can include different forms of professional training, e.g. medical, teacher or military training, in which the training aims at acquiring specific professional skills. However, I will leave these forms of professional training out of consideration.

2 References to Ryle's distinction between single- and multi-track dispositions can also be found in Kazepides (1979: 158) and Bohlmeijer (1987: 147–8).

3 Training is also a key notion in Wittgensteinian accounts of upbringing (see MacMillan 1985; Atkinson 1982; Spiecker 1984).

4 This idea, of course, was already mooted by Richard Peters: '. . . learning habits in an intelligent way can be regarded as providing an appropriate basis, in the moral case, for the later stage when rules are followed or rejected because of the justification that they are seen to have or lack' (1974: 326).

5 For more comprehensive accounts of Aristotle's views on moral and civic education and development, see Sherman 1989, Crittenden 1990 and Curren 1992.

6 In this view training of habits is necessary for teaching or instruction. Burnyeat (1980) characterizes the starting-point and the last stage of moral development as respectively 'the that' and 'the because'. The child first learns or comes to see what is noble and just, not by experience or by induction, but by being habituated to

noble and just conduct. This knowledge of 'the that' becomes second nature to him or her: 'This is not yet to know *why* it is true, but it is to have *learned that* it is true in the sense of having made the judgment your own, second nature to you' (1980: 74). Such a young person has acquired the capacity to enjoy noble and just conduct for their own sake, but does not yet understand why they are so. The road to full virtue ends when the person of virtue and practical wisdom understands 'the because' of these beliefs or convictions (see also Tobin 1989).

7  For other Aristotelian views of moral stages, see Crittenden 1990: 120; Tobin 1989.

8  Other postulates are veracity, unicity, authenticity. Dialogues are characterized by a *mutual* contra-factual anticipation of these postulates by the participants (Habermas 1971; De Boer 1980). The caretaker's attitude towards the infant can also be characterised as 'adopting the intentional stance', which Dennett describes as the strategy of interpreting the behaviour of an entity (person, animal, artifact, whatever) by treating it *as if* it were a rational agent (1996: 35).

9  The way in which the young child is 'taught' or 'instructed', which feelings or emotions it should have, is nicely demonstrated in research regarding the phenomenon of 'social referencing'. Social referencing is generally described as the treating of other persons as a source of information regarding the social or physical environment. This phenomenon can be met with in infants as young as eight months, but is more common in two-year old children. When, for example, the young child is confronted with unknown stimuli – such as a noisy object or a stranger who enters the room – the child will often adjust his or her feelings and emotions towards the stimulus to those of the caretaker. For example, by looking worried – often in an exaggerated way – the caretaker 'invites' the young child to have the same feelings and behaviour towards the stimulus (Thompson 1987).

# References

Aristotle (1985) *Nichomachean Ethics* (Ethica Nicomachea), trans. T. Irwin, Cambridge: Hackett.

Atkinson, C. (1982) 'Beginning to learn', *Journal of Philosophy of Education* 16, 1: 69–75.

Bohlmeijer, J. (1987) 'Gewoontevorming' ('Habituation'), *Pedagogische Verhandelingen*, Special Issue: 143–150.

Bok, S. (1996) *Common Values*, Columbia/London: University of Missouri Press.

Burnyeat, M. F. (1980) 'Aristotle on learning to be good', in A. O. Rorty (ed.) *Essays on Aristotle's Ethics*, Berkeley: University of California Press.

Crittenden, P. (1990) *Learning To Be Moral: Philosophical thoughts about moral development*, New Jersey/London: Humanities Press International.

Curren, R. (1992) 'Education and the origins of character in Aristotle', in M. Buchmann and R. Floden (eds) *Philosophy of Education 1992*, Normal, Ill.: Philosophy of Education Society.

De Boer, T. (1980) *Grondslagen van een kritische psychologie* ('Foundations of a Critical Psychology'), Baarn: Ambo.

Dennett, D. C. (1996) *Kinds of Minds: Towards an understanding of consciousness*, London: Orion Books.

Flanagan, O. (1991) ~~*Varieties of Moral Personality: Ethics and psychological realism*~~, Cambridge, Mass.: Harvard University Press.

Habermas, J. (1971) 'Vorbereitende Bemerkungen zu einer Theorie der kommunikativen Kompetenz', in J. Habermas und N. Luhmann, *Theorie der Gesellschaft oder Sozialtechnologie*, Frankfurt a.M.: Suhrkamp.

Kaye, K. (1982) *The Mental and Social Life of Babies: How parents create persons*, London: Methuen.

Kazepides, T. (1979) 'The alleged paradox of moral education', in D. B. Cochrane, C. M. Hamm and A. C. Kazepides (eds) *The Domain of Moral Education*, New York: Paulist Press.

Kohlberg, L. (1981) 'Education for justice: A modern statement of the Socratic view', in L. Kohlberg, *Essays on Moral Development: vol. 1, The Philosophy of Moral Development: Moral stages and the idea of justice*, San Francisco: Harper and Row.

MacMillan, J. (1985) 'Rational teaching', *Teachers College Record* 86: 411–22.

McClellan, J. E. (1976) *Philosophy of Education*, Englewood Cliffs: Prentice-Hall.

Melden, I. (1971) 'Moral education and moral action', in C. M. Beck, B. S. Crittenden and E. V. Sullivan (eds) *Moral Education: Interdisciplinary approaches,* New York: Newman Press.

Oakeshott, M. (1962) *Rationalism in Politics and Other Essays*, London: Methuen.

Oakley, J. (1992) *Morality and the Emotions*, New York: Routledge.

Okin, S. M. (1996) 'Feminism, moral development, and the virtues', in R. Crisp (ed.) *How Should One Live? Essays on the virtues*, Oxford: Clarendon Press.

O'Leary, P. (1993) 'Ethical attentiveness', *Studies in Philosophy and Education* 12, 2–4: 139–51.

Passmore, J. (1980) *The Philosophy of Teaching*, London: Duckworth.

Peláez, M. and Gewirtz, J.L. (1995) 'The learning of moral behavior. A behavior-analytic approach', in W. Kurtiness and J. Gewirtz (eds) *Moral Development: An introduction*, Boston/London: Allyn and Bacon.

Peters, R. S. (1974) *Psychology and Ethical Development*, London: Unwin University Books.

Ryle, G. (1963) *The Concept of Mind*, London: Hutchinson.

Scheffler, I. (1965) *Conditions of Knowledge: An introduction to epistemology and education*, Chicago/London: The University of Chicago Press.

—— (1991) 'Moral education beyond moral reasoning', in I. Scheffler, *In Praise of Cognitive Emotions and Others Essays in the Philosophy of Education*, New York/London: Routledge.

Sherman, N. (1989) *The Fabric of Character: Aristotle's theory of virtue*, Oxford: Clarendon Press.

—— (1997) *Making a Necessity of Virtue. Aristotle and Kant on virtue*, Cambridge: Cambridge University Press.

Shotter, J. and Gregory, S. (1978) 'On first gaining the idea of oneself as a person', in R. Harré (ed.) *Life Sentences*, London/New York: Wiley.

Siegel, H. (1997) *Rationality Redeemed? Further dialogues on an educational ideal*. London: Routledge.

Sorabji, R. (1980) 'Aristotle on the role of intellect in virtue', in A. O. Rorty (ed.) *Essays on Aristotle's Ethics*, Berkeley: University of California Press.

Spiecker, B. (1984) 'The pedagogical relationship', *Oxford Educational Review* 10, 2: 203–10.

—— (1990) 'Forms of trust in education and development', *Studies in Philosophy and Education* 10, 2: 157–64.

—— (1988) 'Education and the moral emotions', in B. Spiecker and R. Straughan (eds) *Philosophical Issues in Moral Education and Development*, Milton Keynes: Open University Press.

Stern, D. (1977) *The First Relationship: Infant and mother*, London: Fontana/Open Books.

Thompson, R. A. (1987) 'Empathy and emotional understanding: the early development of empathy', in N. Eisenberg and J. Strayer (eds) *Empathy and Its Development*, Cambridge: Cambridge University Press.

Tobin, B. M. (1989) 'An Aristotelian Theory of Moral Development', *Journal of Philosophy of Education* 23, 2: 195–211.

Williams, B. (1985) *Ethics and the Limits of Philosophy*, London: Fontana/Collins.

# 16

# TRUST, TRADITIONS AND PLURALISM

## Human flourishing and liberal polity

*Kenneth A. Strike*

## Introduction

In *Political Liberalism* (1993: 59) John Rawls claims that people have two moral powers, the capacity for a sense of justice and the capacity for a conception of the good. Rawls's liberalism notwithstanding, the second moral power is described in a way suggestive of a communitarian outlook. Rawls associates the second moral power with the idea of a comprehensive doctrine which he characterizes as a tradition. He sees people as formed through their community membership, and this is part of his account of how people develop the second moral power. However, this account of human flourishing is embedded in a liberal outlook which insists on a plurality of traditions and communities whose members are accorded equal rights by a state which must treat them impartially. The net effect is to privatize human flourishing. Only the right is a matter of public concern. The good belongs to individuals or private associations.

I do not criticize this view here. I believe that there must be substantial restraints on making conceptions of the good into public conceptions. Nevertheless, privatizing human flourishing may have undesirable consequences. One consequence for public schools is that in moral education attention is focused on identifying moral content that has public standing.[1] However, the neutrality expected of the liberal state may have a chilling effect on engagement with views of human flourishing.

This educational privatization of human flourishing makes sense if those private associations that develop conceptions of, and the capacity for, human flourishing do so well. However, we need to remind ourselves that the academic subjects schools teach are not just instrumental goods. They are what MacIntyre calls practices with goods internal to them and virtues required to realize these goods. These goods are among the components of human flourishing. Public schools cannot privatize them without making intellectual practices into mere instrumentalities.

In this chapter, I am concerned with how the goods, virtues, and standards associated with academic disciplines are taught. My focus is on human flourishing, not on the public ethic. I argue that to teach intellectual practices so as to transmit their associated goods and virtues, teachers should play roles which I shall call *exemplar* and *elder*. I shall argue that trust is a requirement for these roles and that trust has both personal and communal aspects. However, the privatization of human flourishing makes it difficult adequately to realize trust in public schools.

My claims for trust depends on the view that the standards, goods, and virtues that are internal to intellectual practices cannot be fully cognized by the uninitiated. Hence, students cannot judge the worth of intellectual practices until they have moved some distance down the path of initiation into them. Here trust substitutes for understanding. It is an epistemological bridge. I am not going to make the necessary epistemological argument here, but it is presupposed. It depends on the criticism of foundationalist epistemologies that has been made by philosophers such as Kuhn (1970), Toulmin (1972) and Lakatos (1970).[2] This critique shows two things of importance. First, 'reason does not go all the way down'. The capacity to reason depends on the internalization of concepts which have histories and must be learned from other people. Reasoning occurs within traditions. Second, experience is dependent on the acquisition of concepts. We cannot experience what we cannot conceive. If so, we cannot fully explain or justify complex intellectual practices to novices. Moreover, students need help in seeing the goods that are internal to such practices. Their attention must be directed. They must be supplied with a vocabulary.

Novices may also be limited in their ability to cognize the worth of intellectual practices because the virtues required by practices may themselves be essential to seeing their point. Dishonest people rarely see the point of honesty or feel the good of integrity. Those who have not formed the disposition to seek rigour in argument are generally unable to experience the satisfaction that results from constructing a powerful but simple proof. Thus, the virtues required to realize the goods internal to practices are often also required to experience them or see their point. Moreover, the possession of these virtues is often part of the good of the practice.

Hence, education requires an initiation into intellectual practices that cannot be rationalized to the novice, because the capacities required to appraise and experience the goods, standards, and virtues associated with these practices are largely developed during the process of mastery. Education is initiation (Peters 1964). Engaging students (who often seem very disengaged (Steinberg 1996)) in the process of initiation may be motivated through appeal to, or manipulation of, external goods. Alternatively it can be mediated by trust. The latter approach, I argue, is more conducive to human flourishing.

KENNETH A. STRIKE

# Two examples of initiation

## *Case 1*

In my first high school chemistry lab we performed an electrolysis of water. Inverted water-filled test tubes slowly filled with gas as the experiment progressed. One filled twice as rapidly as the other. We were told that this was because water is two parts hydrogen to one part oxygen. Then we were given wooden splints. These were lit and extinguished leaving a spark. The splint was inserted into the oxygen where it burst into flame, then went out. We were told that the splint flamed because it was put into pure oxygen, and went out because the oxygen was consumed. Later the teacher told us that this experiment was evidence for the particulate theory of matter, and that what happens in chemical interactions is the recombination of atoms.

Is the experiment evidence to the novice? The phenomena can be explained by the particulate theory of matter and the oxygenation theory of combustion. Does this make it evidence? Suppose we take another theory of combustion, the phlogiston theory. Can modern theories better explain the phenomena than this nineteenth century account? Are no other accounts possible? These topics were not discussed, but the evidence for a scientific theory is not just that it can explain some phenomena, but that it can explain them better than rivals.

More importantly, the teacher's description of the experiment would hardly be intelligible apart from the particulate theory of matter. The teacher's interpretation of the experiment assumes the conclusions for which it was supposed to be evidence. Also, there are many things ignored in the experiment. Why is the volume of gas emphasized instead of the production of gases from a liquid? Why not focus on the flame and heat instead of the volume of material? Many of the most manifest features of the experiment are viewed as irrelevant, at least for the moment. Why?

These observations suggest that even if the experiment is in some sense evidence for the conclusions drawn, it cannot be evidence for the novice who lacks the prerequisite interpretive concepts. This case is better understood in this way. The teacher is saying to students, 'Here is how chemists think. Here is the vocabulary they use. Here is how they see these phenomena. It is the volume of gas that is important. It is the fact that combustion is accelerated by one of these gasses until it is gone that counts. Ignore the smoke, flame and heat. We'll get to these in a bit. If you will only acquire this vocabulary, talk like chemists talk, see it as we see it, we can help you to make sense of this, eventually in all of its details. If you won't, we can't help you. You must trust me (us) for a while'. The explanation is not an argument. It is an initiation, one that will not work unless the student trusts the teacher.

This case emphasizes acquisition of the concepts and standards of judgement of an academic practice. Now consider one that emphasizes its goods and virtues.

*Case 2*

Mrs Smith was my ninth grade algebra teacher. To enter Mrs Smith's class was to enter the Temple of Mathematics. Equations were objects of reverence. There were no attempts to make math fun or 'relevant'. There was no discussion of how math helped one get a good job. Rather, Mrs Smith was able to point to the goods that made math intrinsically valuable.

I recall a demonstration in which she 'proved' that $1 = 0$. We were invited to discover what went wrong. We checked the proof line by line. Everything seemed OK. We were invited to inspect a particular line. No one could see what was wrong. Finally we were told, 'Why, here you've multiplied by 0'. This was done in a way so as to suggest 'Isn't it fascinating that multiplying by zero can be so hard to see, yet it has such an effect on an otherwise power-ful proof?' Through Mrs Smith's evident engagement with this paradox, and her insistence that it had to be resolved and understood, we had been given a small window on what motivated mathematicians. When, years later, I became engaged with Godel's proof and Russell's paradox, I had only to look to Mrs Smith to understand how mathematicians could find fascination in problems that challenged the ideals and central convictions of the field.

I do not recall that Mrs Smith used terms like elegance, simplicity, paradox or power to describe mathematics, but I do know that she showed us that these things were what motivated her about mathematics. These were words I acquired later for an experience to which she had pointed. Moreover, in her world, consistency and rigour were paramount, contradictions and fuzzi-ness not tolerated, resolving paradoxes obligatory. Mrs Smith exemplified the virtues required to realize the goods of math. In doing so, she was beginning the process of initiation into the goods internal to mathematics and their associated virtues.

One thing that made Mrs Smith's pointing and exemplifying successful was the integrity of her stance. It was apparent that this was how she felt about math. In effect, her message to us was this. 'Here is what I see in math. There are goods internal to its practice. There are virtues required to realize these goods. Let me help you see them'. The success of the message depended on students understanding the math well enough to have some rudiment of the experience she sought to mediate, but it also depended on our trust in Mrs Smith. She was able to point us towards these goods and virtues and to show us that they enriched her life. These two examples both involve teaching languages of judgement and appraisal, languages essential to cognizing the goods, virtues and standards of disciplines. They also involve pointing to the goods internal to the practice, and helping students to look for what the language describes. They constitute an initiation, not an argument. They do not make sense as attempts to persuade students of the good of mathe-matics. They make sense as ways of helping students to conceptualize and experience goods that other human beings have tested and found valuable.

The initiation can only succeed if the teacher is trusted. The teacher's best 'evidence' for her practice is that its values and forms of argument have been realized in her life and in the lives of others. Mrs Smith was able to show us what mathematics contributed to her life. She could do this because she was able to point to the goods of math and because she was an exemplar of its virtues. She was able to show us the beauty of a proof and the enticement of a puzzle. She exemplified the virtues of an insistence on rigour and clarity. She was not satisfied until we got to the bottom of things. She was able to show us that these goods and virtues enriched her life.

Here we can ask two further questions. The first is whether the virtues acquired in the mastery of a discipline transfer to other areas of life. The second is whether they should. Much that has been written about the value of intellectual pursuits assumes that the virtues and habits of mind acquired through them do transfer. If so, it may be that success in transmitting the goods and the virtues of academic disciplines has import not just for human flourishing, but for the public ethic as well. Perhaps people who acquire a sense of intellectual integrity and a respect for reasoned argument are also better citizens. However, the justification for teaching academic subject matter in a way that develops the virtues internal to it should not depend on whether those virtues transfer to the public ethic. It should be enough that they help to enrich life. To say otherwise is to devalue human flourishing at the expense of justice.

It should not be assumed uncritically that capacities that are virtues in the context of some academic discipline are virtues in all contexts. To take a trivial example, an appreciation of the importance of rigour in mathematics may not be a virtue when transferred to balancing one's checkbook. Here getting the balance close enough may be fine and spending hours searching for the missing penny a vice. Virtues and vices are contextual. We need ways to assess the contribution that academic pursuits and their associated goods and virtues make to a full picture of a good life. This is a point to which I shall return below.

### Affiliation, practices and traditions

In this section, I take a deeper look at the claim that the process of initiation into the goods, virtues or standards associated with academic subject matters cannot be fully rationalized to students, and thus, that initiation must be mediated by trust. Here I rely substantially on Alasdair MacIntyre's (1984) account of practices, traditions, and the virtues. I use this account to argue that trust is not just a relationship between a teacher and a student, but a relationship between a teacher, a student and a community. There are two different kinds of communities involved, communities of practice and communities constituted by a tradition.

MacIntyre characterizes a practice as:

any coherent and complex form of socially established cooperative human activity through which goods internal to that form of activity are realized in the course of trying to achieve those standards of excellence which are appropriate to, and partially definitive of, that form of activity, with the result that human powers to achieve excellence, and human conceptions of the ends and goods involved, are systematically extended.

(MacIntyre 1984: 187)

Examples of practices include complex games and sports (e.g. chess and football), academic disciplines (e.g. mathematics or biology), the arts (e.g. musical performance, dancing, and painting), and many occupations (e.g. farming or engineering). It is, of course, to this picture of practices that my argument has appealed throughout.

There are authoritative standards associated with a given practice. MacIntyre claims:

A practice involves standards of excellence and obedience to rules as well as the achievement of goods. To enter into a practice is to accept the authority of those standards and the inadequacy of my own performance as judged by them. It is to subject my own attitudes, choices, preferences and tastes to the standards which currently and partially define the practice.

(MacIntyre 1984: 190)

MacIntyre gives an initial account of the virtues that connects them to practices and, thus, suggests their role in human flourishing: 'A virtue is an acquired human quality the possession and exercise of which tends to enable us to achieve those goods which are internal to practices and the lack of which effectively prevents us from achieving any such goods (ibid: 191)'. He says two things about goods internal to practices. First, goods are internal to a practice in that they can only be 'specified' within the context of that practice. Second, they can only be identified and recognized by the experience of participation in the practice (ibid. 188–9). The first of these aspects of internality I take to mean that the goods, virtues, and standards of a practice are bound up together so that they cannot be described or understood apart from each other. By the second aspect MacIntyre means to call attention to the fact that we cannot experience such goods except through participation in the practice.

Consider the motivation to learn. Again, it follows that it is difficult for a novice to be persuaded to master a practice through an argument that appeals to an understanding of its internal goods. The novice does not yet understand these goods. However, the novice may be persuaded to master a practice by an argument that appeals to external goods. (And, as MacIntyre suggests, doing so may be one way to get the student to come to have the experience of the practice's internal goods.)

Here, however, I think MacIntyre is wrong if he means to suggest that all that is necessary to engage novices with a practice is to begin with an external inducement. When external goods are overly relied on to motivate, they can come to substitute for intrinsic goods, not point to them. Additionally, the consistent and pervasive use of extrinsic motivation may well convey a message of social approval of these motives and of disapproval of intrinsic motivation. Finally, merely getting a novice to go through the motions of a practice may be insufficient to produce an experience of its goods. Experience is mediated by concepts. The experience of the internal goods of a practice may often require someone who can help the learner to acquire the language necessary to articulate the goods, virtues, and standards of a practice and who can direct attention towards the relevant features of the practice. This takes us back to the picture of the teacher as one who initiates by showing, helping the student to acquire the language appropriate to a practice, exhibiting its virtues, and who shows mastery through criticism of performance. This is the teacher as exemplar.

This again points to the importance of trust. Teachers may employ extrinsic rewards without asking for trust. Students have little problem understanding fun or getting a job. However, the teacher can not function as an exemplar, cannot point to what is intrinsically valuable, without asking for trust. The message here must always be, 'Do it my way, think about it as I do, pay attention to these aspects, here's what you should be seeing and beginning to experience. Trust me and you may come to experience it as I do.'

To trust the teacher in this way is to acknowledge the teacher as an authority. The teacher is someone whose role is achieved in virtue of mastery of the practice, who is thus capable of being an exemplar of its goods, virtues, and standards, and whose task is to guide the initiation of the novice into the practice. This occurs through the process of exemplification, through getting the student to engage in the activities required to master the practice, by using its vocabulary, by drawing attention to its goods, and by applying the standards of excellence appropriate to the practice to the performance of the novice. Such appraisal is not only part of how the novice learns to perform competently, but is also how the novice learns to articulate and internalize a practice's standards and their associated virtues. Given this, the relations between teacher and student with respect to any practice will have some features of an apprenticeship wherein a novice learns the practice under the supervision of an accomplished practitioner whose role is to exemplify and whose authority is justified in virtue of mastery. This mastery is not just a matter of technical competence, but requires the teacher to exemplify the practice's characteristic virtues and to be motivated by the experience of its goods. A mathematics teacher who can solve problems and prove theorems, but who has no love of an elegant proof and no disposition to rigour, may teach math skills, but such a teacher cannot initiate students into the practice of mathematics in a way that contributes to human flourishing.

The object of the student's trust is not just a teacher, but a community. The goods, virtues, and standards of a practice live in the activities and shared understandings of the community engaged in that practice. If so, initiation into a discipline is initiation into a community of shared standards, virtues and goods. To accept these goods and standards is an act of affiliation, of joining. Affiliation may have a complex relationship with trust. Trust may be a bridge to affiliation. The trust extended to a teacher may come to be transferred to the community the teacher represents. Students who have formed a bond with a teacher for reasons unrelated to the subject matter being learned, may be led to affiliate and, thereby, to trust the teacher's community and discover its goods. But affiliation may also be a reason for trust. Students who begin to form a connection with a community of practice may find that their sense of affiliation, of being a member, is a reason for trusting other members and other teachers. In this case affiliation may abet a process of discovering the goods to which we have become committed in virtue of affiliation. In either case, the ultimate object of trust is not the teacher. It is the community and the community's goods, virtues, and standards. The teacher must be viewed as the community's representative whose essential responsibility is to represent the community with integrity.

This view extends the notion that the teacher is an exemplar by adding to it a picture of the teacher's role in the community and a view about the source of the teacher's authority. The teacher is someone who exemplifies the goods, virtues, and standards of an intellectual practice and who has a certain role in a community by virtue of this capacity. The role is that of elder. An elder is someone whose authority in a community depends on their embodying and exemplifying its goods, virtues, and standards. Authority is justified by virtue of a recognition that the elder exemplifies the community's values. The right to teach and the authority it implies is thus dependent on having and being able to display valued excellences.

Practices can themselves be appraised. Students need to have some conception of the goods internal to a practice to judge it. However, they also need some framework, from which perspective they can make comparative judgements about the worth of these goods compared to the goods internal to other practices. Perhaps the goods internal to some practices do not fit into a well elaborated, coherent and praiseworthy view of a good human life, or they may not fit into a coherent view of life in association with others. Individuals and communities attempting to create worthwhile lives for themselves must select practices that provide a mix of goods that are reasonably achievable, and which also develop the virtues required for a satisfactory shared life.

Thus practices can be appraised by their effects on the characters of those individuals who pursue them. The virtues acquired through mastery of a practice may form character so as to affect many areas of life. It may well be that some dispositions that are virtues in the context of a given practice are vices in the larger context of social life. Sports are often judged in this way.

Advocates of American football, for example, will claim that it develops such socially desirable character traits as co-operation and discipline. Opponents argue that it can produce vices such as brutality and subservience to authority.

MacIntyre argues that the appraisal of practices must occur within a tradition. A tradition is characterized as an argument extended through time (MacIntyre 1988: 12). Traditions involve agreement on certain fundamental positions which are defined and redefined as a consequence of internal deliberations and external criticism. Presumably, there will be communities organized around both practices and traditions. Sports teams, scientific societies, orchestras and garden clubs are illustrative of communities organized around practices. Religions, philosophies, and cultures illustrate communities organized around traditions.

If MacIntyre is right, if students are to be able to judge practices, they must also be initiated into praiseworthy frameworks capable of providing perspectives on the nature of a good life and on the virtues required for co-operation in a just society. Much of the preceding discussion of initiation into practices can be generalized to how students acquire such frameworks. However, the public schools of liberal democracies may face limitations in initiating students into them. Public schools in liberal states have an obligation to respect the diversity of traditions in their societies. This may lead them to try to promote practices apart from any tradition that interprets and judges practices. In the next section, I will argue that an attempt to transmit practices while viewing traditions as private matters is likely to result in practices being pursued largely for instrumental reasons, and thus to a diminishment of their role in human flourishing. Once again I will use the lens of trust to approach this matter.

## Traditions and the conditions of trust

How is trust achieved? There are obvious things to say. Trust may be earned by being trustworthy. In part, being trustworthy is a matter of relating to one's students with care and decency. However, an important element of being trustworthy is being a faithful representative of one's practice, its goods, standards, and virtues, teaching with integrity. There is a paradox here. Integrity may make one trustworthy, but it may not, at the outset, be a large factor in whether the novice student sees the teacher as trustworthy. The disability the novice faces in cognizing the standards, virtues, and goods of a field is also a disability in judging whether a teacher is representing a field faithfully. Teachers, thus, are likely to be trusted (or not) for reasons that are independent of whether they exemplify their fields well. Trust may be influenced by the extent to which the child's parents or community trust the school, or by whether the teacher is someone with whom the child can identify. Thus, rightly or wrongly, race or ethnicity can be significant factors in trust.

The relationship between trust and traditions is similarly complex. Traditions provide resources for the appraisal of the goods and virtues internal to practices. Students may come to school with some degree of affiliation with a tradition. They may be members of a religious group or a culture that has its own standards of appraisal. They will have other elders and exemplars in their lives. These diverse frameworks are not always benign as far as schooling is concerned. Some may devalue the life of the mind. Some may be suspicious of secular knowledge. Some may affirm visions of human flourishing that are base or shallow. Some may view certain forms of knowledge as the impositions of an alien culture. Thus a student's framework may be a source of distrust.

Consider an illustration.

### Case 3

Len was a sophomore in high school. Dr Johnson was his biology teacher. Len had been raised in a fundamentalist church. His religion was his tradition, his pastor and his religious teachers his first elders and exemplars, his church his first object of trust. Len's religion conveyed three messages about education. First, all knowledge is God's knowledge. Second, faith stands in judgement of secular knowledge. Len has been brought to view certain forms of secular knowledge with considerable suspicion. Evolution was the chief sinner. Third, jobs are vocations, and being a student is the vocation of a teenager. Academic conscientiousness is a religious duty.

Len's tradition placed two obstacles in the path of any attempt by Dr Johnson to initiate him into the goods, standards, and virtues of biology, one obvious and one subtle. The obvious one is the hostility to evolution. The subtle one is the tendency to view work, including intellectual work, as a duty more for the love of God rather than something valued through an attachment to the goods of the life of the mind. These obstacles were counterbalanced by two positive factors: a duty to one's work and a conviction that even scientific truth reveals the mind of God.

Dr Johnson viewed evolution as central to modern biology. He made it central in his teaching. His classes were not only taught what the theory claimed, but shown that its assumptions were central to how biologists think. The first time Dr Johnson taught evolution he said something like this. 'Many people reject evolution because it is inconsistent with their faith. This may be true of some of you. I respect your beliefs, and I will not require you to believe in evolution. Nevertheless, I regard the evidence for evolution as overwhelming. Moreover, evolution is central to how biologists think about the world. Thus, I will teach it extensively, I will present the evidence for it, and I will assume it in my discussions of other issues. I will expect you to know it. Moreover, I will not waste class time discussing creationism since it is not credible.'

This example illustrates the complexities of trust. Dr Johnson has done what he can to earn Len's trust. He has treated him with kindness. He has refrained from embarrassing him because of his creationist convictions. He has avoided making Len's grade depend on accepting evolution. Dr Johnson has also shown considerable integrity in teaching his discipline. In this respect he has earned Len's trust.

However, he is unlikely to receive it. Len's tradition provides Len with strong reasons to distrust evolution. Dr Johnson's desire faithfully to represent his field has made this worse. He has emphasized evolution. Moreover, he has shown Len that evolution is woven into the fabric of modern biology and, indeed, into the whole of modern science. Now Len has reasons to feel alienated from the whole of science.

There is little in Len's tradition to balance this distrust. There is no attachment to the goods of the life of the mind. The view that knowledge reveals the mind of God is unlikely to work in the case of evolution. There remains only a duty to conscientiousness, but, in this case, Len is likely to view this as a duty to endure Dr Johnson.

Dr Johnson has done what he can while respecting his discipline. He has tried to relate to Len with kindness, and he has shown respect to Len's beliefs without suggesting that he agrees with them. This, and Len's need to do his work conscientiously, may enable Len to attend to what Dr Johnson says and to consider the evidence fairly. However, Dr Johnson cannot adequately teach Len so long as Len cannot trust the community and the work of modern biology. He may learn what they say, but he cannot affiliate. He cannot make the standards, virtues, and goods of the practice his. Len thus faces limits in incorporating science, and perhaps the life of the mind, into his conception of human flourishing. Here the communal aspects of trust become crucial. In order to teach so as to promote human flourishing, teachers must ask students not only to learn a subject, but to engage and, perhaps, affiliate with communities whose goods and standards they can only glimpse. Students in turn may appraise these opportunities to affiliate from the perspective of frameworks that are receptive or unreceptive to the goods and virtues of the subject.

Public schools, however, cannot affirm some particular tradition as the basis of the education they seek to provide. Indeed, they face formidable obstacles in even putting different traditions on the table for discussion. Public sensitivity about religious and cultural differences has a strong chilling effect here. Teachers are in a weak position to counter dysfunctional frameworks by offering praiseworthy alternatives. Moreover, the teachers in a given school are themselves unlikely to share any common framework. As a consequence they will be limited in their ability to articulate the purposes of education in terms of any larger vision of the nature of human flourishing. They will be unable to do so collectively, restrained from doing so as individuals, and limited in their ability to promote open discussion of praiseworthy alternatives. Public schools that seek to be neutral between competing traditions are thus apt to be morally incoherent as far as visions of the good life are concerned. Moreover, one of the sources of trust is necessarily absent from such schools. Students cannot trust teachers nor can teachers trust one another on the basis of membership in a community forged by a shared tradition and engaged in a commonly understood educational project.

One consequence may be an instrumental conception of schooling. Teachers face restraints on their ability to locate the practices they seek to transmit in a larger picture of human flourishing, but they face no similar obstacles in explaining that people who are competent in disciplines such as math or science have good job prospects. In the United States, it is currently popular to believe that students can be engaged with their school work if we have high standards and high stakes tests, and it may well be true that achievement scores will go up as a consequence of high stakes tests. Proposals of this sort are, though, monuments to our inability to help students to see the purposes of their education in the context of a coherent vision of human flourishing which values the goods internal to intellectual practices.

Finally, to attempt to promote engagement with learning through high stakes testing may well be to teach an instrumental evaluative frame to students, which will make affiliation difficult because it does not attend to those goods that are internal to the discipline. It is imaginable that we could create an educational system in which test scores would rise and genuine education, the sort of education that involves affiliation with communities and the internalization of their goods and standards, could wane.

Here it may be useful to contrast US public schools with US Catholic schools. In a recent discussion of Catholic schools Bryk, Lee, and Holland (1993: 35–41) argue that Catholic schools are no longer narrowly sectarian institutions. Since Vatican II, they have become rooted in a humane neo-scholasticism developed by such writers as Gilson and Maritain and derived from interpretations of Aquinas and Aristotle. This tradition sustains schools that value academic knowledge, not just instrumentally, but also because of the way in which it fits into a conception of human flourishing. Catholic schools also value academic knowledge for everyone, and have in many places become successful educators of minority, non-Catholic youth. Finally, Catholic schools often succeed in establishing caring communities and transmitting a sense of social justice to their students. In contrast Bryk, Lee and Holland (ibid. 318–9) claim that public schools are characterized by an ethos that is individualistic, competitive, materialistic and lacking in concern for the common good. Ironically, they claim, Catholic schools are more successful in realizing the aspirations of common schools to produce good citizens than are public schools.

If my argument is correct, the fact that Catholic schools have a sense of community rooted in a praiseworthy tradition while public schools have privatized human flourishing in some measure, accounts for these differences. Public schools cannot articulate a meaning for education beyond its instrumental uses. They lack moral coherence. They make trust a personal matter between individual teachers and students, because they cannot establish the conditions of community that allow trust to be a bridge of affiliation to larger communities and their larger purposes. They thus erode the conditions required for an education conducive to human flourishing. They may even erode the conditions in which the values and virtues required for citizenry can be developed.

The point of this argument is not to affirm neoscholastic Catholicism as a solution to the ills of education. While I think it is on the whole praiseworthy, I am somewhat deterred by the fact that I do not believe in the Catholic faith, a rather different, but not trivial matter. I think one must regard with suspicion any attempt to root public education in neoscholasticism or any other religious tradition. Nor am I advocating a rush to privatization, which in the US context may be more likely to make schools subservient to the ethos of the market than to praiseworthy traditions. Not all traditions that might benefit from privatization are equally praiseworthy or conducive to liberal citizenship. The point is rather that we need to find ways to make praiseworthy traditions more real in the education of our children. If we cannot, we will promote an instrumental conception of the role of intellectual practices in human flourishing.

Thus I am left with a question: How can we make praiseworthy traditions more important in the education of our children while appropriately respecting the diversity of traditions? Any answer will have to balance conflicting interests. We need to find ways to be both liberals and communitarians. This may require compromises and some muddling through. However, an education that contributes to a conception of human flourishing in which the life of the mind has a part depends on a better answer to my question than the privatization of human flourishing now permits.

## Notes

1 The institutional framework and vocabulary I assume in this paper is American. In the United States the most common type of school is the *public school*, i.e. a government operated and financed school typically available to and attended by the children of a given geographical area. The argument I shall make can, I believe, be recast for systems with different characteristics, but I will not attempt to do so.

2 Three useful and classic sources for arguments of this sort are Kuhn 1970, Lakatos 1970 and Toulmin 1972.

## References

Bryk, A., Lee, V. and Holland, P. (1993) *Catholic Schools and the Common Good*, Cambridge, Mass.: Harvard University Press.

Kuhn, T. (1970) *The Structure of Scientific Revolutions*, Chicago: University of Chicago Press.

Lakatos, I. (1970) 'Falsification and the methodology of scientific research programs', in I. Lakatos and A. Musgrave (eds) *Criticism and the Growth of Knowledge*, London: Cambridge University Press.

MacIntyre, A. (1984) *After Virtue*, Notre Dame, Ill.: University of Notre Dame Press.

—— (1988) *Whose Justice? Which Rationality?*, Notre Dame, Ill.: University of Notre Dame Press.

Peters, R. S. (1964) *Education as Initiation*, London: Evans.

Rawls, J. (1993) *Political Liberalism*, New York: Columbia University Press.

Steinberg, L. (1996) *Beyond the Classroom: Why school reform has failed and what parents need to do about it*, New York: Simon and Schuster.

Toulmin, S. (1972) *Human Understanding*, Princeton, N.J.: Princeton University Press.

# Part 7

# CONCLUSION

# 17

# THE VIRTUE APPROACH TO MORAL EDUCATION

## Pointers, problems and prospects

*David Carr and Jan Steutel*

## Virtue ethics and modern accounts of moral education

In his introduction to a valuable recent reader on virtue ethics, Daniel Statman (1997: 25) lists a number of areas – animal ethics, vegetarianism, medical ethics, psychological ethics, political philosophy – in which the ethics of virtue is beginning to find serious practical application. Even if, as seems likely, the omission is more a matter of oversight than design, it is surely nevertheless striking (notwithstanding earlier passing observations on the educational implications of virtue ethics) that education in general, and moral education in particular, should find no place on this list. To be sure, *Virtue Ethics: A critical reader* is a collection of mainstream philosophical papers and it is not, in our experience, common for 'pure' philosophers to have much contact with theorists attempting to apply philosophical ideas and analyses to the practical problems and concerns of field professionals in such areas as education and teaching. Indeed, the present project, which features mainstream philosophers and educational philosophers in more or less equal doses, is a relatively pioneering one in this respect. All the same, it seems strange that education and moral education should fail to receive any mention in virtue-theoretical dispatches: first, given the general interest shown by all great moral philosophers – Socrates, Plato, Aristotle, Augustine, Aquinas, Hume, Kant, Mill and so on – in questions of moral knowledge and moral formation; second, given the very particular interest in the developmental processes of moral formation of the generally acknowledged founding father of virtue ethics, Aristotle, and his principal ethical heirs.

That said, we believe that Statman's oversight – assuming it to be such – is otherwise readily excusable in the light of a surprising dearth of contemporary educational philosophical work on virtue theory. Given the enormous amount of current interest among educational philosophers in contemporary 'post-analytical', communitarian, virtue-theoretical, feminist and other critiques of rationalist liberal enlightenment ethics, it is possible that some might find this remark surprising. But despite these trends – even the enormous reverence for Aristotle that they have engendered – books and papers attempting virtue theoretical analyses of moral education as such are, whilst by no means unknown, surprisingly few and far between.

There is also little evidence that the virtue-theoretical work on moral education which has been done – even by such prominent contemporary virtue ethicists as Alasdair MacIntyre (1987; 1991) – has had much impact on theorizing processes of moral development, beyond propagating a general skepticism about the very possibility of common school moral education. Indeed, it may well be that the most conspicuous alternative conception of moral education to have emerged so far by way of criticism of liberal-rationalist models is that of feminist proponents of 'ethics of care' (Gilligan 1982; Noddings 1984). This approach, despite having features in common with virtue ethics, has arguably much less impressive philosophical credentials. Apart from this, perhaps the most influential attempt to turn Aristotelian virtue theory to the purposes of moral education was made over a period of years by the founding father of British post-war analytical philosophy of education, Richard Peters (1981). But Peters seems, somewhat dubiously, to have regarded the Aristotelian emphasis on moral training and character development as a potential addition or supplement, more than an alternative to what was then fast becoming – under the leadership of Lawrence Kohlberg – the prevailing post-war moral educational orthodoxy of cognitive development theory.

Despite the time-honoured interest of many past moral and political philosophers in questions of moral development and learning, it would appear that twentieth-century research and enquiry into moral development has continued to be mostly the disputed territory of competing psychological theories. In the early part of the century, such learning theorists as Watson and Thorndike had enormous influence on the (moral and other) educational thinking of Dewey, Russell and others (see Perry 1967), and the psychoanalytic thought of Freud and Reich had a similar impact on the progressive educational-therapeutic work of Homer Lane (1954), A. S. Neill (1965) and their followers. Post-war work on moral development took a somewhat more philosophical turn with the emergence of cognitive development theory and the values clarification movement (Kirschenbaum 1977; Simon and Olds 1976) – partly in reaction to behaviourist and psychotherapeutic views – but these ideas were again, by and large, brainchilds of ethically minded psychologists.

In turn, the influential moral educational approaches of the ethics of care (Gilligan 1982; Noddings 1984) and character education (Lickona 1996) – albeit driven, to a greater or lesser extent, by social and political concerns – have never the less drawn theoretical inspiration from psychological research and enquiry. Of all these, however, there can be no doubt that the Piaget (1932) inspired work of Kohlberg (1981) and his cognitive developmental followers has occupied the centre stage of theorising about moral education for most of the post-war period.

With the benefit of hindsight it seems likely that the extraordinary success of Kohlberg's work related in a large part to the way it chimed in with post-war social and political aspirations. The forces of reason, justice, truth and individual freedom having finally triumphed over the collectivist barbarism and insanity of fascism, there seems to have been something of a grass roots determination, in both defeated and victorious free economies, to create the kind of brave new world of liberal-democratic sweetness and light which would forever prevent any relapse into totalitarian nightmare. In the light of this climate of socio-political optimism, it is hardly surprising that education came to be seen by many as the key to the promotion of the sweet reasonableness – as well as the economically competitive edge – which might hasten the new order.

Thus, at the same moment that social and political philosophers returned afresh to the task begun by their enlightenment predecessors of tracing the ground rules of liberal democracy, a relatively new breed of philosophers of education – concerned to lay the foundations of a liberal programme of education which might equip young people for responsible, impartial and open-minded democratic participation – emerged under the inspiration of (most notably) Richard Peters (1986) in Britain and Israel Scheffler (1973) in the United States. To the large extent that any such overall educational ambition would appear to presuppose an adequate theory of moral education, much was written on this topic by such educational philosophers as Peters (1981); but there can be no doubt that Kohlberg's cognitive theory of moral development and education seemed to many to be the moral educational holy grail for which other liberal educationalists had so far unsuccessfully sought.

Despite the fair share of criticism which Kohlberg's theory was bound to attract from some philosophical quarters, what is more striking is the almost unprecedented level of support it secured from early analytical educational philosophers, who mostly welcomed his account as broadly along the right lines. As already indicated, for example, Peters proposed to draw on Aristotle largely by way of supplement for what he took to be certain motivational short-comings of an otherwise sound theory. The agreement is perhaps less surprising given the extent to which Kohberg's theory is a basic pick and mix of such post-enlightenment philosophical influences as Kantian deontology, the Kant-inspired structuralist epistemology of Piaget, Deweyan pragmatism, the critical theory of Habermas, Rawlsian contractualism, non-cognitivist constructivism and others (as well as, allegedly, a Platonic account of justice). So far as this is so, Kohlberg's account is – as indicated in several places in this volume – prey to precisely the kinds of objection which have been raised against the received modern moral rationalisms of deontology, utility and so on.

The theoretical difficulties of the varieties of enlightenment ethics which seem to have informed the modern (and modernist) Kohlbergian moral educational orthodoxy have, of course, been aired fairly comprehensively in the extensive recent literature of moral and social theory (including Crittenden's contribution to the present volume). The present work, however, has been addressed primarily to a set of rather more practical concerns concerning the nature and processes of moral education. Hence, it may be more appropriate – by way of summary of the moral educational implications of virtue ethics which have received expert detailed treatment at the hands of the distinguished contributors to this collection – to devote what remains of this concluding chapter to a brief overview of the main respects in which virtue ethics might be regarded as offering a more promising perspective than its rivals on the educational practicalities of moral formation. In so doing, however, we shall also acknowledge some of the difficulties which a virtue theoretical approach has been thought to raise for the general enterprise of moral education.

## The ethical centrality of character

Most contributors to this volume have had something to say about the primacy of character in ordinary moral appraisals, and about the way in which any such focus on character appears somewhat at odds with the largely normative construal of right action of modern ethics of duty and utility. On the one hand, it is the main intent of utilitarianism to give moral weight to the consequences rather than the motives of action. On the other, though Kant's ethics does allow some room for notions of character and intention – which has prompted some to try to develop a Kantian virtue ethics – modern deontologies have usually regarded such features of moral agency as secondary to rational, complicit or other, obedience to rules and principles.

It appears to be central to virtue ethics in what we earlier called the narrow sense, that assessments of the moral rightness or otherwise of actions are derivative of our common notions of what it is to be a good person, rather than vice versa. While neither strict obedience to universalizable principles nor maximization of utility seem essential to our understanding of moral goodness – persons may well score highly on such tests without their actions having great moral significance – appreciation of moral goodness, understood more aretaically, enters into any true understanding of what it is for an action to be morally right. From this point of view it is not just that traditional virtue ethics is more obviously in tune with (and less distortive of) our ordinary moral intuitions than Kantian deontology or utilitarianism, but that it offers a much more robust and lifelike picture of moral life. In so far as this is so, virtue ethics has clear advantages over the theoretical bases of rival accounts of moral education.

First, it is reasonable to suggest that insofar as it is generally proper to construe education as a matter of initiating young people into a recognition of the intrinsic rather than merely extrinsic or instrumental significance of any form of knowledge, experience or understanding – as a highly influential modern movement in educational philosophy has claimed (Peters 1966) – it should be a crucial aim of moral education to assist young people to an appreciation of the value *for its own sake* of moral engagement. Just as science and history are concerned with acquainting pupils with the potential of scientific or historical explanation to enrich our understanding of the world and our place in it, so it should be the crucial task of moral education to show the ways in which personal life stands to be enriched or enhanced by the possession of such qualities as honesty, temperance, courage, fairness and charity

It is arguable that a virtue-ethical conception of moral education can acknowledge more easily than any of its rivals a substantial distinction between the intrinsic purposes of education and the extrinsic goals of socialization or training. On such a view, moral education is more a matter of the cultivation of those excellences of moral and other character commonly called virtues – bringing pupils to an appreciation of the worthwhileness of moral and other enterprises for their own sakes – than of training in obligations or imposition of prohibitions. (Issues along these lines are explored by Strike in his contribution to this volume.)

Second, in so far as this is so, the virtue-theoretical focus on character is less crudely reductive than any of its rivals. For a start, one may easily distinguish the virtue-theoretical approach from the sort of learning-theoretical or behaviour modificatory approaches that were influential in the early part of the century, and which have perhaps regained some ground in current movements towards character education. Although virtue theory allows a large role for basic moral training, it also sees this as preparatory to the critical appreciation of moral reasons and principles, and therefore as very much more than social conditioning.

Virtue ethics also scores over deontological and other rationalist accounts of the basis of moral education in offering a clearer view of the way in which motivational factors must enter into any real appreciation of principles. On this view, there is an internal relation (a relation which is promised, but not delivered, by cognitive developmental universalization of prescription) between moral reason and moral motivation, such that no one could be said fully to have grasped a moral reason – or to have acquired the relevant moral virtue – who is not at least favourably inclined to pursue what the reason enjoins.

Further, just as virtue ethics seems to score over any view that attempts to locate moral education in the mastery of cognitive process, so it seems to have the edge over any account which seeks to ground it in the acquisition of some cognitive content.

One might say, for example, that a moral, or morally educated, person is someone who believes certain things – has grasped certain moral truths – just as it might be one view of a historically educated person that they have acquired a body of historical facts. As an historically educated person knows that the Battle of Hastings was in 1066, or that Charles I succeeded James I, so the morally educated person believes that capital punishment is barbaric and that abortion is murder. The obvious problem with this point of view is not that there are no moral facts as there are (arguably) historical facts. It is still an open philosophical question whether there are moral facts. To the degree that we might regard failure to grasp obvious moral facts as a particular kind of moral failure, it might be considered a serious objection to the kinds of constructivist moral theories underlying contemporary ideas of moral education as the mastery of cognitive processes, that they subjectivise moral judgement to the extent of leaving small room for the idea of moral fact. The trouble is not even that moral positions on abortion and capital punishment are contested, for the historically educated will also dispute the facticity of alleged historical truths. The problem is rather that although our moral appraisals are based to some extent on what agents believe (the fanatical racist is by that token surely beyond any moral pale) it is clearly possible, indeed far from uncommon, for us to have considerable *moral* regard for people who hold moral beliefs quite contrary to our own.

Indeed, what seems to give the lie to the widespread relativist assumption that moral agency is a function of conformity to the beliefs of one's own cultural constituency, is the observation that the Christian crusader may well have *less* moral respect for his brutal and fanatical co-believers than for his infidel foe whose beliefs he does not share. This seems to indicate that to whatever extent morality would seem to involve at least trying to discern a set of correct beliefs about what is right and good, it is upon the *dispositions* rather than the beliefs of agents that our moral assessments seem critically to turn: the criteria which determine for me that the local Moslem shopkeeper is a good and decent man are that he is honest, fair, courageous, tolerant, charitable and kind – while the racist bigots who persecute him in the name of 'white' Christian culture are none of these. What, in short, seems to support the ordinary intuition that there are objective perspective-independent grounds for our moral assessments is not the facticity or otherwise of moral belief, but the observation that there are features of human make-up – ordinarily called virtues – which constitute a distinctive kind of human excellence irrespective of whether what is believed by their possessors is true or false. Of course, matters are not quite so simple since, as already indicated, the holding of certain false beliefs – such as that people are humanly superior or inferior by virtue of pigmentation – cannot be other than morally corrosive. But the very order of fit here between belief and virtue is in itself telling: what costs moral suspicion on racist dogma is that it is a function of special pleading and bigotry – and that, therefore it could make little ethical sense to try to justify such qualities on the grounds that they are validated by some 'alternative' system of moral thought.

## Naturalism, communitarianism and rival traditions

Such considerations point to distinct virtue-theoretical possibilities for avoiding, not only the motivational shortcomings of the cognitive developmental account, but any subjectivism or relativism latent in either this view or any of its modern philosophical rivals. Indeed, as indicated by Haldane and other contributors to this volume, post-war interest in virtue ethics emerged in the spirit of a new ethical naturalism, which was to a great extent motivated by abhorrence of the modern non-cognitivist orthodoxies of emotivism and prescriptivism.

A quarter of a century ago, however, this dispute became a three-cornered contest in which both the naturalist objectivism of virtue ethicists (Geach 1977; Foot 1978) and the non-cognitivist individualism of prescriptivists (Hare 1952) were challenged by a neo-Wittgensteinian conventionalism (Mounce and Phillips 1969) which sought to relativize moral judgement and commitment to local social practice. The new naturalism of the virtue theorists held its ground against both relativism and subjectivism – as well as opposing any consequentialist naturalism – in insisting, very much in the name of Aristotle, that the virtues are objective features of human character and conduct necessary for human flourishing, irrespective of personal preference or local cultural affiliation. As one leading light of the new virtue ethics put it, 'men need the virtues as bees need stings' (Geach 1977: 17).

However, this early naturalist defence of the virtues – and any associated view of moral education focused more on the promotion and cultivation of character dispositions than upon cognitive content or process – seems to have been seriously eroded by more recent 'post-modern' or communitarian developments in virtue ethics. MacIntyre's epochal *After Virtue* (1981) took its cue from the pioneering reflections on the ethical bankruptcy of received deontic usage of such neo-naturalists as Elizabeth Anscombe, and also fuelled an enormous revival of philosophical interest in virtue ethics and the nature of virtues. All the same, its emphasis on the social provenance and culturally-conditioned character of virtue, and its denial of any 'natural' cross-cultural basis for evaluating human moral response, may have seemed complete capitulation to just the kind of moral relativism that the new Aristotelians of the sixties and seventies had so vehemently opposed. But although MacIntyre rejects the so-called enlightenment moral project, there is good reason to doubt that he regards moral relativism as a consequence of any such rejection (MacIntyre 1988; 1992).

Thus, though MacIntyre holds that there is (for human beings anyway) no God's-eye moral conception – only the partial and partisan perspectives of rival traditions – he appears inclined to a neo-Hegelian conception of truth as a matter of moral progress via a synthesis of the theses and antitheses of rival traditions. Although we can never be sure that we have got things morally right, such progress is consistent with coming to recognize – as slave owners, racists, misogynists and so on – that we once had things badly morally wrong.

MacIntyre's view is also consistent with believing, as a subscriber to one moral tradition, that the views of that tradition are right (or at least on the right lines) and the views of other traditions are wrong. For example, a Catholic is more or less bound to believe that both liberal advocates of abortion on demand and New Guinea cannibals are in the grip of corrupt moral traditions. Since the idea of sitting in judgement on other moral traditions would more than likely be unacceptable on some (normative) accounts of moral relativism, MacIntyre's rival-traditions view is presumably (at least to this extent) less morally omnitolerant than such views.

However, as indicated in the introduction and elsewhere in this collection (see especially Haldane's contribution), the consequences of any such rival-traditions view for theorising moral educational provision in contemporary conditions of cultural pluralism are at least as devastating, if not more so, than those of moral relativism. For if, as MacIntyre and others argue, there can be no such thing as a consistent socio-culturally neutral conception of moral formation – and, more-over, moral formation can only be regarded coherently as a matter of protracted Aristotelian initiation into a particular set of cultural practices – it follows that there can be no question of a common school conception of moral education of the kind envisaged by some post-war philosophers of liberal education. Indeed, MacIntyre (1987) has explicitly extended this argument to education in general, arguing that the entire post-war ideal of a liberal education, as distinct from general forms of basic socialization and particular specialist forms of vocational training, can no longer be regarded as a viable or coherent educational goal.

It seems to be the logical implication of MacIntyre's view that moral educa-tion is only coherently pursuable in contexts in which the main agencies of moral formation – school and community – profess and are in a position to nurture and reinforce a coherent common set of moral and/or religious values. It has long been common – on something like MacIntyrean grounds – for particular religious constituencies and denominations in developed democracies to make their own provision for the education of their members, and demands for separate schooling from Moslem and other minority communities in the UK and elsewhere seem to be on the increase. However, any such rival-traditions conception of schooling may also have dangerously socially divisive implications – as we know all too well from the experience of religious sectarian educational apartheid in Northern Ireland and elsewhere – and for many people the new communitarian arguments are a postmodern counsel of despair regarding any prospect of a socio-culturally unfragmented and tolerant society.

It is easy to see how considerations such as these might well be enough for some to reject virtue ethics – at least in its communitarian rival-traditions form – in favour of a revised liberal-rational or other conception of moral education. But there are also reasons why we should perhaps not be so hasty. First, let us suppose that MacIntyre's virtue ethics is (wholly) right. In that case, no liberal-rationalist cognitive developmental, or other moral educa-tional rival of virtue ethics, is tenable. Thus, if we want to sustain any coher-ent conception of moral education, we have little option other than to bite the bullet of MacIntyre's communitarian conclusions, and, if needs must, their pessimistic socially divisive consequences.

However, MacIntyre could be wrong, or only partially right. Indeed, even liberal opponents of the rival-traditions account frequently acknowledge the importance for moral growth of communitarian or familial initiation of individuals into traditions and practices of value and virtue. Thus, one strategy – adopted, possibly under Rawlsian influence, by some contributors to this volume – is to try to weld an Aristotelian conception of moral nurture to a more general liberal-enlightenment conception of moral principle, in the interests of what we described in the introduction to this volume as an ethics of virtue in a broad sense. The overall aim would be, in short, to have the liberal cake, but eat it communitarianly.

It is still not obvious, however, that this would be either the only strategy, or the most coherent one. Indeed, since it would appear to be the liberal conception of morality as rational principle which distorts our ordinary understanding of the life of virtue – rather that vice versa – it might make more sense to derive our conception of liberal-democratic association from virtue ethics, rather that our conception of virtue from liberal ethics. Indeed, some recent work in virtue theory is proceeding in this direction, by attempting to show how rational reflection upon the nature of the life of virtue may coherently explain and justify liberal-democratic ideas about freedom and justice (Nussbaum 1990; Slote 1993). Thus, although any such project might appear to be threatened by the radical communitarian view of the incommensurability of rival traditions, not all virtue ethicists accept that view as an essential ingredient of virtue ethics.

Thus, whilst taking the communitarian point that virtue needs to be nurtured in a particular cultural soil, many virtue ethicists regard development of the critical capacities required for objective evaluation of social context as crucial to mature acquisition of virtue. Some virtue theorists (Nussbaum 1988; Carr 1996) have argued that despite the local cultural form that virtues are bound to assume, it is never the less reasonable to suppose there are general non-relative forms of virtue underlying local variation. This would go some way to vindicating the neo-naturalist claim that our cross-cultural moral evaluations have a distinct virtue-ethical basis. Moreover we have already seen how MacIntyre himself (as distinct from his interpreters) seems to hold that there can be internal or inter-cultural criticism of the views of a particular tradition, and it is a virtue-theoretical commonplace that the route to moral objectivity is less a matter of ascent to Platonic universals, more one of Aristotelian sensitivity to, and perception of, the particular.

## Virtue and reason: the interplay of cognition, perception and affect

It should be clear from the last section, however, that virtue ethics is by and large committed to some, not necessarily relativist, version of communitarianism. This has arguably radical consequences for theorising the moral-educational roles and relationships of community, home and school. There can be little doubt that the post-war analytical philosophy of liberal education inclined to a fairly sharp distinction between socialization and education, which were seen as the separate spheres of home and formal schooling. Philosophers such as Richard Peters and Paul Hirst for the most part assigned to schools the tasks of providing young people with the intellectual capacities required to make rational sense of the world, and of equipping them with vocationally relevant theoretical and practical skills. The heavy cognitive emphasis in all of this has been too often remarked to need further elaboration here, and it was nowhere more apparent than in the use of cognitive-theoretical ideas from Piaget and Kohlberg in developing highly rationalist dilemma-solving approaches to moral education. Morality was, in short, assumed to be largely a matter of Kantian (or sometimes utilitarian) initiation into contractually or other grounded rules and principles, and – though Peters and others did appear to recognize a need for Aristotelian behaviour training for the effective 'stamping-in' of the rules – scant recognition was given to the motivational aspects of moral engagement.

It is interesting that virtually the only significant recognition of the importance of emotional or affective factors in the development of morality at that time was to be found in the work of psychoanalytically-influenced educational 'progressives' working, often enough, with disturbed children (Lane 1954; Neill 1965). Despite the fact that Peters and other liberal educationalists roundly criticized such educationalists for confusing education with therapy – a rather telling criticism in the context – the psychoanalytic progressives at least showed keen appreciation that in the absence of properly ordered affect, any explicit formal or informal teaching of moral rules or principles could only be so much wasted toil.

What was wrong with 'problem' children was not that they could not intellectually grasp (say) the principle of respect for persons, but that they had never in their abused lives any experience of what such respect might mean. To put the difference between liberal traditionalists and psychotherapeutic progressives crudely, the former believed one might only come to care for others via an intellectual grasp of a principle of respect for persons; the latter, that one could only grasp the principle if one had already acquired an other than purely rational appreciation of what it means to care for others. Since any such appreciation must depend upon well-ordered affect, this was precisely what was denied to children of radically dysfunctional family circumstances.

Arguably, however, the liberal traditionalist educational orthodoxy of the day, and the psychoanalytic progressivism of which it was critical, were equally grounded in a problematic dualism of cognition and affect (a dualism also, one suspects, characteristic of contemporary so-called 'ethics of care'), which virtue ethics has always sought to avoid. As we have seen, mainstream virtue ethics – following Aristotle and the Greeks in general – does not generally observe the sharp division of reason from passion or feeling which seems to be the post-enlightenment ethical heritage. Thus, though there may be a clear enough sense in which affective life is *pre-rational* – it does not necesssarily require the ordering of experience under general rules or principles – feelings and emotions are nevertheless not to be regarded as purely passive unconceptualised responses to the world, in need of rational control or suppression.

It is not just that it is hardly possible to make sense of such emotions as pride, jealousy or envy in other than cognitive terms – by reference to some appraisal of things as thus and so – but that forms of affect seem themselves to be as much ways of perceiving or registering experience as of reacting to it. As several contributors to this volume have argued, emotions, passions and feelings are sources of information about the world – ways of *perceiving* – which are necessary to the development of capacities for the principled organization of experience in terms of the received rational categories of this or that established form of human enquiry. It should be clear that if we were incapable of the characteristic range of human affect, we would also be incapable of the kinds of rational appreciation of the world that we have, and, in particular, of the realms of moral, aesthetic and other value. To this extent, it is not hard to understand that children whose affective sensibilities have been impaired or disordered by abuse or neglect are liable to find any subsequent principled appreciation of moral or other values difficult if not impossible.

If this is so, the division of labour observed by post-war pioneers of liberal educational traditionalism (and more popularly) between home and/or community and school, allocating nurture and socialization to the former and education proper to the latter, is no longer tenable for moral education, if not more generally. If moral education is more than just the intellectual grasp of principles, then as far as schools have a moral educational responsibility, they must be concerned with more than intellectual aspects of personal formation. Perhaps more obviously, if home and community are deeply implicated in the nurture and basic socialization of the child, they are to that extent crucially contributory to processes of moral education. In fact these considerations about the joint responsibility of home, community and school for the development of such crucial aspects of personal development as moral formation have increasingly come to be acknowledged by educational professionals, and problems of 'partnership' between school, home and community are among the most live issues of contemporary educational debate.

Thus, as well as increased appreciation of the importance of early, particularly nursery, schooling, and much greater upper school attention to the personal and social aspects of development – in addition to the academic and the vocational – there has been a marked trend in the UK and elsewhere towards much greater community involvement of schools, particularly in areas of social deprivation. It is nowadays widely recognized (though not always by politicians and media) that where problems of the disaffection and delinquency of the young are rife, there are usually social causes for which schools as separate institutions cannot alone compensate. There has therefore been recently more encouragement than ever before of parental assistance and support for their children's learning in schools, as well as the involvement of professional educational expertise in helping parents to acquire the skills of good parenting.

Thus, even at this very general level, the insights of virtue ethics are in tune with the fairly obvious conclusion that positive moral and other human development is as much, if not more, a matter of right affective nurture and good example and support from parents and community, than of the disinterested mastery of rational principles of duty and obligation.

## Virtue education: training, example and narrative

Such observations lead naturally enough to a brief consideration of the main learning-theoretical and pedagogical features and requirements of a virtue approach to moral education. As the contents of this volume have amply shown, it could be argued that a virtue of the virtue approach is that it charts the complexity of human moral life and response more accurately than any other way of thinking about moral development and education. While reflex psychological and character education approaches focus mainly on behaviour shaping or training, the ethics of care concentrates on emotional development, and liberal educational and cognitive developmental approaches dwell primarily on the rational-intellectual aspects of moral understanding, virtue ethics regards moral development as a matter of crucial interplay between all these dimensions of human being, and it has been the concern of all the great virtue theorists from Aristotle to the present to give a coherent account of this interplay. However, as we have learned from various contributors to this volume, there is still an enormous amount of conceptual (and perhaps also empirical) work to be done on the psychology of virtue, in order to reach a clearer understanding of the harmonization of reason, affect and behaviour in virtuous conduct, as well as, from a moral educational viewpoint, what might constitute appropriate and effective moral-educational strategies for the promotion of such conduct.

For now, however, we must remain content with drawing attention to some areas of pedagogical importance, interest and concern to anyone attracted to a virtue ethical approach to moral education. First, it is clear from the Aristotelian origins of virtue theory that moral life is a *practical* sphere of human enquiry and conduct, in which training and habituation have an important part to play, and we have already seen how the virtue-ethical emphasis on virtues as practices meshes well with growing recognition that sound early-years training is crucially contributory to subsequent moral development.

But where Aristotle in one place notably compares the acquisition of virtue to the mastery of skill (as several contributors to this volume have indicated), he elsewhere takes great pains to distinguish the practical wisdom of virtue (*phronesis*) from the practical cleverness of skill (*techne*), precisely because virtuous conduct requires the kind of sensitive independent judgement which cannot be secured by mechanical adherence to general rules or precepts. It is therefore important for virtue-ethical moral educationalists to be clearer about the relation between moral habituation and the development of autonomous moral judgement – in the interests, among other things, of developing a view of the former which is not inhibitory of the latter – and some of the contributions to this volume are of course addressed to this problem.

We have also seen how virtue ethicists are increasingly inclined to regard the proper cultivation of affect as crucial to the development of the situation-sensitive dispositions of Aristotelian virtue. In this respect, training in virtues is to be conceived less on the pattern of mindless drilling in mechanical routines, more on that of the cultivation and refinement of certain natural human capacities and sensibilities for self- and other-regard. What might assist the development of such natural proclivities into full-grown virtues? A key factor for virtue ethicists is the modelling of conduct through the example of others. Such modelling has often been regarded with a degree of suspicion by liberal educationalists, as sailing close to the winds of indoctrination, but it is difficult to see how any coherent moral development might occur in the absence, for good or ill, of some such parental and other exemplification. There is therefore much conceptual and other work for virtue ethics to do, in charting the practically-feasible and morally-acceptable parameters of such modelling, particularly in relation to our current conceptions of the ethics of good parenting and teacher professionalism.

There is also a time-honoured view that the literary heritage of human culture has an important part to play in the development of moral sensibilities, and it is surely significant that virtue ethicists have recently made much of the importance of narrative in general for the formation of personal and cultural moral identity. Given much current incautious postmodern talk of all human knowledge as myth or narrative, however, such ideas need handling with caution. Indeed, this seems wrongheaded whether meant to imply that scientific theories are mere fairy tales, or that fairy tales can contain no truth. However, virtue-ethical interest in the moral-educational potential of literature – especially in as far as good literature is seen as an effective route to objective appreciation of the human condition – may once again seem closer to received wisdom than any artificially constructed cognitive developmental curriculum of moral dilemma resolution. To this end, urgent conceptual and empirical work needs to be done within the broad remit of virtue theory on the effects of literature and other media on the moral formation of young people.

Many of these points may seem no more than glorified common sense, recommendations for courses of action which we might pre-theoretically have regarded part of any sensible research programme into moral education. But the claim of a virtue-theoretical approach to moral education is not that it is original, rather that it reflects a basically correct view of the nature of moral development. To that extent, it is less a criticism of virtue ethics that it is largely faithful to our common sense intuitions about moral growth and education, and more an objection to most, if not all, of its contemporary rivals that they represent only partial or distorted accounts of the rich complexities of moral life.

# References

Carr, D. (1996) 'After Kohlberg: Some implications of an ethics of virtue for the theory and practice of moral education', *Studies in Philosophy and Education* 15, 4: 353–70.

Foot, P. (1978) *Virtues and Vices and Other Essays in Moral Philosophy*, Berkeley/ Los Angeles: University of California Press.

Geach, P. T. (1977) *The Virtues*, Cambridge: Cambridge University Press.

Gilligan, C. (1982) *In a Different Voice: Psychological theory and women's development*, Cambridge, Mass.: Harvard University Press.

Hare, R. M. (1952) *The Language of Morals*, Oxford: Oxford University Press.

Kirschenbaum, H. (1977) *Advanced Values Clarification*, La Jolla: University Associates.

Kohlberg, L. (1981) *Essays on Moral Development*, vols. I–III, New York: Harper and Row.

Lane, H. (1954) *Talks to Parents and Teachers*, London: Allen and Unwin.

Lickona, T. (1996) 'Eleven principles of effective character education', *Journal of Moral Education* 25, 1: 93–100.

MacIntyre, A. C. (1981) *After Virtue*, Notre Dame: University of Notre Dame Press.

—— (1987) 'The idea of an educated public', in Haydon, G. (ed.) *Education and Values: The Richard Peters lectures*, London: Institute of Education (University of London).

—— (1988) *Whose Justice, Which Rationality?* Notre Dame: Notre Dame Press.

—— (1991) *How To Appear Virtuous Without Actually Being So*, Lancaster: Centre for the Study of Cultural Values (University of Lancaster).

—— (1992) *Three Rival Versions of Moral Enquiry*, Notre Dame: Notre Dame Press.

Mounce, M. O. and Phillips, D. Z. (1969) *Moral Practices*, London: Routledge and Kegan Paul.

Neill, A. S. (1965) *Summerhill*, London: Gollancz.

Noddings, N. (1984) *Caring: A feminist approach to ethics*, Berkeley: University of California Press.

Nussbaum, M. (1988) 'Non-relative virtues: an Aristotelian approach', in P. A. French, T. E. Uehling and H. K. Wettstein (eds) *Midwest Studies in Philosophy. vol. XIII. Ethical Theory: Character and virtue*, Notre Dame: Notre Dame Press.

Nussbaum, M. (1990) 'Aristotelian social justice', in R. Douglass, G. Mara and H. Richardson (eds) *Liberalism and the Good*, London.

Perry, L. (1967) *Four Progressive Educators*, London: Collier-Macmillan.

Peters, R.S. (1966) *Ethics and Education*, London: George Allen & Unwin.

—— (1981) *Moral Development and Moral Education*, London: George Allen and Unwin.

Piaget, J. (1932) *The Moral Judgement of the Child*, New York: Free Press.

Scheffler, I. (1973) *Reason and Teaching*, Indianapolis: Bobs-Merrill.

Simon, S. and Olds, S. (1976) *Helping Your Child Learn Right From Wrong: A guide to values clarification*, New York: Simon and Schuster.

Slote, M. (1993) 'Virtue ethics and democratic values', *Journal of Social Philosophy* 24: 5–37.

Statman, D. (1997) *Virtue Ethics: A critical reader*, Edinburgh: Edinburgh University Press.

# INDEX

Alston, W. P. 128
Ames, R. T. 202
Annas, J. 112, 114
Anscombe, G. E. M. 9, 32, 139, 143, 8157–9, 247
Aquinas 109, 121, 160, 163, 235, 241
Arendt, H. 115
aretaic ethics 7–13, 16–7; agent and act version of 9–12, 17, 55–6, 156; replacement and reductionist version of 9
aretaic notions 8, 22, 33; and the conceptualization of moral norms 8, 26–31
Ariston of Chios 112
Aristotle *passim*; on *akrasia* 144–5, 148; on emotions 28, 43–6, 132; on *eudaimonia* 15–6, 29, 42, 59, 70, 76, 88, 158–9, 200–1, 207; on habituation 44–5, 56–60, 68–9, 76–8, 114, 143, 205–6, 215–7; on the mean 35, 39, 52, 80, 131–2, 200, 207; on *phronesis* 12, 27, 35–9, ch. 4, 68–70, 77–8, 112-14, 134, 145–8, 174–5, 181; on pleasure and pain 26–7, 53, 55, 59, 67, 205; on self-control 53, 132, 144; on teaching 35, 56–8, 68, 78, 174; on the unity of virtue 69–70, 109, 112, 145–6
Arnold, M. 43
Atkinson, C. 218, 220
Augustine 117, 163–4, 241
Austen, J. 208, 213

Austin, J. L. 32

Badhwar, N. K. 194
Baier, K. 16
Barnes, J. 46, 61, 79
Baron, M. W. 84
behaviourism 3, 47, 205, 210, 242, 245, 252
Beiner, R. 110
benevolence 82–6, 89–92; and moral imagination 207–8; as a natural virtue 85; conflicts with justice 83–6, 90–2
Bentham, J. 93, 199
Berlin, I. 83
Blasi, A. 118, 120
Blum, L. 47, 182
Bodenhamer, G. 79
Bohlmeijer, J. 220
Bok, S. 214
Brandt, R. B. 10, 82, 119, 130
Broadie, S. 112, 117
Brown, L. M. 182
Bryk, A. 235
Burke, E. 191
Burnyeat, M. F. 114, 217, 220
Burton, R. 120, 122

Callan, E. xiii, 13
Cannon, W. 43
care (ethics of) 3, 121–2, 174, 177–81, 232, 242, 250, 252